ADVANCE PRAISE FOR
WE SURVIVED THE HOLOCAUST

"There are many ways that contemporary students learn, different paths by which they can engage with the complexities of history, much especially a history as difficult and painful as the history of the Holocaust.

We Survived the Holocaust: The Bluma and Felix Goldberg Story is a deeply engaging moving story of two Polish Jews who endured and survived slave labor camps, concentration camps, death camps and death marches to then meet in freedom in another type of camp—a displaced persons camp—and rebuild their lives in the United States, bearing witness, telling their story and embodying the human capacity for resilience and regeneration. It speaks to some of the most important of our values and offers a message that is at once timeless, but so timely in the world of war, antisemitism and racism that has characterized 2022. Simply but not simplistically told and beautifully illustrated, the complex story of the Goldbergs is now accessible to readers of all ages, and even to those who don't like to read!"

—Michael Berenbaum, Distinguished Professor of Jewish Studies, Director of the Sigi Ziering Institute: Exploring the Ethical and Religious Implications of the Holocaust, American Jewish University, Los Angeles

"The graphic style of *We Survived the Holocaust* reminds me of both *Maus* and those rare drawings secretly made by the concentration camp prisoners to preserve the memory of what happened to them. This is a book for 21st century young readers for whom words are not enough to bring the horrors of the Holocaust to life."

—Michael Bazyler, Holocaust legal scholar, Chapman University, author of the award-winning *Holocaust, Genocide and the Law: A Quest for Justice in a Post-Holocaust World*

"*We Survived the Holocaust* makes the story of Bluma and Felix Goldberg come alive for a new generation of readers, many of whom will welcome this version of a Holocaust story. Indeed, the powerful drawings of Tim Ogline and the moving text by Frank Baker make this old story new again—a much needed and appreciated feat in these scary times. Whether you are a classroom teacher wanting to teach the Holocaust or a fan of graphic novels, you will want to have this book in your collection. You won't be able to put it down. Nor should you."

am Kist, Professor Emeritus, Kent State University
Author, *Curating a Literacy Life*

T0043536

"*We Survived the Holocaust* is an extremely powerful graphic novel that can help readers from middle schoolers to adults visualize and understand the atrocities of the Holocaust. Written by Frank Baker and illustrated by award-winning graphic artist Tim Ogline, this is an important personal portrayal of the horrific challenges Bluma and Felix Goldberg managed to survive in cattle cars, concentration camps, and death marches.

Frank Baker, through interviews with the Goldberg children, presents an engaging and informative overview of World War I and World War II, conditions in Europe under the Nazi regime, and what life was like for the Goldbergs from early childhood until they passed away decades later in South Carolina. Ogline's compelling illustrations tell the personal survival stories of Bluma and Felix Goldberg in more realistic and forceful ways than can be portrayed through text-only titles.

In the book, Bluma is quoted as saying, 'In a way we fear that maybe that's why we survived—so we can tell the story.' I cannot think of a more powerful way for the Goldberg's story to be told than through the graphic novel, *We Survived the Holocaust – The Bluma and Felix Goldberg Story*. I highly recommend this title to readers from young adults–adults. As a former school librarian and current educator of school librarians, I hope that this title will be on the shelves of all middle and high school libraries. The stories of how the Goldbergs, and other Jews, survived the Holocaust should never be forgotten by current and future generations."

—Dr. Karen Gavigan, Interim Director, School of Information Science, University of South Carolina

"The story of Bluma and Felix Goldberg successfully walks that fine line, capturing the human experience while also doing justice to the scale and monstrosity of the Holocaust, yet without resorting to horrific imagery. Here, the reader sees the forest and the trees. The detail provided about the broader context and the First World War is a welcome addition, as is the legacy the Goldbergs continued to build with their family and community in the U.S. If any graphic novel has ever captured the profound love that so many survivors felt for their adopted homeland, this is it. Tim Ogline's detailed maps and landscapes help to create a true work of art."

—Doyle Stevick, Ph.D., Executive Director, The Anne Frank Center, University of South Carolina, editor of *Holocaust Education: Promise, Practice, Power and Potential* and *Research in Teaching and Learning About the Holocaust: A Dialogue Beyond Borders*

"*We Survived the Holocaust* is generationally necessary. This critical story of Bluma and Felix Goldberg told in graphic novel form ensures today's generation doesn't forget yesterday's history. Remembrance and reverence lies within these pages."

—Anthony Zuiker, Creator of *CSI*,
Television Writer, Producer, Author, and Publisher

"Who will tell the story of the Holocaust survivors once the last of them has been buried? In this powerful graphic novel, Frank Baker offers an inspiring story, one that includes unforgettable drama and an ending that embodies the powerful reason why we embrace the mantra to 'never forget.' This story is full of riveting details. A Polish Jew named Felix Goldberg comes face to face with Dr. Joseph Mengele before being shipped to a work camp. He was responsible for bringing out the bodies of men who had died of starvation and malnourishment under the slave labor conditions. Not far away, another young Polish Jew is deported to Bergen-Belsen concentration camp under terrifying conditions. Forced to work in a concentration camp, Bluma Tishgarten steals food to keep her sister alive. After being liberated, Felix and Bluma met and fell in love, emigrating to Columbia, South Carolina in 1949. Through hard work, they build a life for themselves and tell their stories of survival, speaking at schools and synagogues. This graphic novel will engage readers of all ages as they encounter the terrors of the past with fresh eyes. With the scourge of intolerance, hate and antisemitism still present in daily life, we must continue to share survivor stories with the next generation."

—Renee Hobbs, Media Education Lab, University of Rhode Island USA

"We are fast losing the generation that lived through the Holocaust, making it more crucial than ever to document their horrific experiences for future generations. The survivors have been in our midst, but often we didn't know the trials and bravery that brought them to our communities. In creating *We Survived the Holocaust* as a graphic novel, Frank Baker engages in a story unsparing in its stark detail, without ever overwhelming the unshakable humanity and hope of Bluma and Felix Goldberg."

—David Kleeman, Children and Media Analyst

"Poignant, timely, engaging, scary, thoughtful, necessary. Necessary. Today, history is being challenged, manipulated, changed or denied to fit the political winds. Frank Baker has made sure that the history of the Holocaust will not be challenged, manipulated or denied. This graphic novel has everything a teacher wants as a resource to teach this necessary period of history. But, what is so exciting about this graphic novel is the connection the story will make with the students. The incredible story combined with the mind blowing graphics will grab the attention of even the most social media distracted student. I taught history for 31 years and I wish I had this graphic novel as a resource when I taught the history of the Holocaust. Teachers and their students need this book. This history has to be taught."

—Perry McLeod, Google Certified Teacher, Apple Distinguished Educator, National Board Certification, Fulbright Scholar/Germany

"The Goldberg story is the American story. Despite all of our obvious problems, it is still a blessed story of inclusion, hope and accomplishment—two people who somehow survived the horrors of the Holocaust to find another life in another land. I highly recommend this heartwarming book."

—Marvin Kalb, former CBS/NBC correspondent, author of the widely acclaimed *Assignment Russia*

"The words 'Never Again' resonate loudly to this day, but the world has been on a slippery slope since World War II. The Holocaust was a carnage of torture and death. This beautifully illustrated and written graphic novel demonstrates the miracle of surviving human devastation. Overcoming the most vile living conditions as the Goldbergs and millions of others have, speaks to an inner strength hard to imagine. This book reminds us to hope that no person should ever live under a brutal dictatorship that has no respect for life. The talent and craft in this book brought us squarely into the awful world of concentration camps and boxcars with a punch to the solar plexus. We must avoid taking that path again. Ever! This blunt, truthful graphic novel is a must read as a reminder we must fight to preserve freedom for all."

—Frances Metzman, Author, Educator and Lecturer at Temple University, Two-time Pushcart Prize nominee

We Survived the Holocaust

THE BLUMA & FELIX GOLDBERG STORY

Published by Imagine & Wonder
Irvington, New York 10533 USA
www.imagineandwonder.com

Scan this QR code with your phone camera
for more titles from Imagine and Wonder.

Your Guarantee of Quality: As publishers, we strive to produce every
book to the highest commercial standards. The printing and binding
have been planned to ensure a sturdy, attractive publication that should
give years of enjoyment. If your copy fails to meet our high standards,
please inform us and we will gladly replace it.
admin@imagineandwonder.com

Cataloging-in-Publication information is available
from the Library of Congress.

Library of Congress Control Number: 2021953079
ISBN #978-1637610206 (Trade Paperback)
ISBN #978-1637610213 (Hardcover)

First Edition

Printed in Canada by Marquis. www.marquisbook.com

We Survived the Holocaust

THE BLUMA & FELIX GOLDBERG STORY

FRANK W. BAKER
with TIM E. OGLINE
and ESTHER GOLDBERG GREENBERG,
KARL GOLDBERG & HENRY GOLDBERG

IMAGINE & WONDER™
Publishers, New York

"The story of our parents,
Bluma and Felix Goldberg, is a difficult one to tell.
Our hope is that people, young and old all over the
world, will be able to feel a personal connection to
our parents by reading their story."

– HENRY GOLDBERG, KARL GOLDBERG,
AND ESTHER GOLDBERG GREENBERG

CONTENTS

*"For the survivor who chooses to testify,
it is clear: his duty is to bear witness for
the dead and for the living. He has no right
to deprive future generations of a past
that belongs to our collective memory.*

*To forget would be not only dangerous
but offensive; to forget the dead would
be akin to killing them a second time."*

– ELIE WIESEL

INTRODUCTION

BY FRANK W. BAKER

In 2000, Felix Goldberg (of blessed memory) handed me the speech he had just delivered at our synagogue in Columbia South Carolina. The occasion was Yom Hashoa — the annual Day of Remembrance — where he had just testified about his harrowing Holocaust experience.

As he stepped off the stage he handed me that speech and said in his unmistakable Polish accent: "Frankie, do something with this"... Little did I know how his words would change my life.

I have known Felix and Bluma Goldberg (and their family) all my life, but it wasn't until

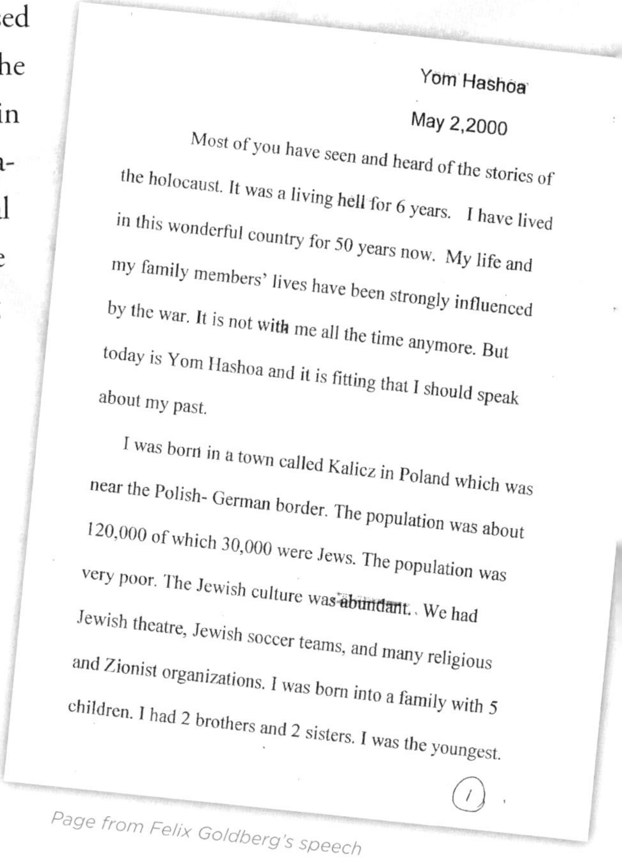

Yom Hashoa

May 2,2000

Most of you have seen and heard of the stories of the holocaust. It was a living hell for 6 years. I have lived in this wonderful country for 50 years now. My life and my family members' lives have been strongly influenced by the war. It is not with me all the time anymore. But today is Yom Hashoa and it is fitting that I should speak about my past.

I was born in a town called Kalicz in Poland which was near the Polish- German border. The population was about 120,000 of which 30,000 were Jews. The population was very poor. The Jewish culture was abundant. We had Jewish theatre, Jewish soccer teams, and many religious and Zionist organizations. I was born into a family with 5 children. I had 2 brothers and 2 sisters. I was the youngest.

1

Page from Felix Goldberg's speech

that day — when he charged me with passing on his story — that I realized how powerful and important that moment was.

The speech was deposited at my work desk where it was slowly lost over the years. But his words — "do something with this"— kept coming back to me. He knew I was an education consultant and that keeping his story alive was vital.

Finally, some years later, after having unearthed the speech, I thought I would publish his story as a small paperback and have copies printed for middle and high school students in South Carolina, where the teaching of the Holocaust was mandated many years ago.

That idea morphed into the idea of creating a website — an educational memorial that would tell his story (and that of his wife). I approached the family with the idea and an outline: the website would tell their story from before World War II, during World War II and after World War II, when they emigrated to South Carolina. The family contributed a box of valuable material much of which is now posted at www.StoriesofSurvival.org.

Two years later, after reading that many young people lack essential knowledge about the Holocaust, I realized that I had to do something more. That's when the idea for this graphic novel was born. I again reached out to the family who endorsed the idea enthusiastically.

This book is more than just the story of how two Polish Jews survived; it is also a cautionary tale of what happens when people standby and allow antisemitism, hate and prejudice to run rampant. We must not be innocent bystanders. We must make our voices heard when we see and experience wrongdoing, whether it occurs at home or halfway around the world.

I am most proud of this work and I hope you, the reader, will get as much out of it, as we've put into it.

– Frank W. Baker
Columbia, South Carolina

A portion of proceeds from the sale of "We Survived the Holocaust" will go to Holocaust education efforts in South Carolina.

PROLOGUE

Dear Reader. As you begin this story I'd like you to think about the following questions as *they may help you gain a better understanding.*

First... *How much do you know about the Holocaust?*
Where did you learn it?

Did you know in 1933 there were just over
9,000,000 Jews living in Europe?

Did you know that Hitler ordered the deaths
of over 6,000,000 Jews?

Did you know that over 11,000,000 people
were exterminated in Hitler's camps during WWII?

Do you know why the Nazis considered Jews to be an *inferior race?*
Are you aware that the *same types of injustices and atrocities* are happening all around the world?

These are *questions you should consider* as you read this true story.

Sadly, there are *people even today who deny the Holocaust ever happened.* Even with all the historical data and evidence, *they refuse to accept this very real part of human history. That is utterly tragic.*

This story is about two people who lived through the horrors of Nazi Germany. *Their story adds to the evidence of the Holocaust.*

NOTE: Words and phrases that you will encounter in the novel are defined and described in the Glossary at the end of the book.

*"I know that they're hearing it every year.
But you still have to remind people."*

– FELIX GOLDBERG

*"In a way, we fear that maybe that's why
we survived—so we can tell the story."*

– BLUMA TISHGARTEN GOLDBERG

REMEMBRANCE

PRESENT DAY

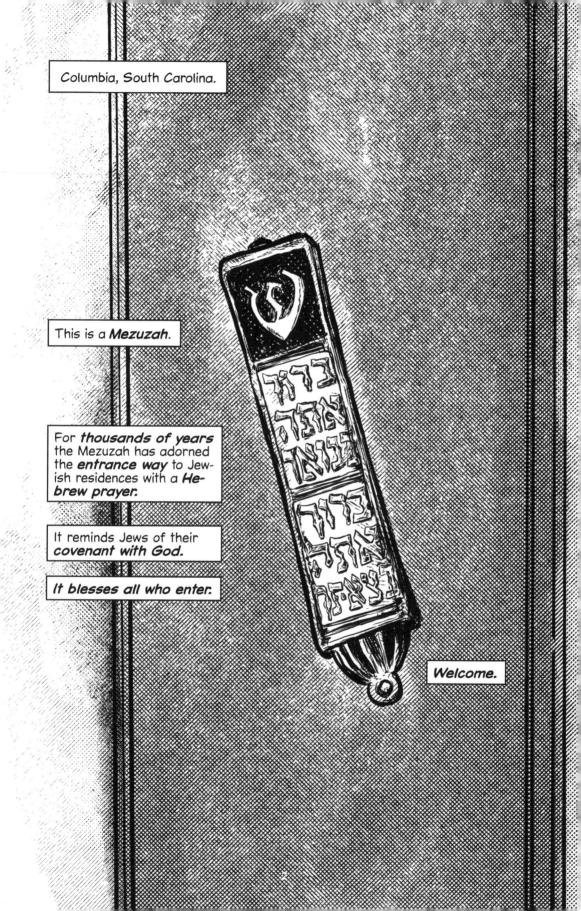

Columbia, South Carolina.

This is a *Mezuzah*.

For *thousands of years* the Mezuzah has adorned the *entrance way* to Jewish residences with a *Hebrew prayer.*

It reminds Jews of their *covenant with God.*

It blesses all who enter.

Welcome.

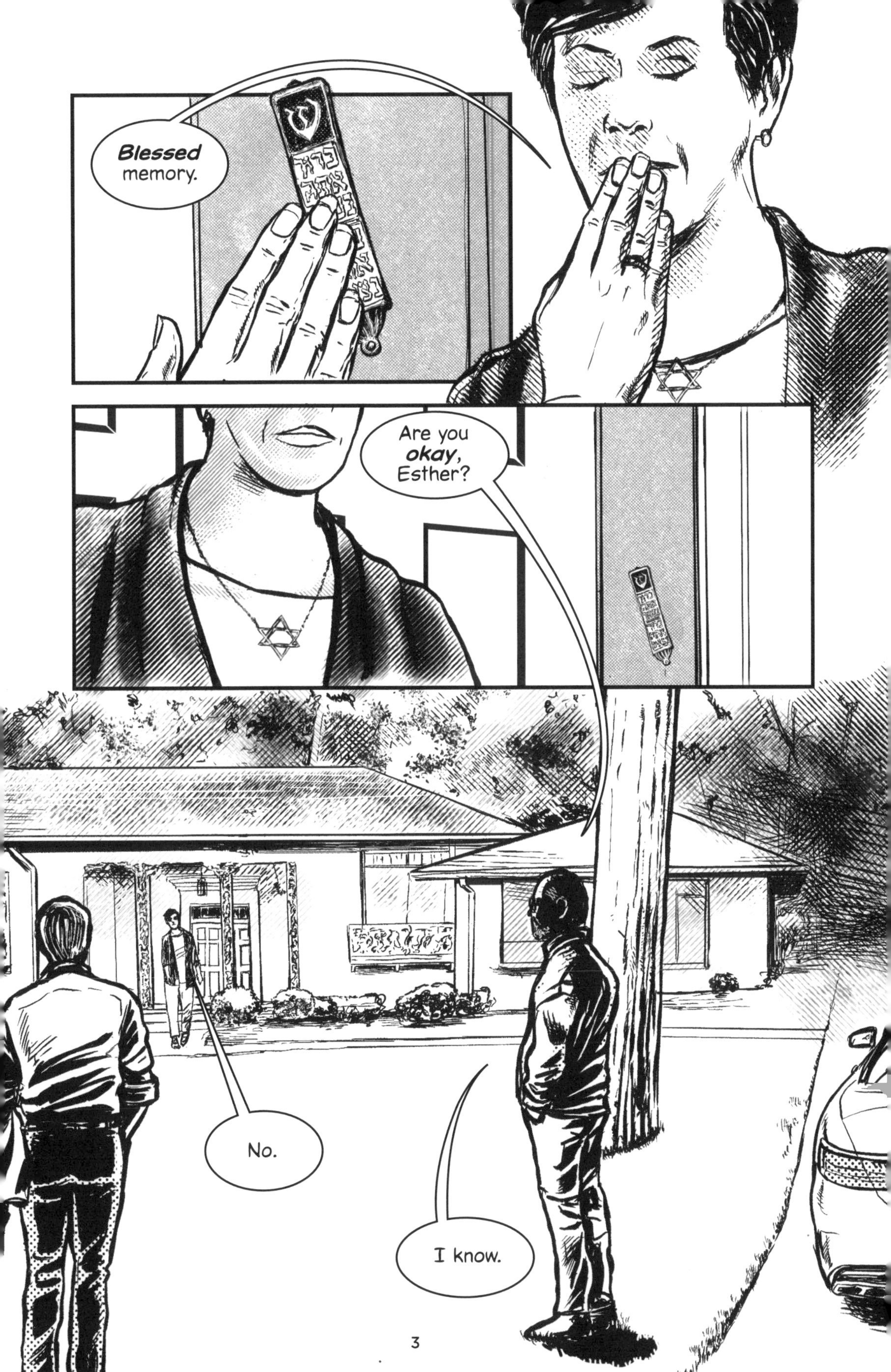

Blessed memory.
Are you *okay*, Esther?
No.
I know.

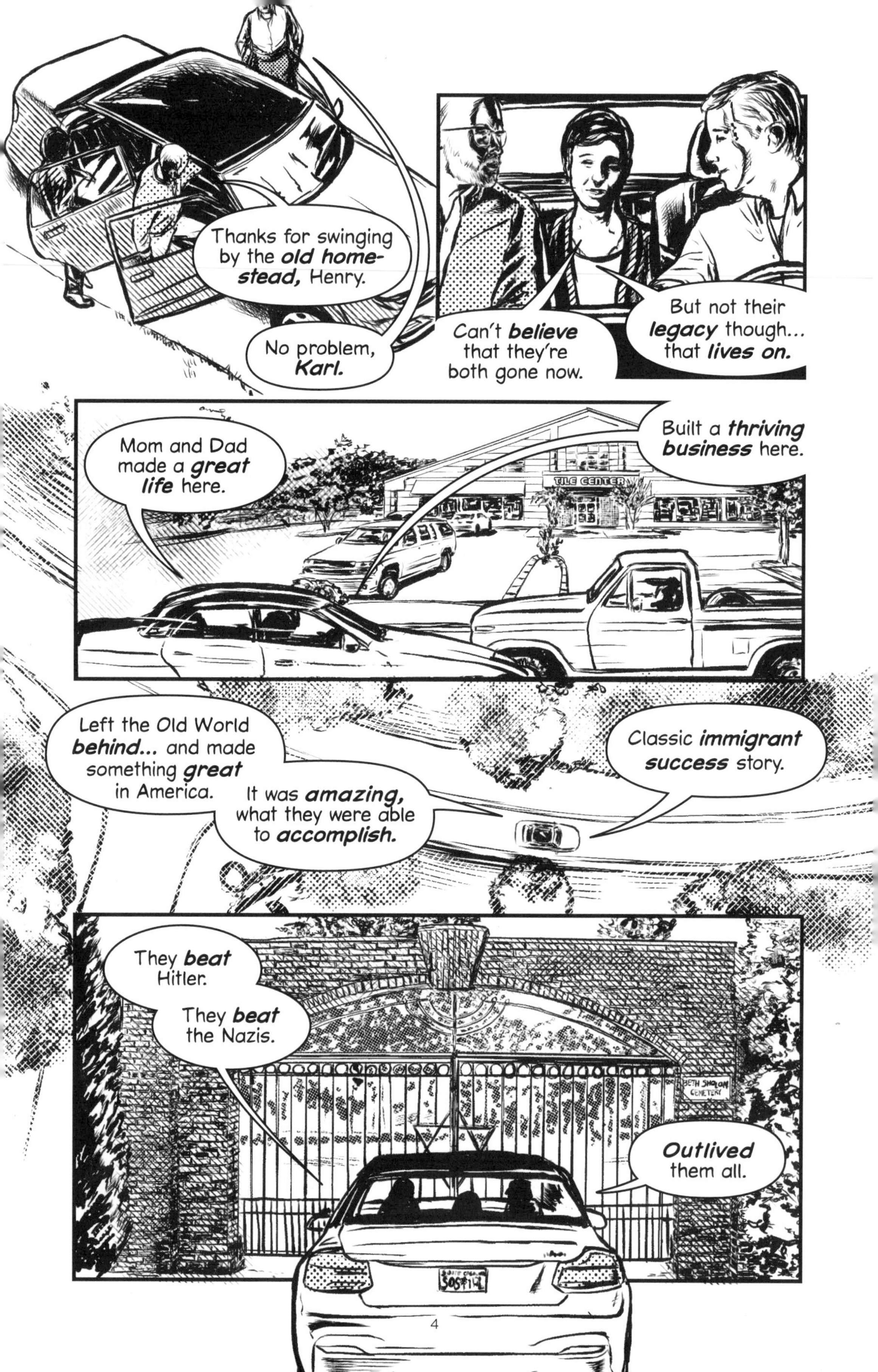

Thanks for swinging by the old homestead, Henry.
No problem, Karl.
Can't believe that they're both gone now.
But not their legacy though... that lives on.
Mom and Dad made a great life here.
TILE CENTER
Built a thriving business here.
Left the Old World behind... and made something great in America.
It was amazing, what they were able to accomplish.
Classic immigrant success story.
They beat Hitler.
They beat the Nazis.
BETH SHOLOM CEMETERY
Outlived them all.

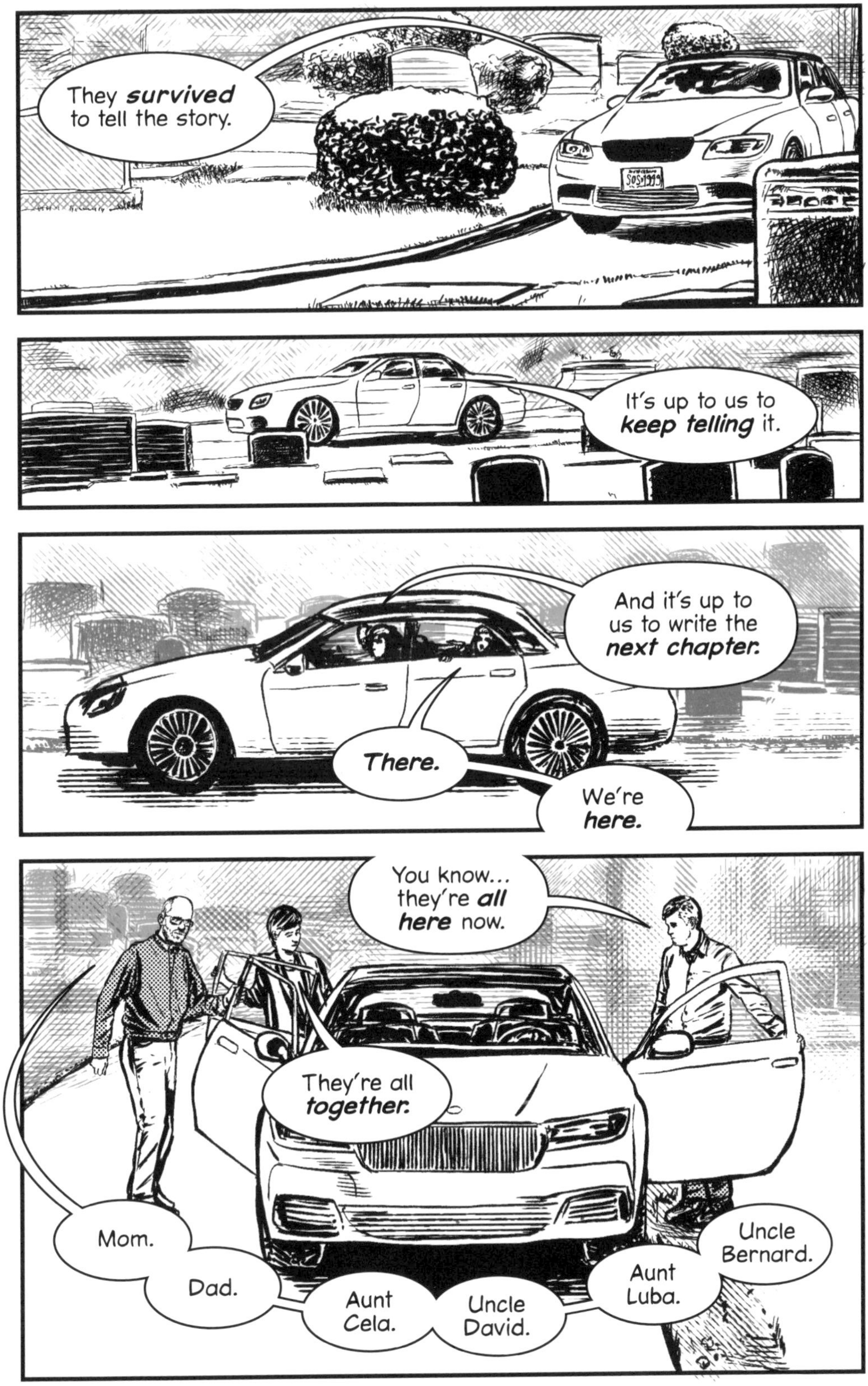
They survived to tell the story.
It's up to us to keep telling it.
And it's up to us to write the next chapter.
There.
We're here.
You know... they're all here now.
They're all together.
Mom.
Dad.
Aunt Cela.
Uncle David.
Aunt Luba.
Uncle Bernard.

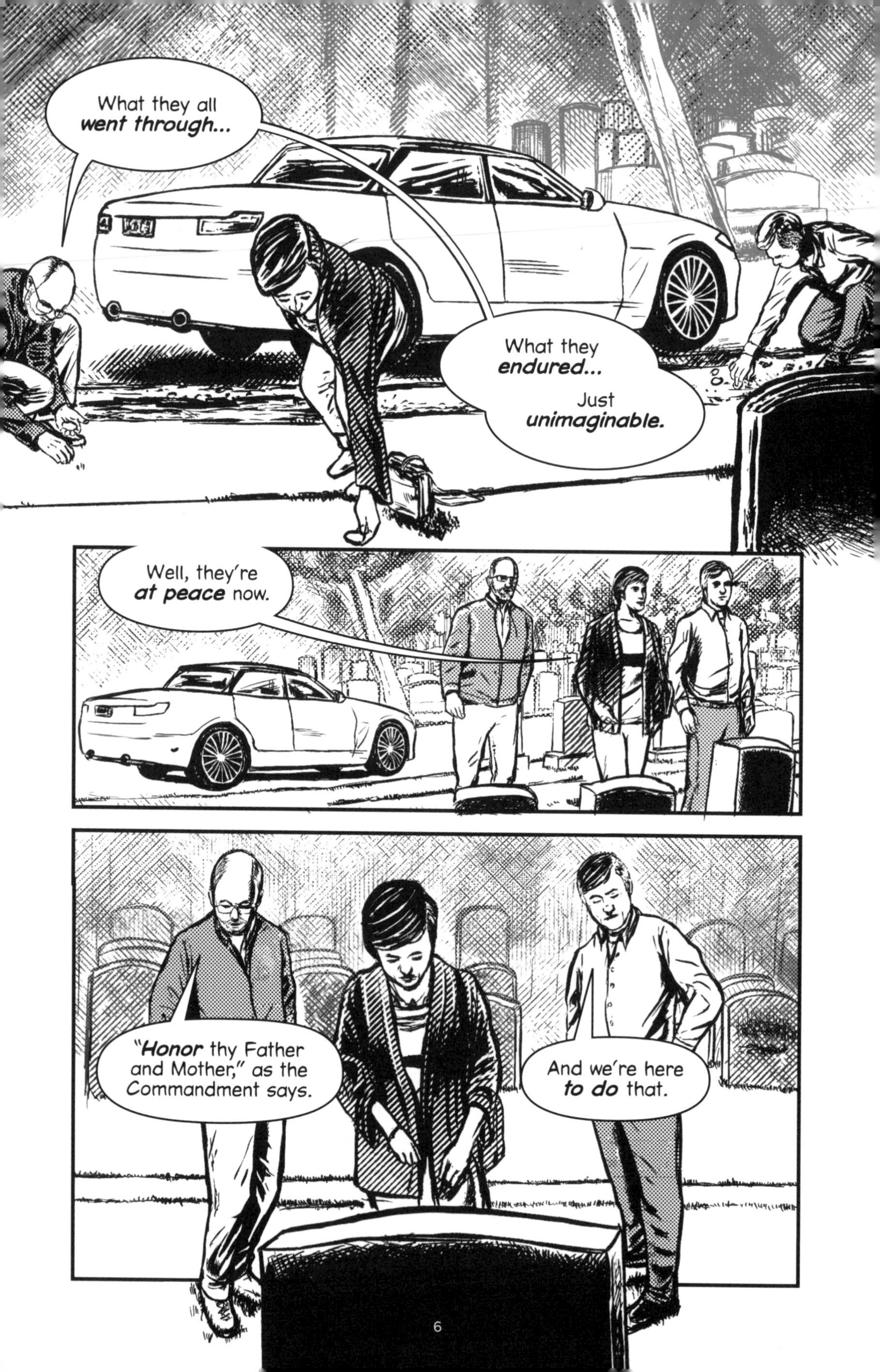
What they all *went through...*
What they *endured...* Just *unimaginable.*
Well, they're *at peace* now.
"*Honor* thy Father and Mother," as the Commandment says.
And we're here *to do* that.

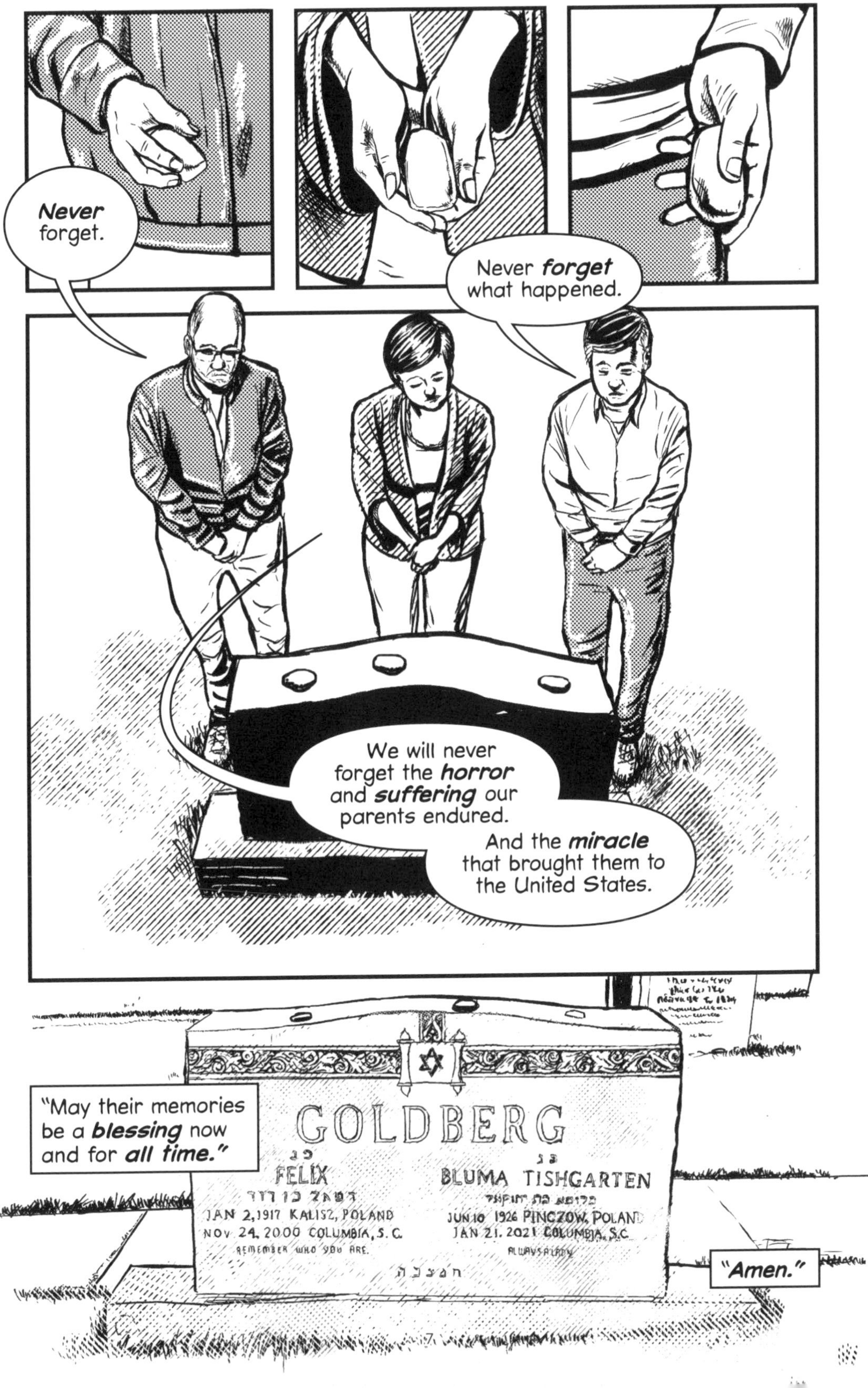

Never forget.
Never *forget* what happened.
We will never forget the *horror* and *suffering* our parents endured.
And the *miracle* that brought them to the United States.
GOLDBERG
FELIX
JAN 2, 1917 KALISZ, POLAND
NOV 24, 2000 COLUMBIA, S.C.
REMEMBER WHO YOU ARE.
BLUMA TISHGARTEN
JUN 10 1926 PINCZOW, POLAND
JAN 21, 2021 COLUMBIA, S.C.
ALWAYS A LADY
"May their memories be a *blessing* now and for *all time.*"
"Amen."

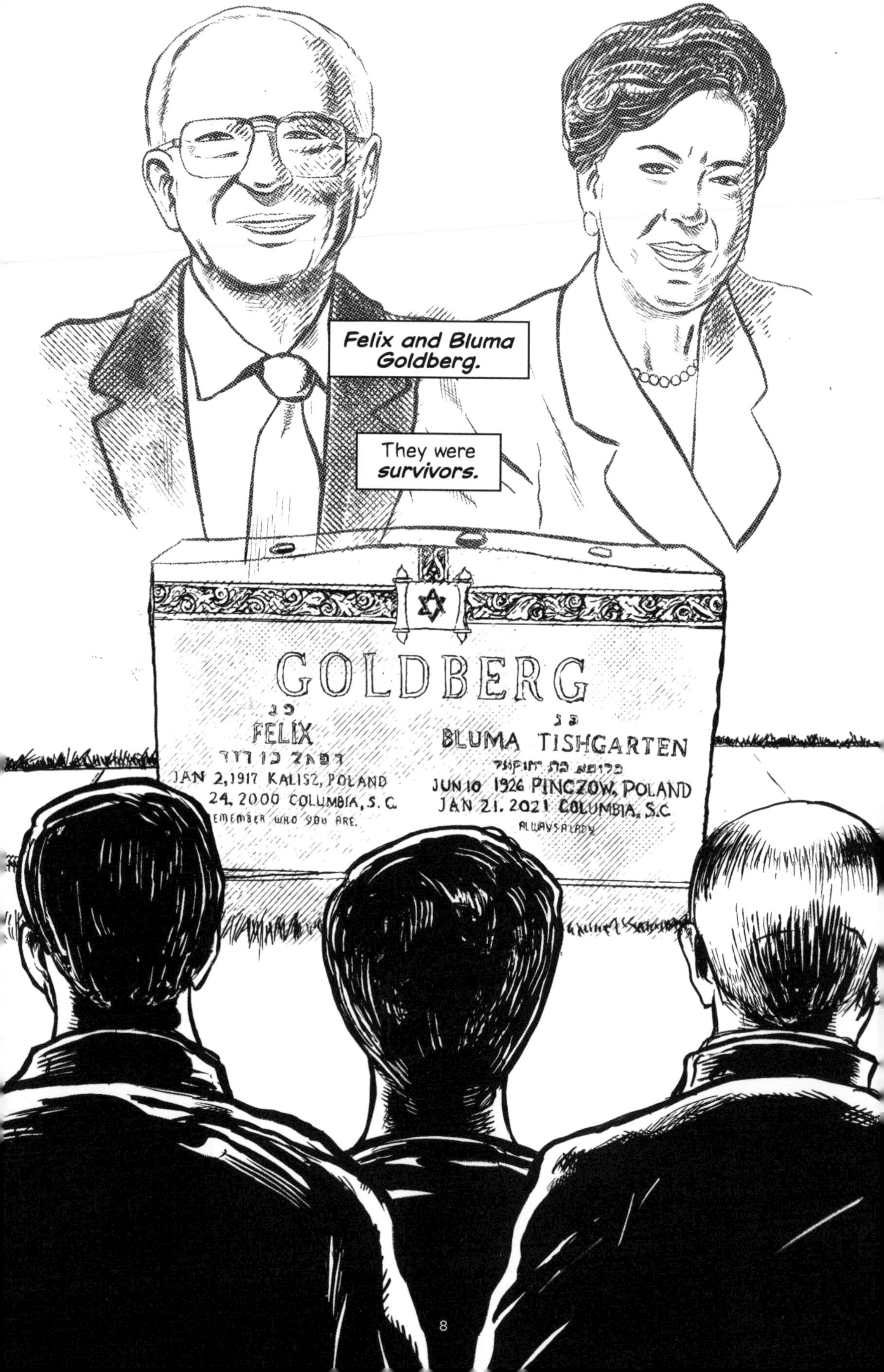
Felix and Bluma Goldberg.
They were survivors.
GOLDBERG
FELIX
JAN 2, 1917 KALISZ, POLAND
24, 2000 COLUMBIA, S.C.
EMEMBER WHO YOU ARE.
BLUMA TISHGARTEN
JUN 10 1926 PINCZOW, POLAND
JAN 21, 2021 COLUMBIA, S.C
ALWAYS A LADY

BEGINNINGS

JANUARY 1917 – SPRING 1939

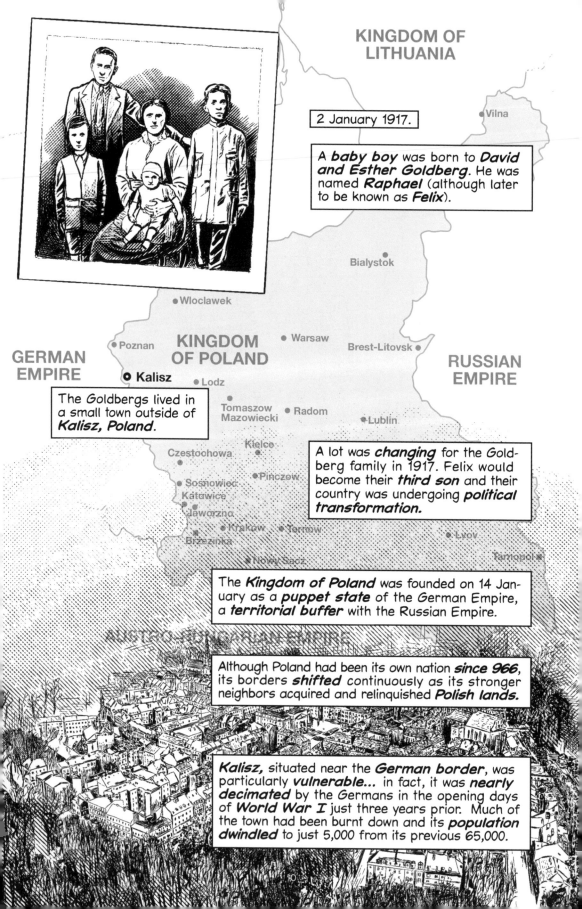

KINGDOM OF LITHUANIA

Vilna

2 January 1917.

A **baby boy** was born to **David and Esther Goldberg**. He was named **Raphael** (although later to be known as **Felix**).

Bialystok

Wloclawek

Warsaw

Brest-Litovsk

KINGDOM OF POLAND

Poznan

GERMAN EMPIRE

Kalisz

Lodz

RUSSIAN EMPIRE

The *Goldbergs* lived in a small town outside of *Kalisz, Poland*.

Tomaszow Mazowiecki

Radom

Lublin

Kielce

Czestochowa

A lot was *changing* for the Goldberg family in 1917. Felix would become their *third son* and their country was undergoing *political transformation*.

Sosnowiec

Pinczow

Katowice

Jaworzno

Krakow

Tarnow

Lvov

Brzezinka

Nowy Sacz

Tarnopol

The *Kingdom of Poland* was founded on 14 January as a *puppet state* of the German Empire, a *territorial buffer* with the Russian Empire.

AUSTRO-HUNGARIAN EMPIRE

Although Poland had been its own nation *since 966*, its borders *shifted* continuously as its stronger neighbors acquired and relinquished *Polish lands*.

Kalisz, situated near the *German border*, was particularly *vulnerable*... in fact, it was *nearly decimated* by the Germans in the opening days of *World War I* just three years prior. Much of the town had been burnt down and its *population dwindled* to just 5,000 from its previous 65,000.

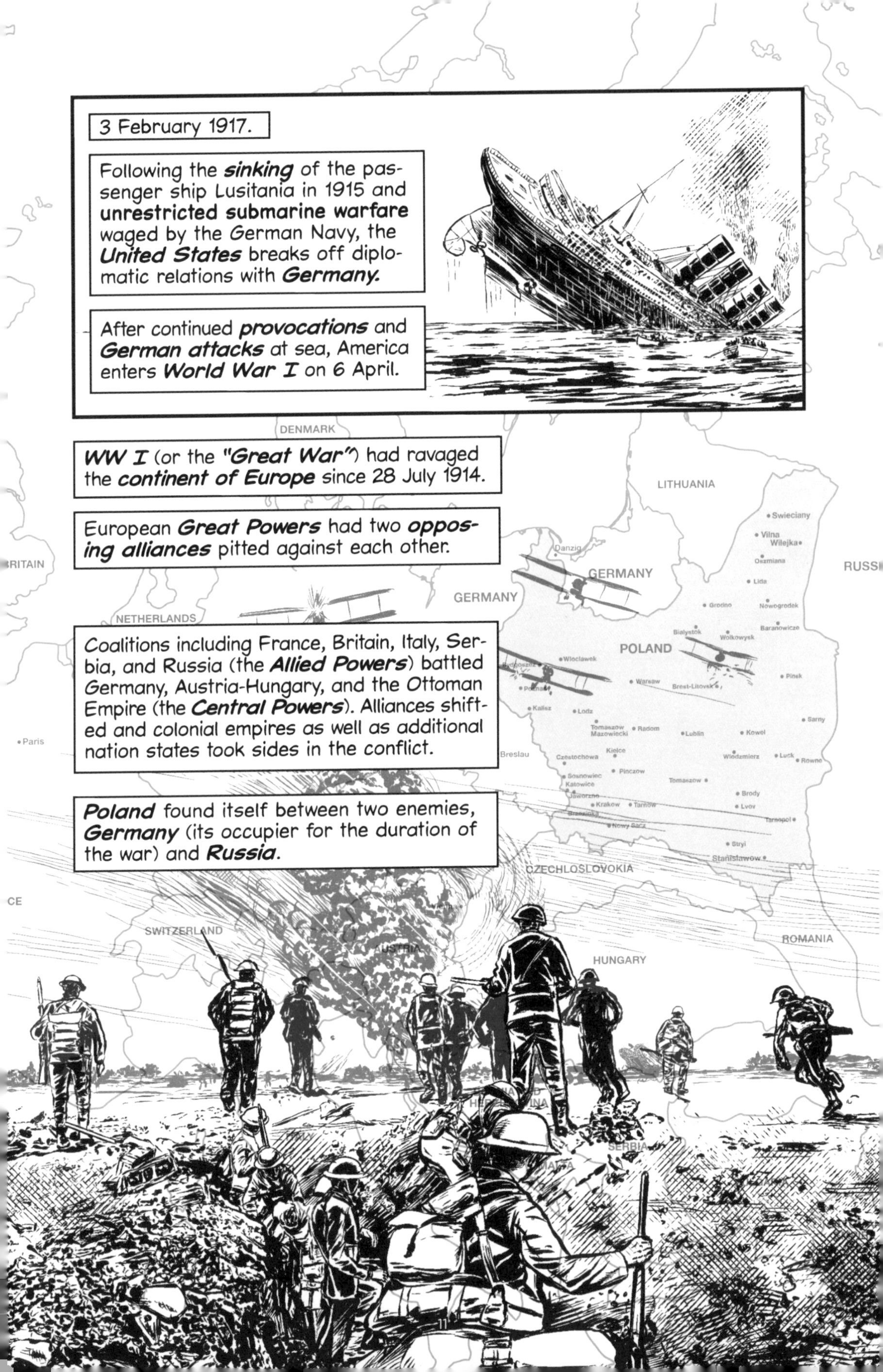
3 February 1917.
Following the ***sinking*** of the passenger ship Lusitania in 1915 and **unrestricted submarine warfare** waged by the German Navy, the ***United States*** breaks off diplomatic relations with ***Germany.***
After continued ***provocations*** and ***German attacks*** at sea, America enters ***World War I*** on 6 April.
WW I (or the ***"Great War"***) had ravaged the ***continent of Europe*** since 28 July 1914.
European ***Great Powers*** had two ***opposing alliances*** pitted against each other.
Coalitions including France, Britain, Italy, Serbia, and Russia (the ***Allied Powers***) battled Germany, Austria-Hungary, and the Ottoman Empire (the ***Central Powers***). Alliances shifted and colonial empires as well as additional nation states took sides in the conflict.
Poland found itself between two enemies, ***Germany*** (its occupier for the duration of the war) and ***Russia***.
DENMARK
LITHUANIA
GERMANY
GERMANY
NETHERLANDS
POLAND
CZECHOSLOVAKIA
SWITZERLAND
AUSTRIA
HUNGARY
ROMANIA
SERBIA

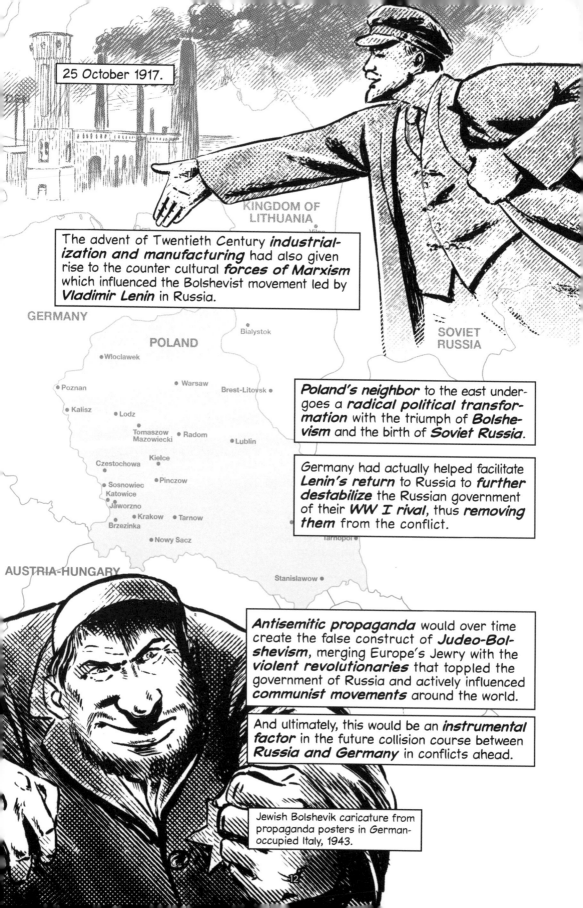

25 October 1917.

KINGDOM OF LITHUANIA

The advent of Twentieth Century **industrialization and manufacturing** had also given rise to the counter cultural **forces of Marxism** which influenced the Bolshevist movement led by **Vladimir Lenin** in Russia.

GERMANY

Bialystok

POLAND

SOVIET RUSSIA

• Wloclawek

• Poznan   • Warsaw   Brest-Litovsk •

• Kalisz   • Lodz

Tomaszow   • Radom   • Lublin
Mazowiecki

Kielce
Czestochowa •

• Sosnowiec   • Pinczow
Katowice
Jaworzno
      • Krakow   • Tarnow
Brzezinka

• Nowy Sacz   Tarnopol •

AUSTRIA-HUNGARY

Stanislawow •

Poland's neighbor to the east undergoes a **radical political transformation** with the triumph of **Bolshevism** and the birth of **Soviet Russia**.

Germany had actually helped facilitate **Lenin's return** to Russia to **further destabilize** the Russian government of their **WW I rival**, thus **removing them** from the conflict.

Antisemitic propaganda would over time create the false construct of **Judeo-Bolshevism**, merging Europe's Jewry with the **violent revolutionaries** that toppled the government of Russia and actively influenced **communist movements** around the world.

And ultimately, this would be an **instrumental factor** in the future collision course between **Russia and Germany** in conflicts ahead.

Jewish Bolshevik caricature from propaganda posters in German-occupied Italy, 1943.

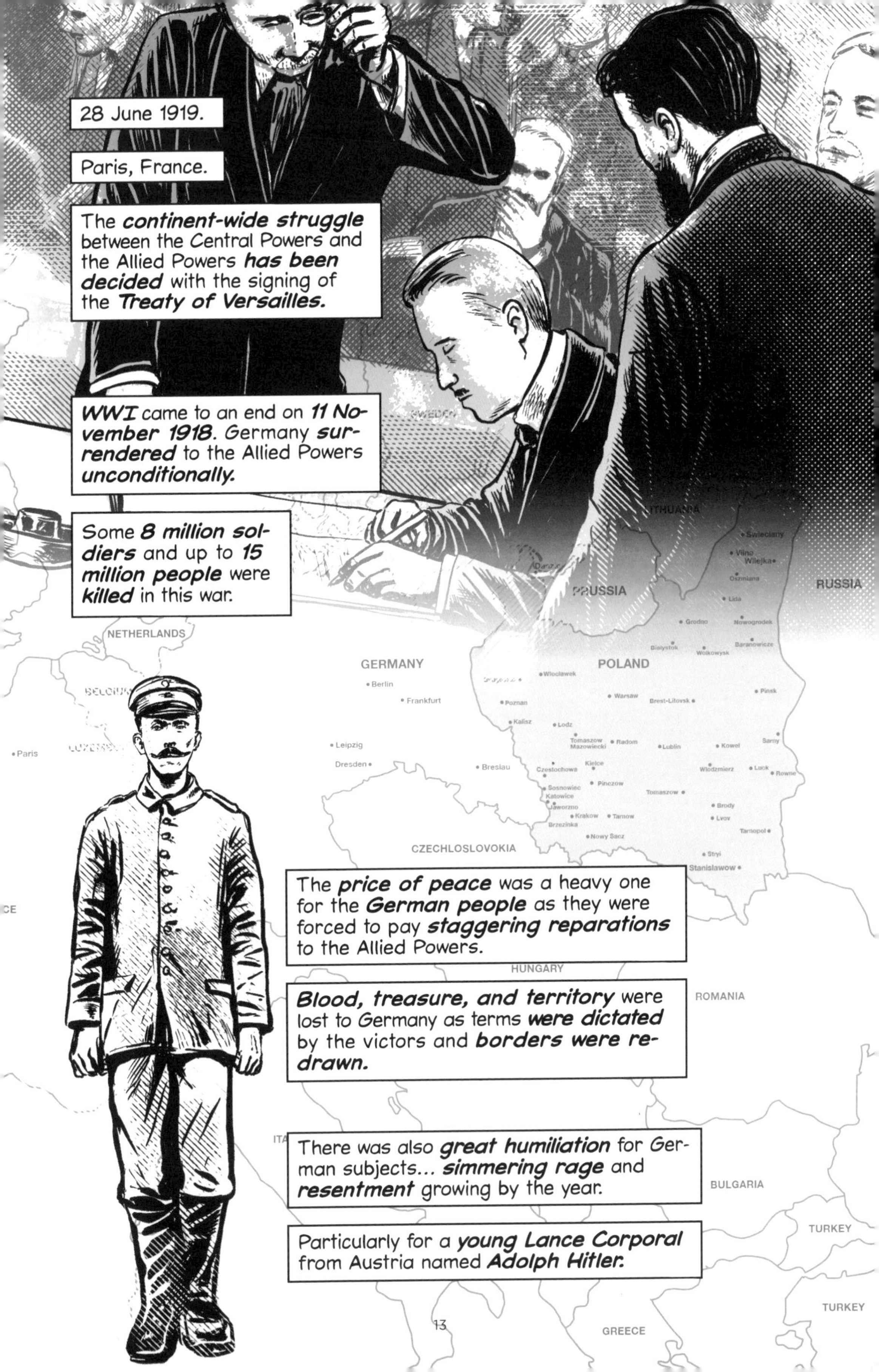
28 June 1919.
Paris, France.
The ***continent-wide struggle*** between the Central Powers and the Allied Powers ***has been decided*** with the signing of the ***Treaty of Versailles.***
WWI came to an end on ***11 November 1918***. Germany ***surrendered*** to the Allied Powers ***unconditionally.***
Some ***8 million soldiers*** and up to ***15 million people*** were ***killed*** in this war.
NETHERLANDS
GERMANY
POLAND
PRUSSIA
RUSSIA
Berlin
Frankfurt
Leipzig
Dresden
Paris
Breslau
Poznan
Kalisz
Lodz
Warsaw
Radom
Lublin
Kowel
Pinsk
Grodno
Wilejka
Oszmiana
Lida
Nowogrodek
Baranowicze
Bialystok
Wolkowysk
Brest-Litovsk
Wloclawek
Tomaszow Mazowiecki
Kielce
Czestochowa
Pinczow
Sosnowiec
Katowice
Jaworzno
Krakow
Tarnow
Brzezinka
Nowy Sacz
Tomaszow
Wlodzmierz
Luck
Rowne
Sarny
Brody
Lvov
Tarnopol
Stryi
Stanislawow
CZECHLOSLOVAKIA
The ***price of peace*** was a heavy one for the ***German people*** as they were forced to pay ***staggering reparations*** to the Allied Powers.
HUNGARY
ROMANIA
Blood, treasure, and territory were lost to Germany as terms ***were dictated*** by the victors and ***borders were redrawn.***
There was also ***great humiliation*** for German subjects... ***simmering rage*** and ***resentment*** growing by the year.
BULGARIA
Particularly for a ***young Lance Corporal*** from Austria named ***Adolph Hitler.***
TURKEY
TURKEY
GREECE

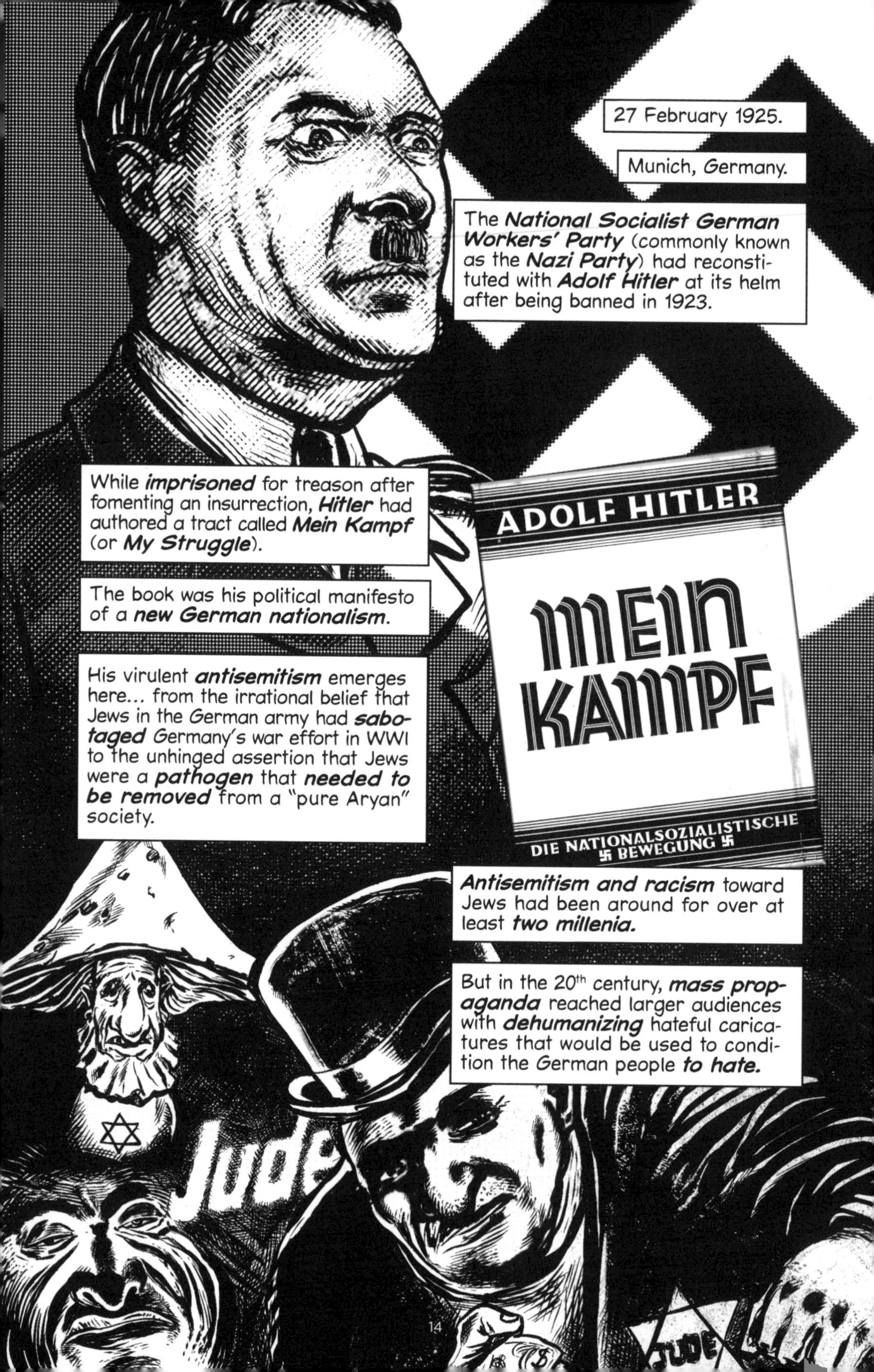
27 February 1925.
Munich, Germany.
The **National Socialist German Workers' Party** (commonly known as the **Nazi Party**) had reconstituted with **Adolf Hitler** at its helm after being banned in 1923.
While **imprisoned** for treason after fomenting an insurrection, **Hitler** had authored a tract called **Mein Kampf** (or **My Struggle**).
The book was his political manifesto of a **new German nationalism**.
His virulent **antisemitism** emerges here... from the irrational belief that Jews in the German army had **sabotaged** Germany's war effort in WWI to the unhinged assertion that Jews were a **pathogen** that **needed to be removed** from a "pure Aryan" society.
ADOLF HITLER
MEIN KAMPF
DIE NATIONALSOZIALISTISCHE BEWEGUNG
Antisemitism and racism toward Jews had been around for over at least **two millenia.**
But in the 20th century, **mass propaganda** reached larger audiences with **dehumanizing** hateful caricatures that would be used to condition the German people **to hate.**
JUDE
JUDE

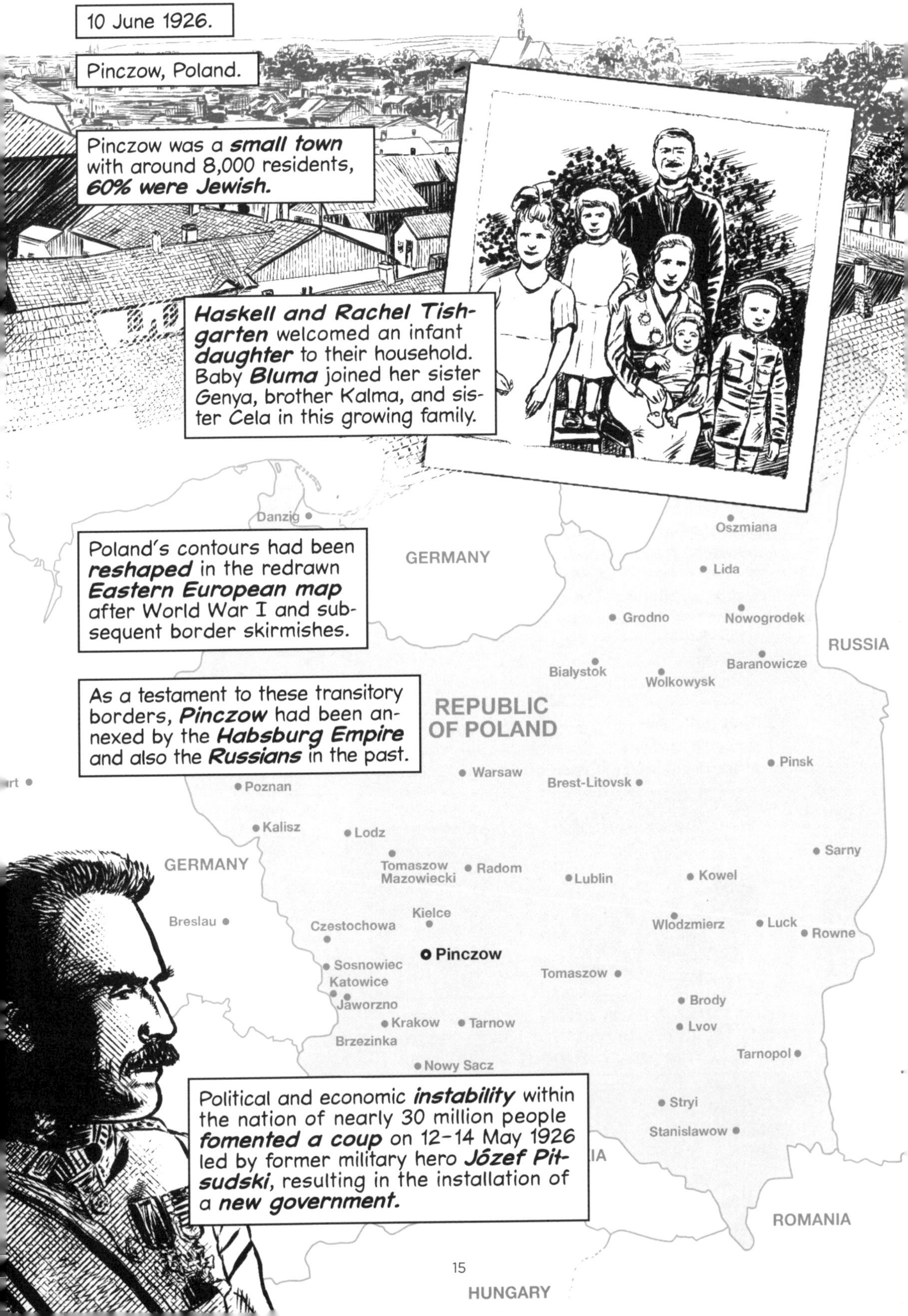

10 June 1926.
Pinczow, Poland.
Pinczow was a **small town** with around 8,000 residents, **60% were Jewish.**
Haskell and Rachel Tishgarten welcomed an infant **daughter** to their household. Baby **Bluma** joined her sister Genya, brother Kalma, and sister Cela in this growing family.
Poland's contours had been **reshaped** in the redrawn **Eastern European map** after World War I and subsequent border skirmishes.
As a testament to these transitory borders, **Pinczow** had been annexed by the **Habsburg Empire** and also the **Russians** in the past.
Political and economic **instability** within the nation of nearly 30 million people **fomented a coup** on 12–14 May 1926 led by former military hero **Józef Pitsudski**, resulting in the installation of a **new government.**
Danzig
GERMANY
Oszmiana
Lida
Grodno
Nowogrodek
RUSSIA
Bialystok
Wolkowysk
Baranowicze
REPUBLIC OF POLAND
Pinsk
Warsaw
Brest-Litovsk
Poznan
Kalisz
Lodz
Sarny
GERMANY
Tomaszow Mazowiecki
Radom
Lublin
Kowel
Breslau
Kielce
Czestochowa
Wlodzmierz
Luck
Rowne
Pinczow
Sosnowiec
Katowice
Tomaszow
Jaworzno
Brody
Krakow
Tarnow
Lvov
Brzezinka
Tarnopol
Nowy Sacz
Stryi
Stanislawow
ROMANIA
HUNGARY

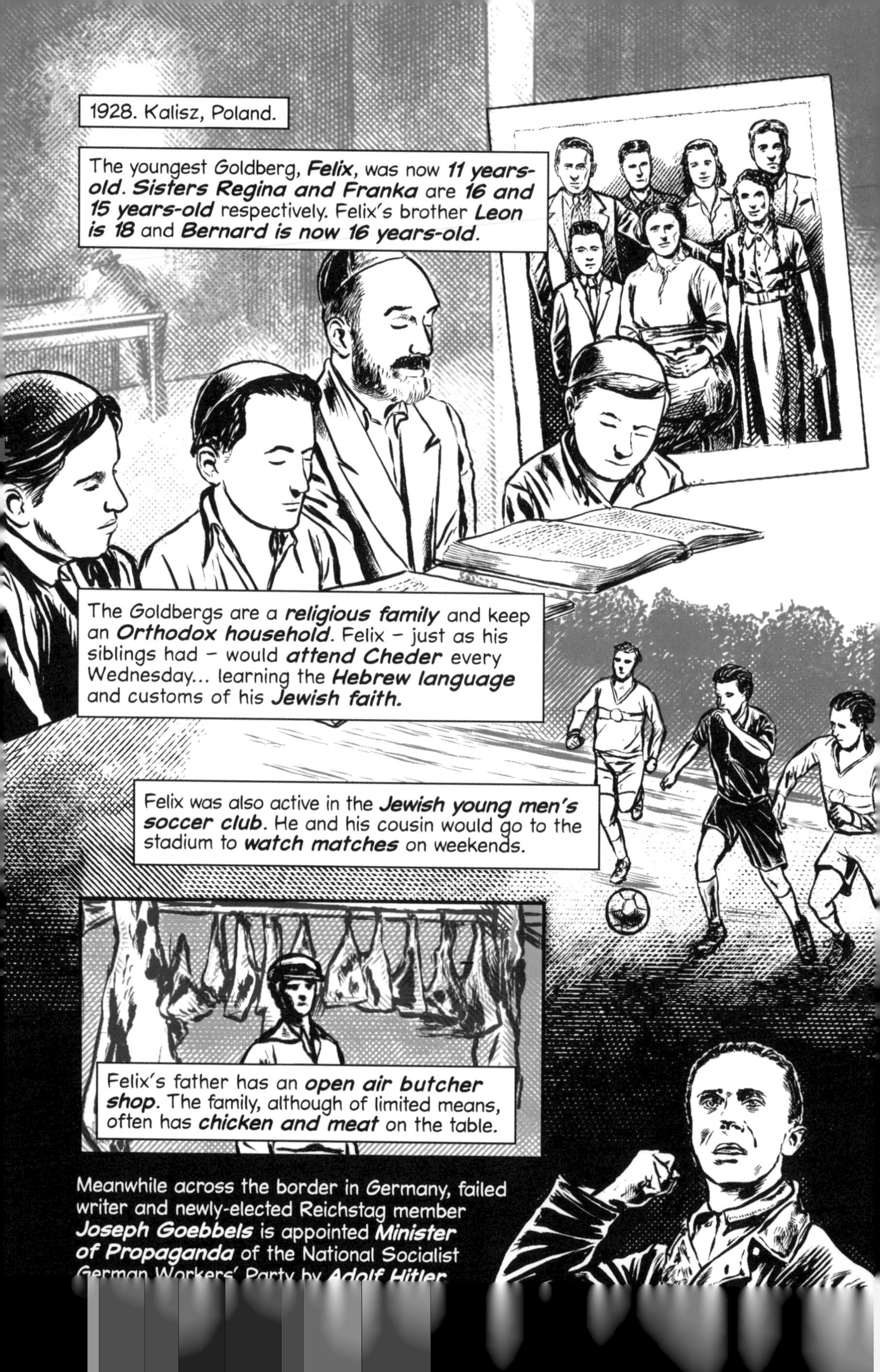
1928. Kalisz, Poland.
The youngest Goldberg, Felix, was now 11 years-old. Sisters Regina and Franka are 16 and 15 years-old respectively. Felix's brother Leon is 18 and Bernard is now 16 years-old.
The Goldbergs are a religious family and keep an Orthodox household. Felix – just as his siblings had – would attend Cheder every Wednesday... learning the Hebrew language and customs of his Jewish faith.
Felix was also active in the Jewish young men's soccer club. He and his cousin would go to the stadium to watch matches on weekends.
Felix's father has an open air butcher shop. The family, although of limited means, often has chicken and meat on the table.
Meanwhile across the border in Germany, failed writer and newly-elected Reichstag member Joseph Goebbels is appointed Minister of Propaganda of the National Socialist German Workers' Party by Adolf Hitler.

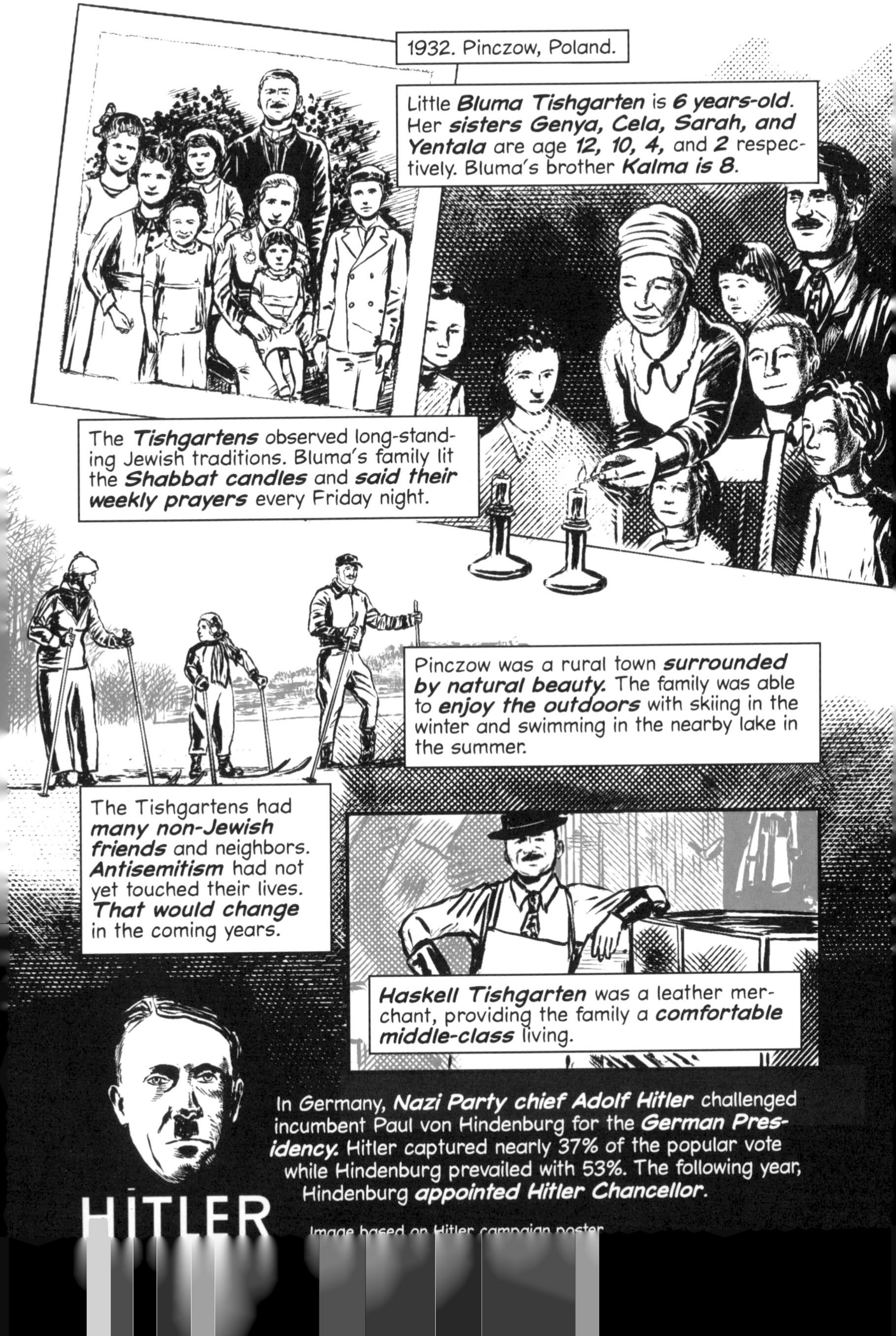
1932. Pinczow, Poland.
Little ***Bluma Tishgarten*** is ***6 years-old.*** Her ***sisters Genya, Cela, Sarah, and Yentala*** are age ***12, 10, 4,*** and ***2*** respectively. Bluma's brother ***Kalma is 8.***
The ***Tishgartens*** observed long-standing Jewish traditions. Bluma's family lit the ***Shabbat candles*** and ***said their weekly prayers*** every Friday night.
Pinczow was a rural town ***surrounded by natural beauty.*** The family was able to ***enjoy the outdoors*** with skiing in the winter and swimming in the nearby lake in the summer.
The Tishgartens had ***many non-Jewish friends*** and neighbors. ***Antisemitism*** had not yet touched their lives. ***That would change*** in the coming years.
Haskell Tishgarten was a leather merchant, providing the family a ***comfortable middle-class*** living.
HITLER
In Germany, ***Nazi Party chief Adolf Hitler*** challenged incumbent Paul von Hindenburg for the ***German Presidency.*** Hitler captured nearly 37% of the popular vote while Hindenburg prevailed with 53%. The following year, Hindenburg ***appointed Hitler Chancellor.***
Image based on Hitler campaign poster

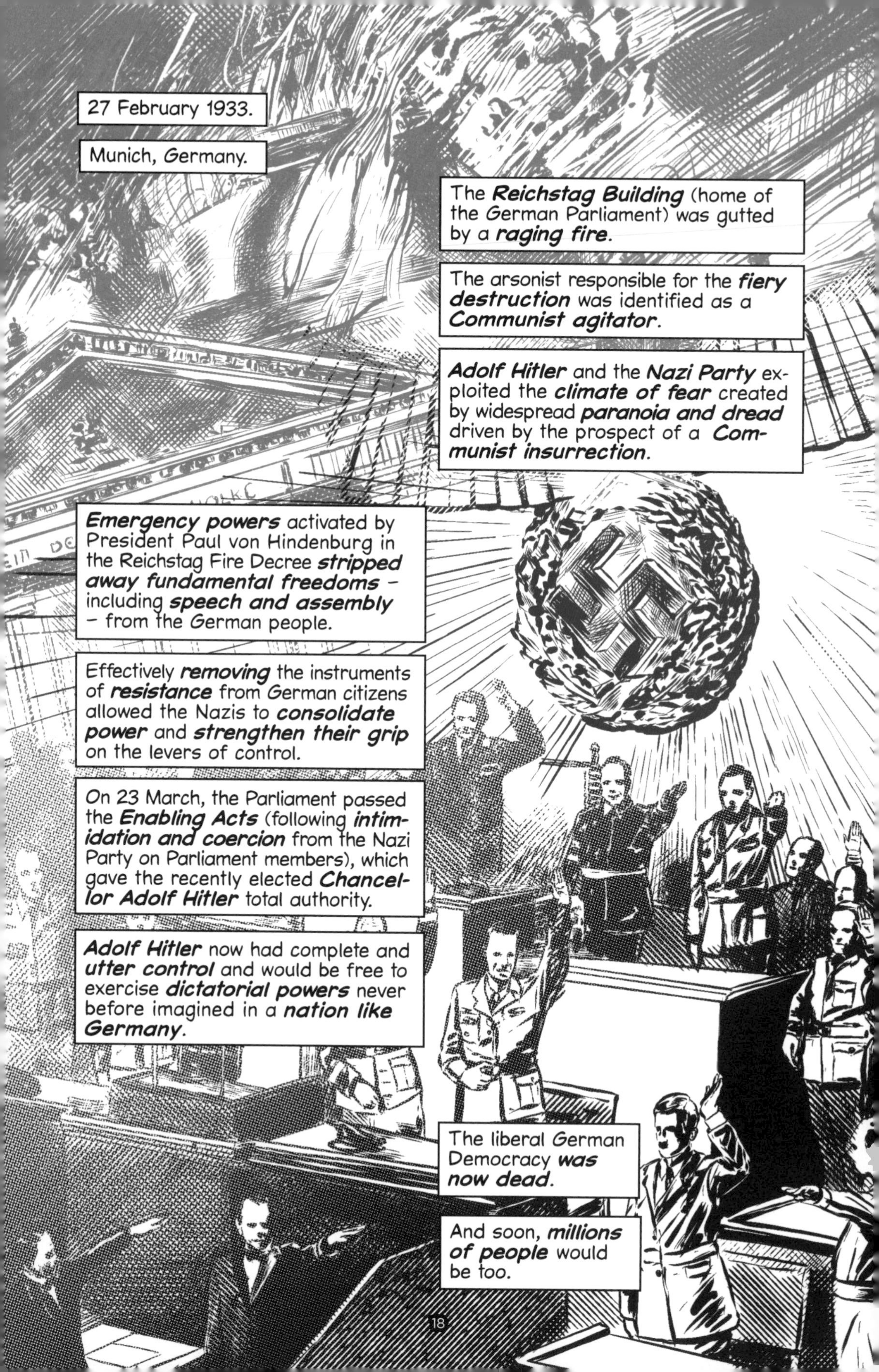

27 February 1933.
Munich, Germany.
The ***Reichstag Building*** (home of the German Parliament) was gutted by a ***raging fire***.
The arsonist responsible for the ***fiery destruction*** was identified as a ***Communist agitator***.
Adolf Hitler and the ***Nazi Party*** exploited the ***climate of fear*** created by widespread ***paranoia and dread*** driven by the prospect of a ***Communist insurrection***.
Emergency powers activated by President Paul von Hindenburg in the Reichstag Fire Decree ***stripped away fundamental freedoms*** – including ***speech and assembly*** – from the German people.
Effectively ***removing*** the instruments of ***resistance*** from German citizens allowed the Nazis to ***consolidate power*** and ***strengthen their grip*** on the levers of control.
On 23 March, the Parliament passed the ***Enabling Acts*** (following ***intimidation and coercion*** from the Nazi Party on Parliament members), which gave the recently elected ***Chancellor Adolf Hitler*** total authority.
Adolf Hitler now had complete and ***utter control*** and would be free to exercise ***dictatorial powers*** never before imagined in a ***nation like Germany***.
The liberal German Democracy ***was now dead***.
And soon, ***millions of people*** would be too.

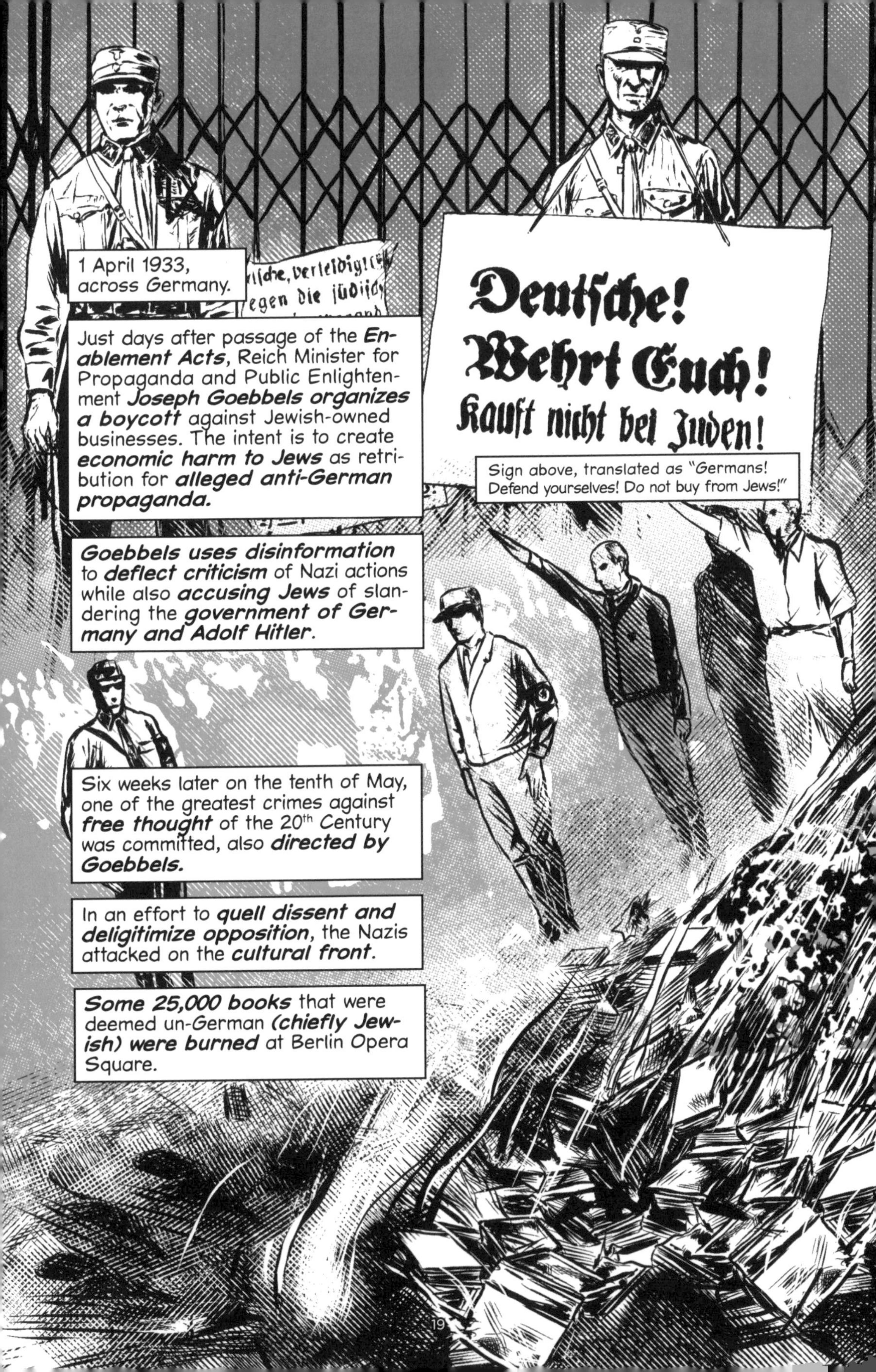
1 April 1933, across Germany.
Just days after passage of the **Enablement Acts**, Reich Minister for Propaganda and Public Enlightenment **Joseph Goebbels organizes a boycott** against Jewish-owned businesses. The intent is to create **economic harm to Jews** as retribution for **alleged anti-German propaganda.**
Goebbels uses disinformation to **deflect criticism** of Nazi actions while also **accusing Jews** of slandering the **government of Germany and Adolf Hitler**.
Deutsche! Wehrt Euch! Kauft nicht bei Juden!
Sign above, translated as "Germans! Defend yourselves! Do not buy from Jews!"
Six weeks later on the tenth of May, one of the greatest crimes against **free thought** of the 20th Century was committed, also **directed by Goebbels.**
In an effort to **quell dissent and deligitimize opposition**, the Nazis attacked on the **cultural front**.
Some 25,000 books that were deemed un-German **(chiefly Jewish) were burned** at Berlin Opera Square.

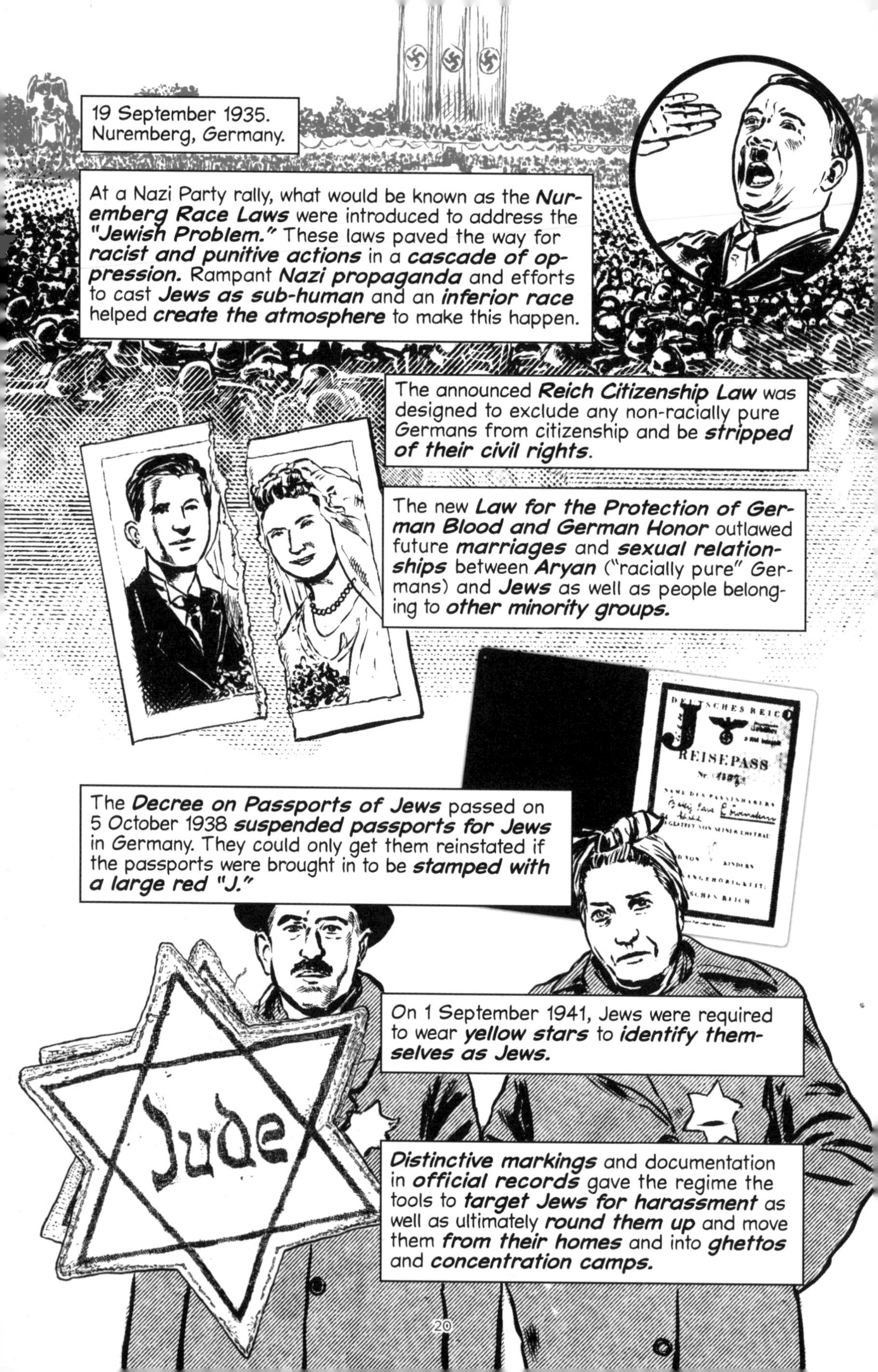
19 September 1935. Nuremberg, Germany.
At a Nazi Party rally, what would be known as the ***Nuremberg Race Laws*** were introduced to address the ***"Jewish Problem."*** These laws paved the way for ***racist and punitive actions*** in a ***cascade of oppression.*** Rampant ***Nazi propaganda*** and efforts to cast ***Jews as sub-human*** and an ***inferior race*** helped ***create the atmosphere*** to make this happen.
The announced ***Reich Citizenship Law*** was designed to exclude any non-racially pure Germans from citizenship and be ***stripped of their civil rights***.
The new ***Law for the Protection of German Blood and German Honor*** outlawed future ***marriages*** and ***sexual relationships*** between ***Aryan*** ("racially pure" Germans) and ***Jews*** as well as people belonging to ***other minority groups.***
DEUTSCHES REIC
J
REISEPASS
The ***Decree on Passports of Jews*** passed on 5 October 1938 ***suspended passports for Jews*** in Germany. They could only get them reinstated if the passports were brought in to be ***stamped with a large red "J."***
Jude
On 1 September 1941, Jews were required to wear ***yellow stars*** to ***identify themselves as Jews.***
Distinctive markings and documentation in ***official records*** gave the regime the tools to ***target Jews for harassment*** as well as ultimately ***round them up*** and move them ***from their homes*** and into ***ghettos*** and ***concentration camps.***

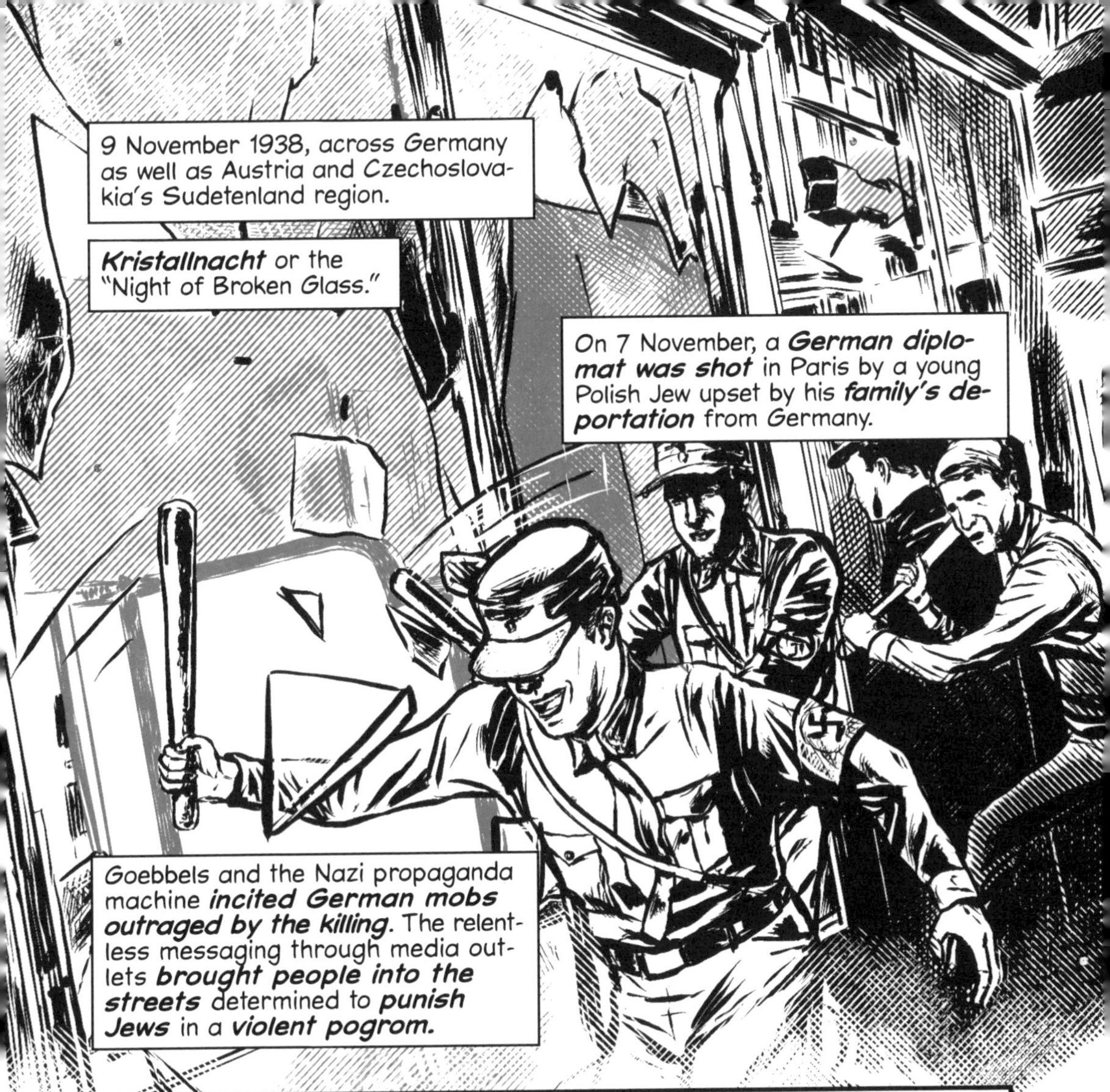
9 November 1938, across Germany as well as Austria and Czechoslovakia's Sudetenland region.
Kristallnacht or the "Night of Broken Glass."
On 7 November, a ***German diplomat was shot*** in Paris by a young Polish Jew upset by his ***family's deportation*** from Germany.
Goebbels and the Nazi propaganda machine ***incited German mobs outraged by the killing***. The relentless messaging through media outlets ***brought people into the streets*** determined to ***punish Jews*** in a ***violent pogrom.***

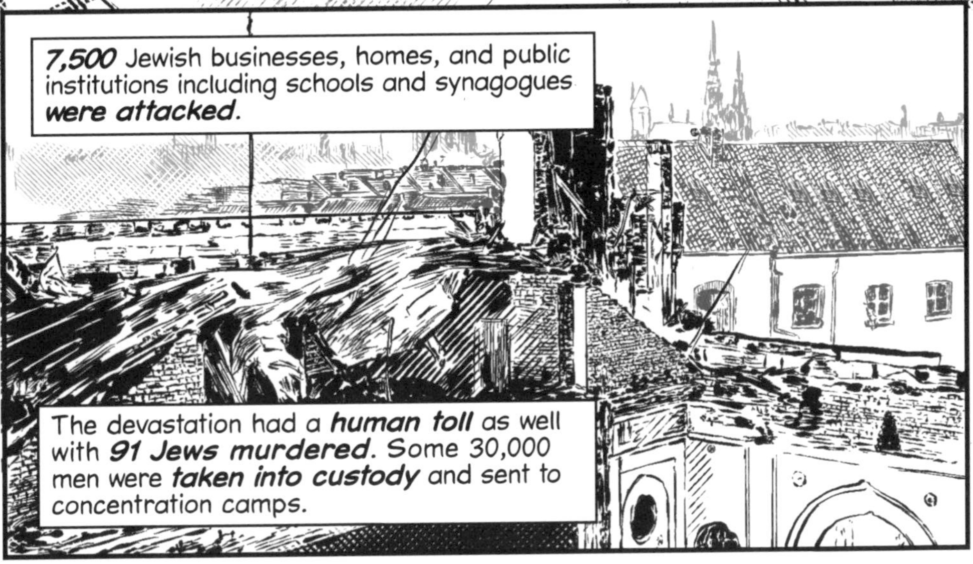
7,500 Jewish businesses, homes, and public institutions including schools and synagogues ***were attacked***.
The devastation had a ***human toll*** as well with ***91 Jews murdered***. Some 30,000 men were ***taken into custody*** and sent to concentration camps.

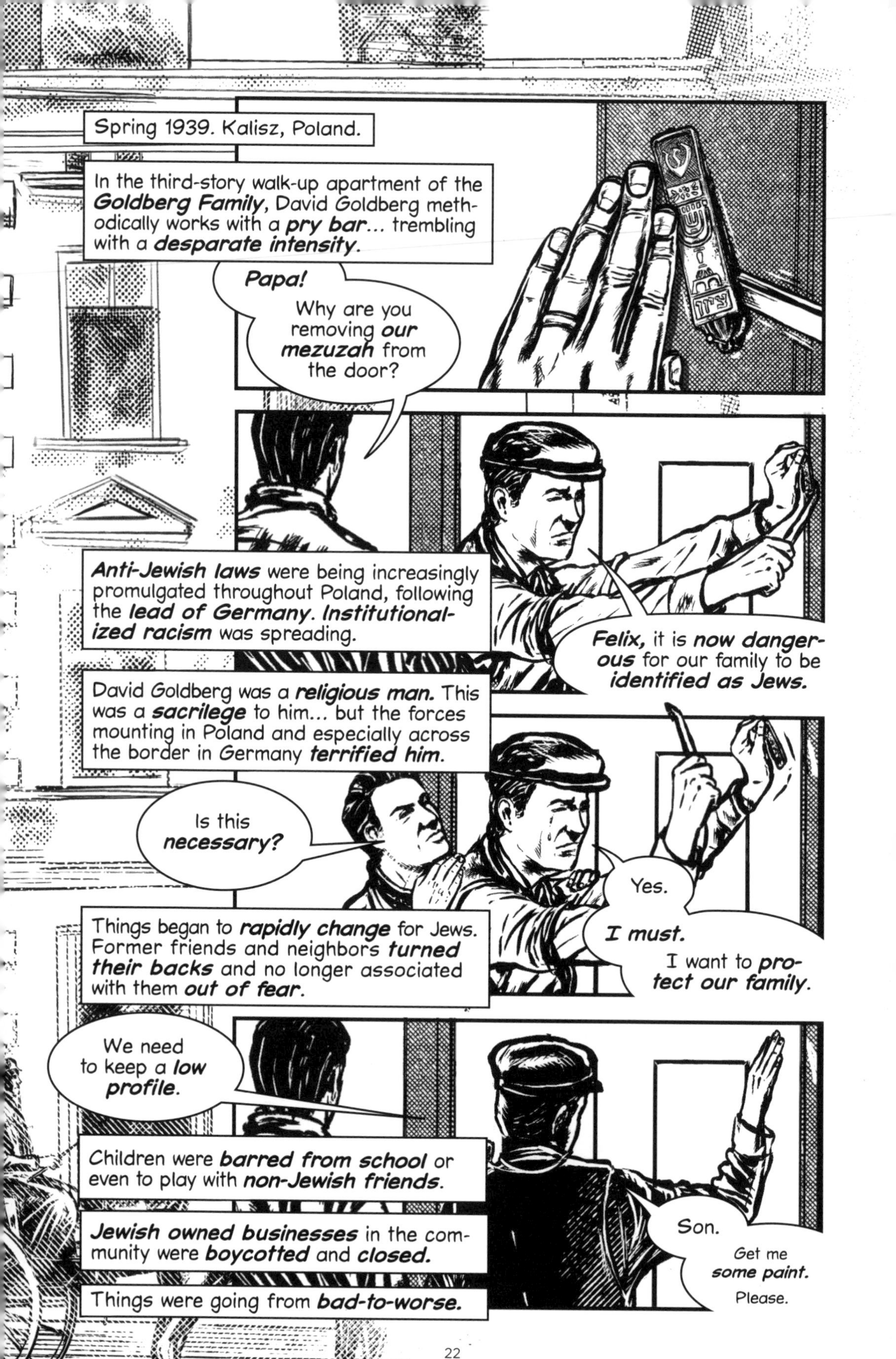

Spring 1939. Kalisz, Poland.
In the third-story walk-up apartment of the **Goldberg Family**, David Goldberg methodically works with a **pry bar**... trembling with a **desparate intensity**.
Papa! Why are you removing **our mezuzah** from the door?
Anti-Jewish laws were being increasingly promulgated throughout Poland, following the **lead of Germany**. **Institutionalized racism** was spreading.
Felix, it is **now dangerous** for our family to be **identified as Jews.**
David Goldberg was a **religious man.** This was a **sacrilege** to him... but the forces mounting in Poland and especially across the border in Germany **terrified him.**
Is this **necessary?**
Yes.
I must. I want to **protect our family.**
Things began to **rapidly change** for Jews. Former friends and neighbors **turned their backs** and no longer associated with them **out of fear**.
We need to keep a **low profile**.
Children were **barred from school** or even to play with **non-Jewish friends**.
Jewish owned businesses in the community were **boycotted** and **closed.**
Things were going from **bad-to-worse.**
Son.
Get me **some paint.** Please.

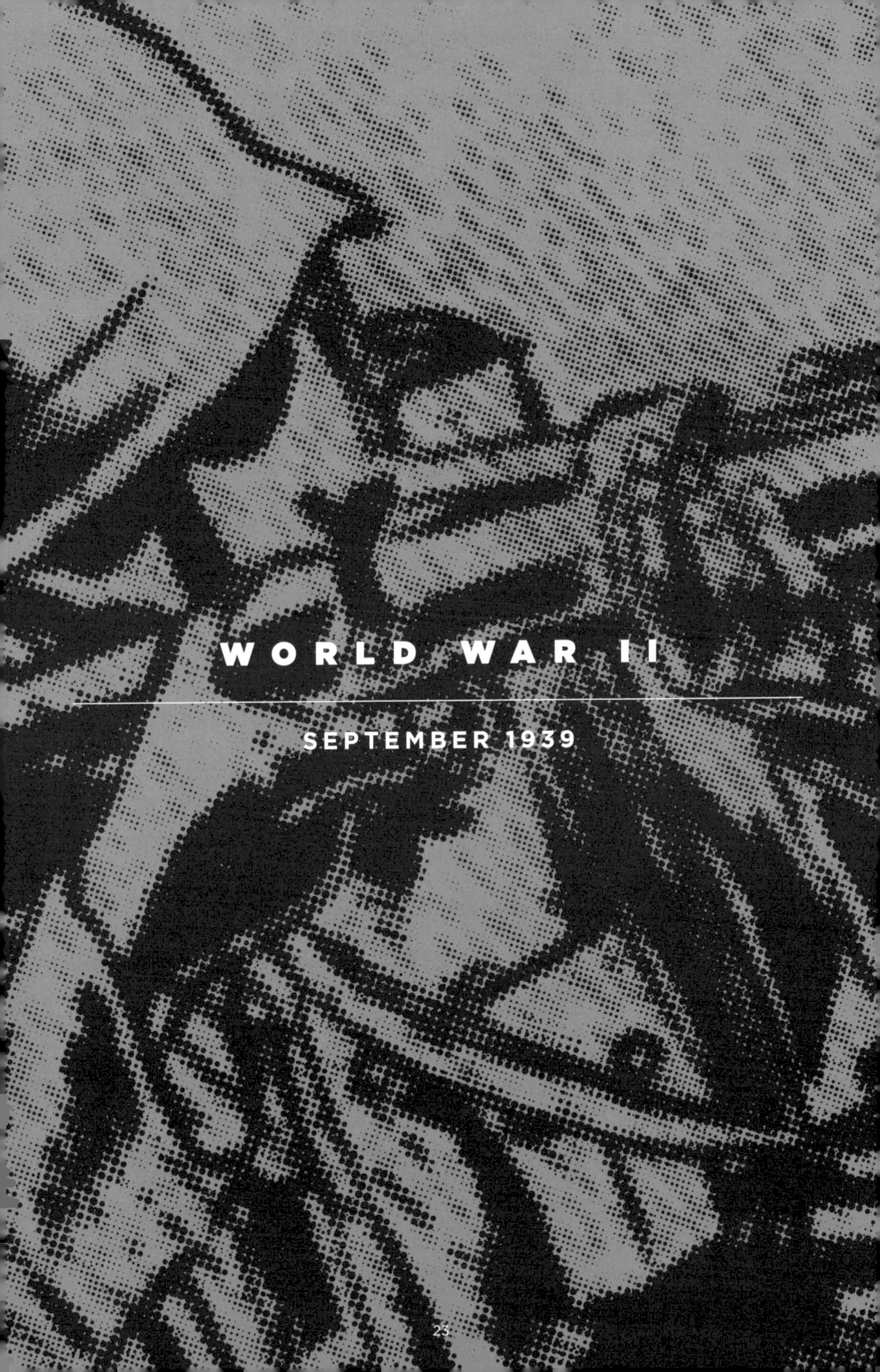

WORLD WAR II

SEPTEMBER 1939

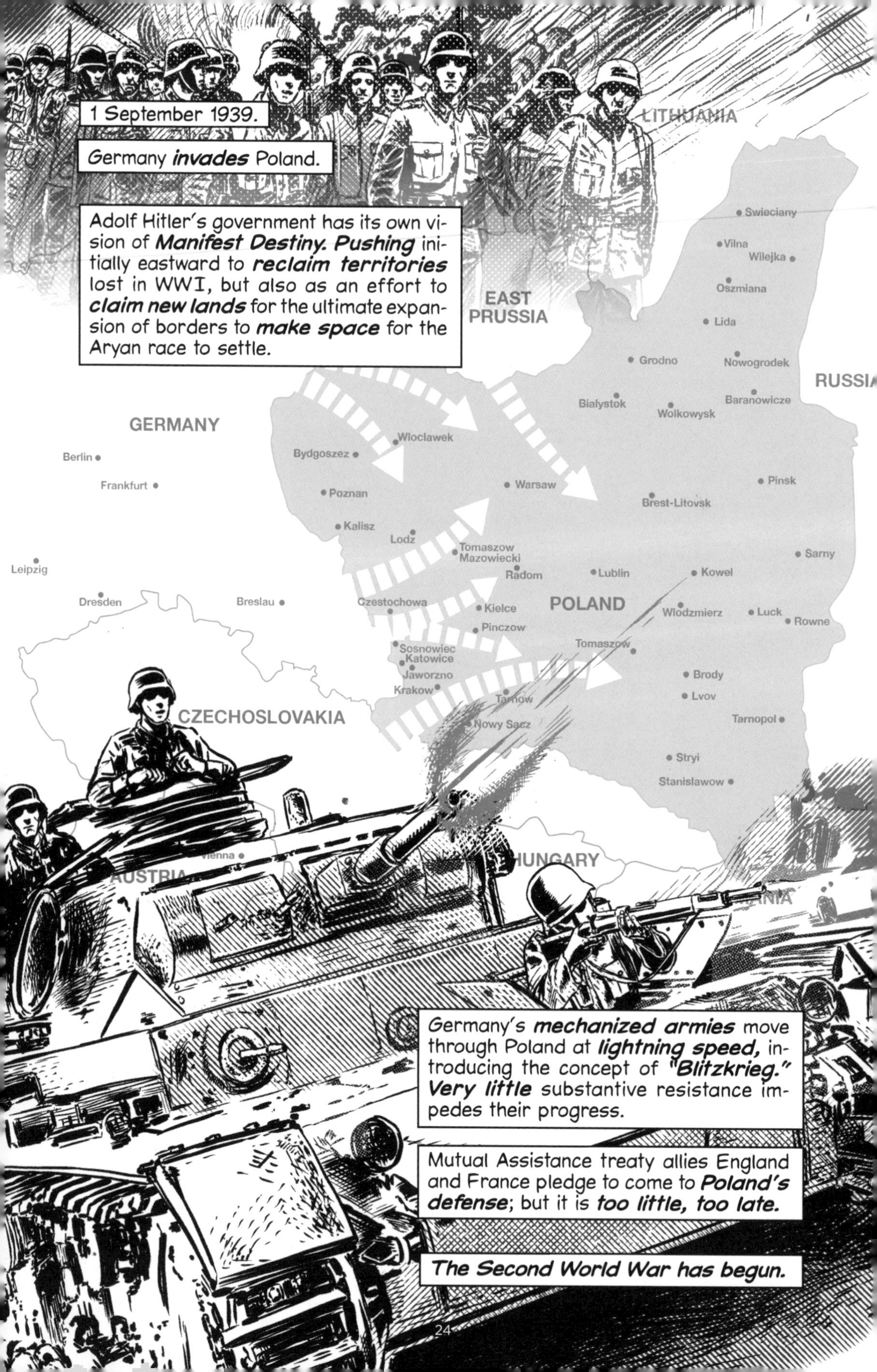

1 September 1939.
Germany invades Poland.
Adolf Hitler's government has its own vision of Manifest Destiny. Pushing initially eastward to reclaim territories lost in WWI, but also as an effort to claim new lands for the ultimate expansion of borders to make space for the Aryan race to settle.
LITHUANIA
EAST PRUSSIA
GERMANY
RUSSIA
POLAND
CZECHOSLOVAKIA
HUNGARY
AUSTRIA
Swieciany
Vilna
Wilejka
Oszmiana
Lida
Grodno
Nowogrodek
Bialystok
Wolkowysk
Baranowicze
Berlin
Frankfurt
Bydgoszez
Wloclawek
Poznan
Warsaw
Pinsk
Brest-Litovsk
Kalisz
Lodz
Tomaszow Mazowiecki
Sarny
Leipzig
Radom
Lublin
Kowel
Dresden
Breslau
Czestochowa
Kielce
Wlodzmierz
Luck
Rowne
Pinczow
Tomaszow
Sosnowiec
Katowice
Jaworzno
Krakow
Brody
Lvov
Tarnow
Nowy Sacz
Tarnopol
Stryi
Stanislawow
Vienna
Germany's mechanized armies move through Poland at lightning speed, introducing the concept of "Blitzkrieg." Very little substantive resistance impedes their progress.
Mutual Assistance treaty allies England and France pledge to come to Poland's defense; but it is too little, too late.
The Second World War has begun.

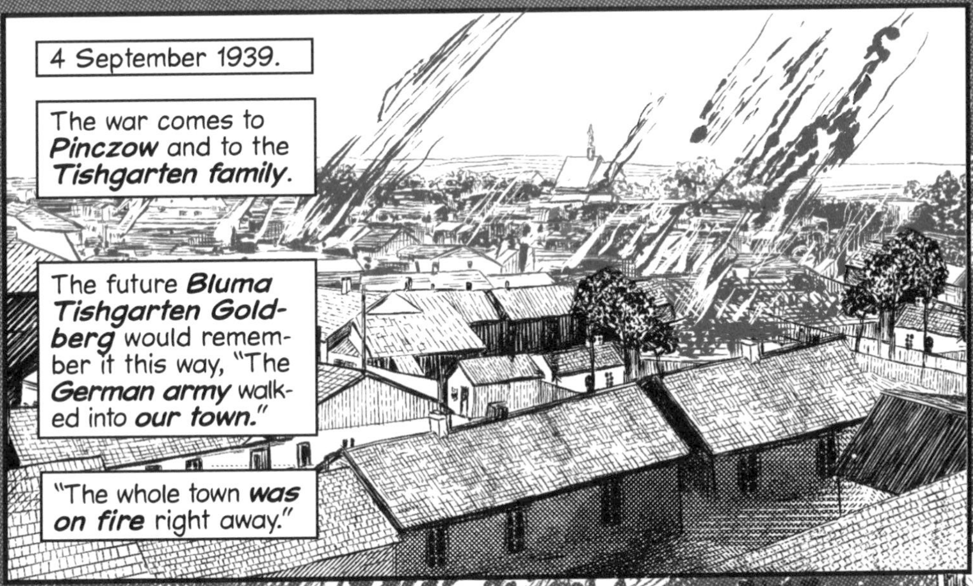
4 September 1939.
The war comes to **Pinczow** and to the **Tishgarten family**.
The future **Bluma Tishgarten Goldberg** would remember it this way, "The **German army** walked into **our town.**"
"The whole town **was on fire** right away."

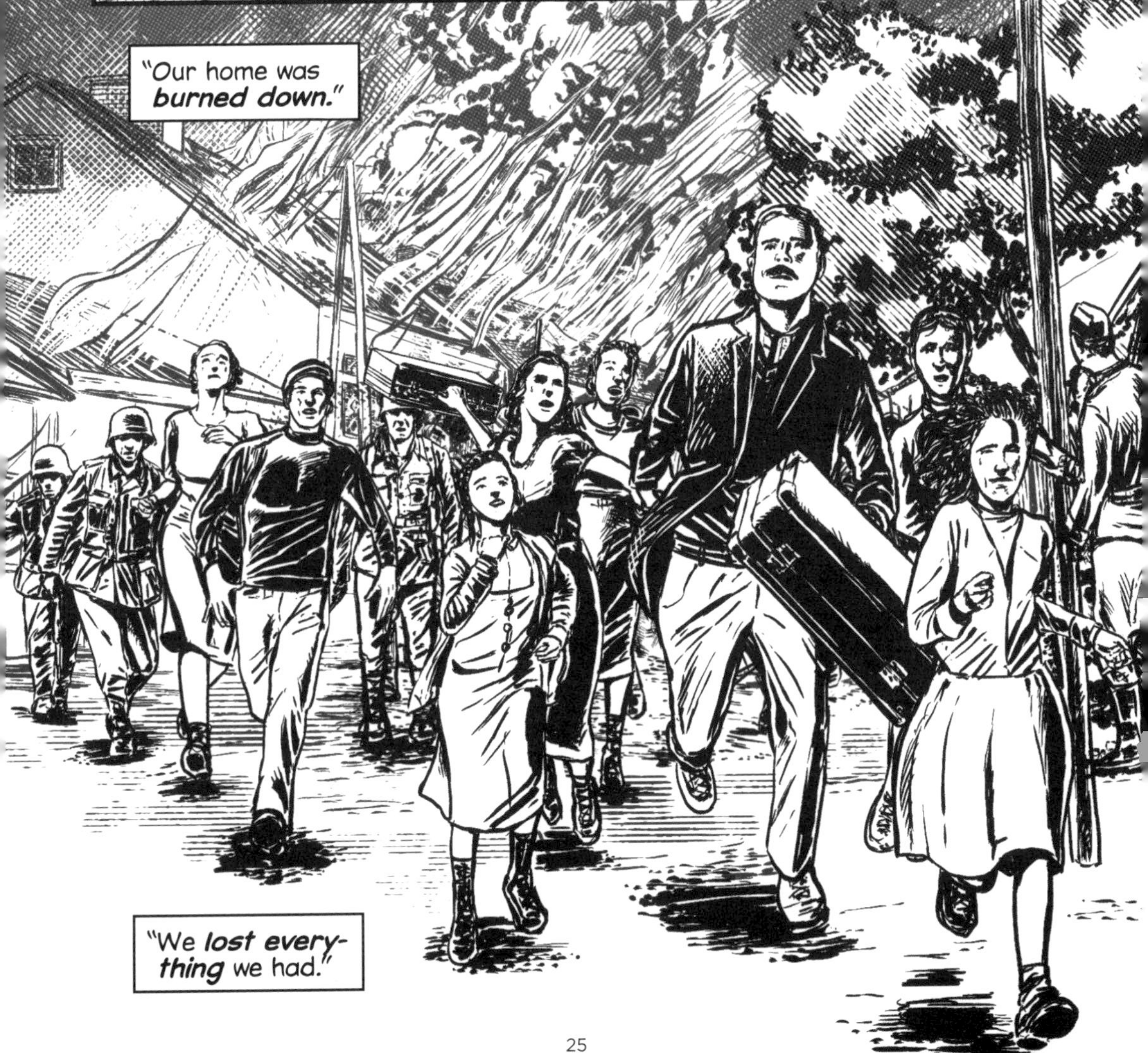
"Our home was **burned down.**"
"We **lost everything** we had."

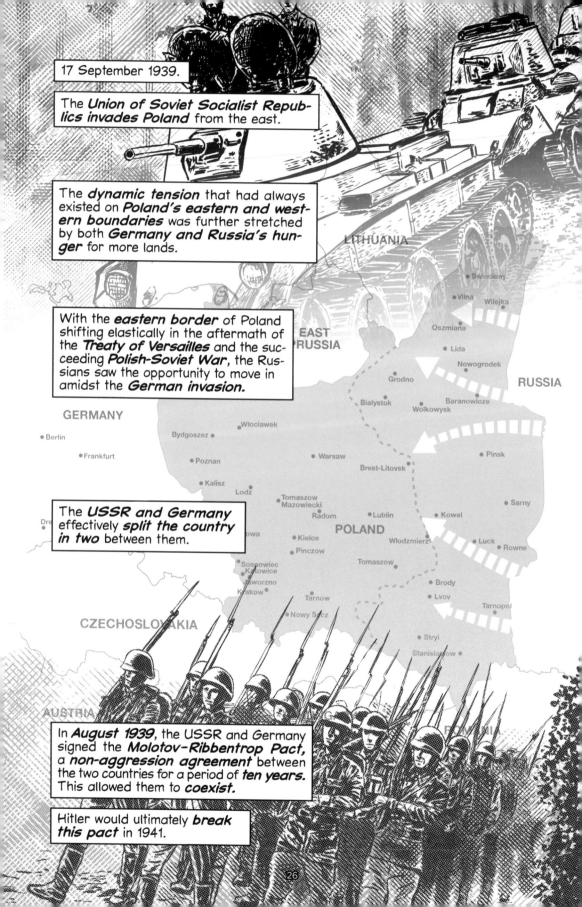

17 September 1939.

The **Union of Soviet Socialist Republics invades Poland** from the east.

The **dynamic tension** that had always existed on **Poland's eastern and western boundaries** was further stretched by both **Germany and Russia's hunger** for more lands.

With the **eastern border** of Poland shifting elastically in the aftermath of the **Treaty of Versailles** and the succeeding **Polish-Soviet War**, the Russians saw the opportunity to move in amidst the **German invasion.**

The **USSR and Germany** effectively **split the country in two** between them.

In **August 1939**, the USSR and Germany signed the **Molotov–Ribbentrop Pact,** a **non-aggression agreement** between the two countries for a period of **ten years.** This allowed them to **coexist.**

Hitler would ultimately **break this pact** in 1941.

LITHUANIA

Swieciany
Vilna
Wilejka
Oszmiana

EAST PRUSSIA

Lida
Nowogrodek

RUSSIA

Grodno
Baranowicze
Bialystok
Wolkowysk

GERMANY

Wloclawek
Bydgoszez

Berlin
Frankfurt
Poznan
Warsaw
Pinsk
Brest-Litovsk
Kalisz
Lodz
Sarny
Tomaszow
Mazowiecki
Radom
Lublin
Kowel
POLAND
Dre
Kielce
Wlodzmierz
Luck
Rowne
Pinczow
Sosnowiec
Tomaszow
Katowice
Jaworzno
Krakow
Brody
Tarnow
Lvov
Tarnopol
Nowy Sacz

CZECHOSLOVAKIA

Stryi
Stanislawow

AUSTRIA

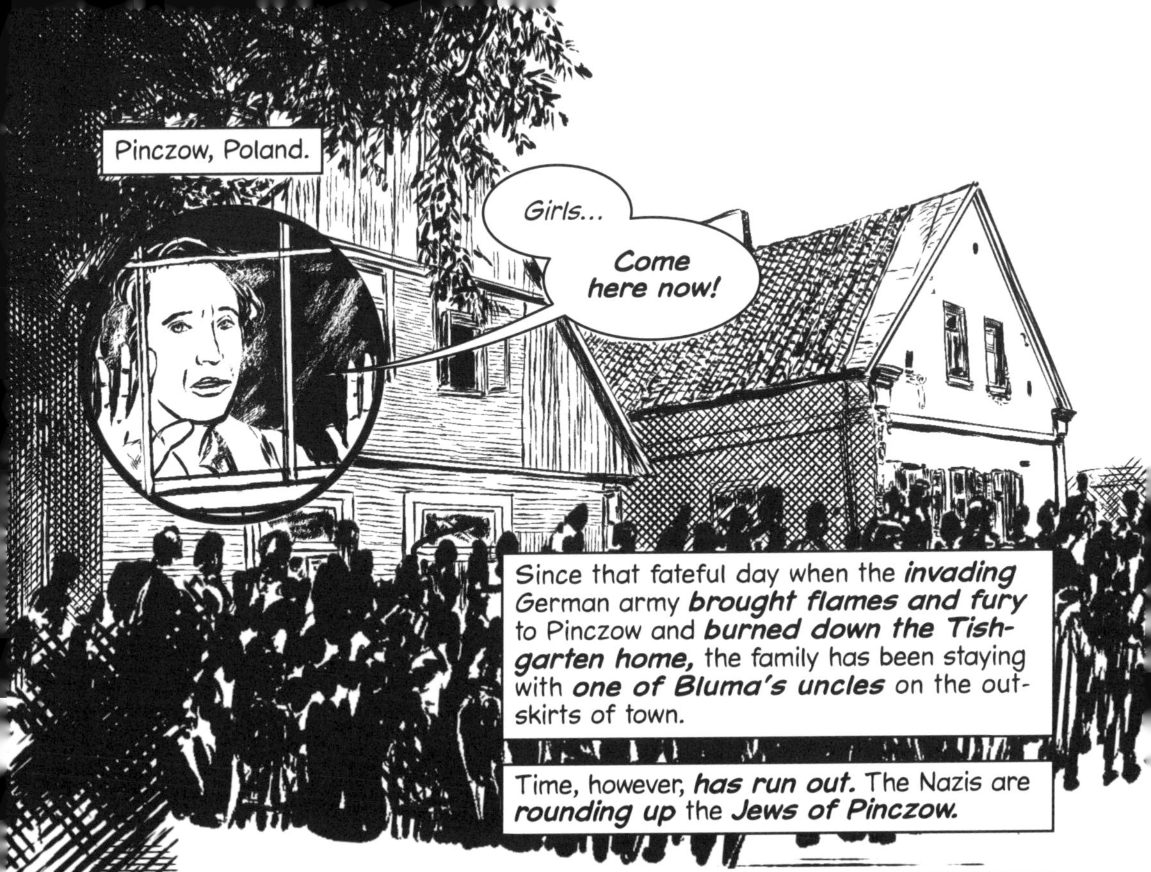

Pinczow, Poland.
Girls...
Come here now!
Since that fateful day when the invading German army brought flames and fury to Pinczow and burned down the Tishgarten home, the family has been staying with one of Bluma's uncles on the outskirts of town.
Time, however, has run out. The Nazis are rounding up the Jews of Pinczow.

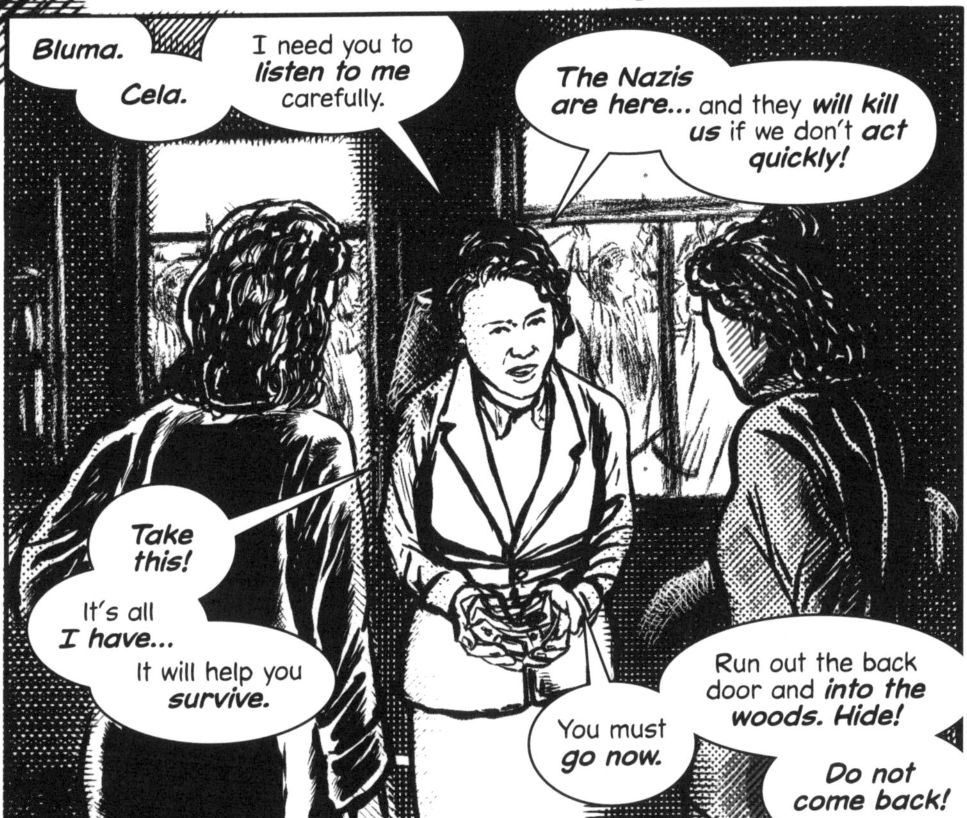

Bluma.
Cela.
I need you to listen to me carefully.
The Nazis are here... and they will kill us if we don't act quickly!
Take this!
It's all I have...
It will help you survive.
You must go now.
Run out the back door and into the woods. Hide!
Do not come back!

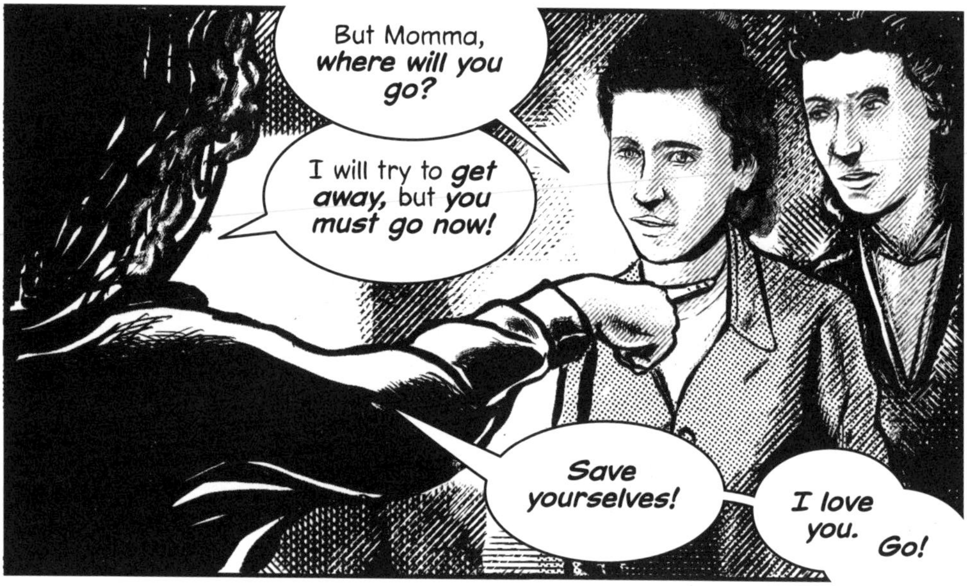
But Momma, where will you go?
I will try to get away, but you must go now!
Save yourselves!
I love you. Go!

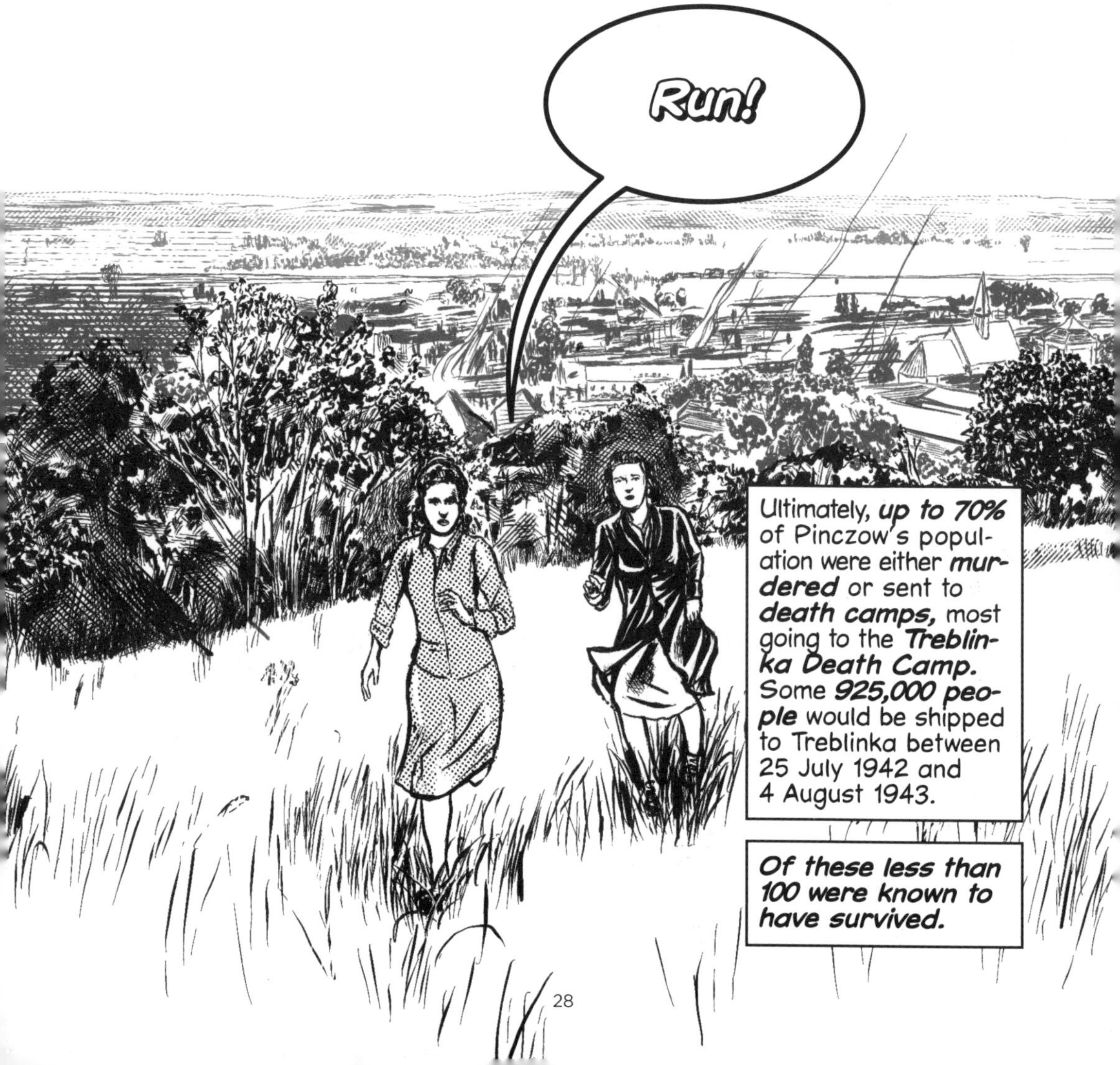
Run!
Ultimately, up to 70% of Pinczow's population were either murdered or sent to death camps, most going to the Treblinka Death Camp. Some 925,000 people would be shipped to Treblinka between 25 July 1942 and 4 August 1943.
Of these less than 100 were known to have survived.

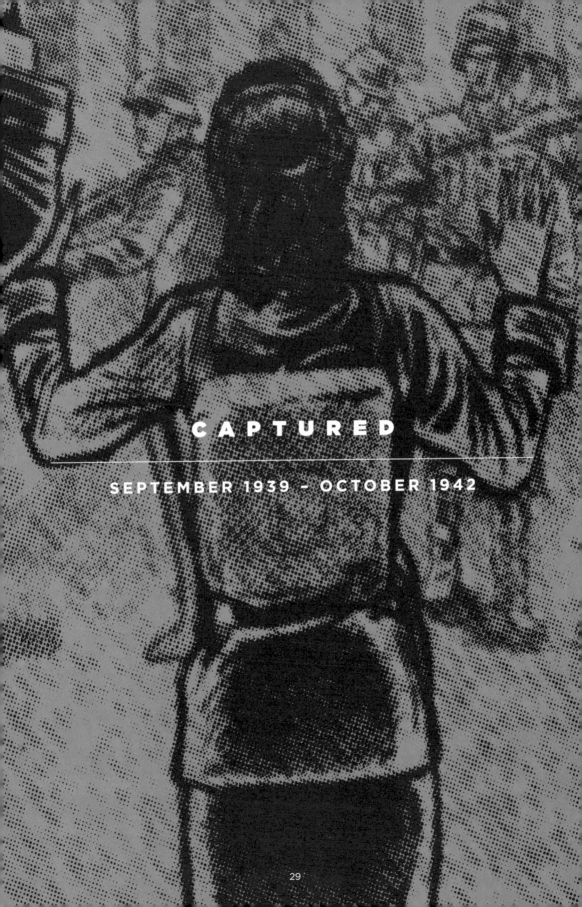

CAPTURED

SEPTEMBER 1939 – OCTOBER 1942

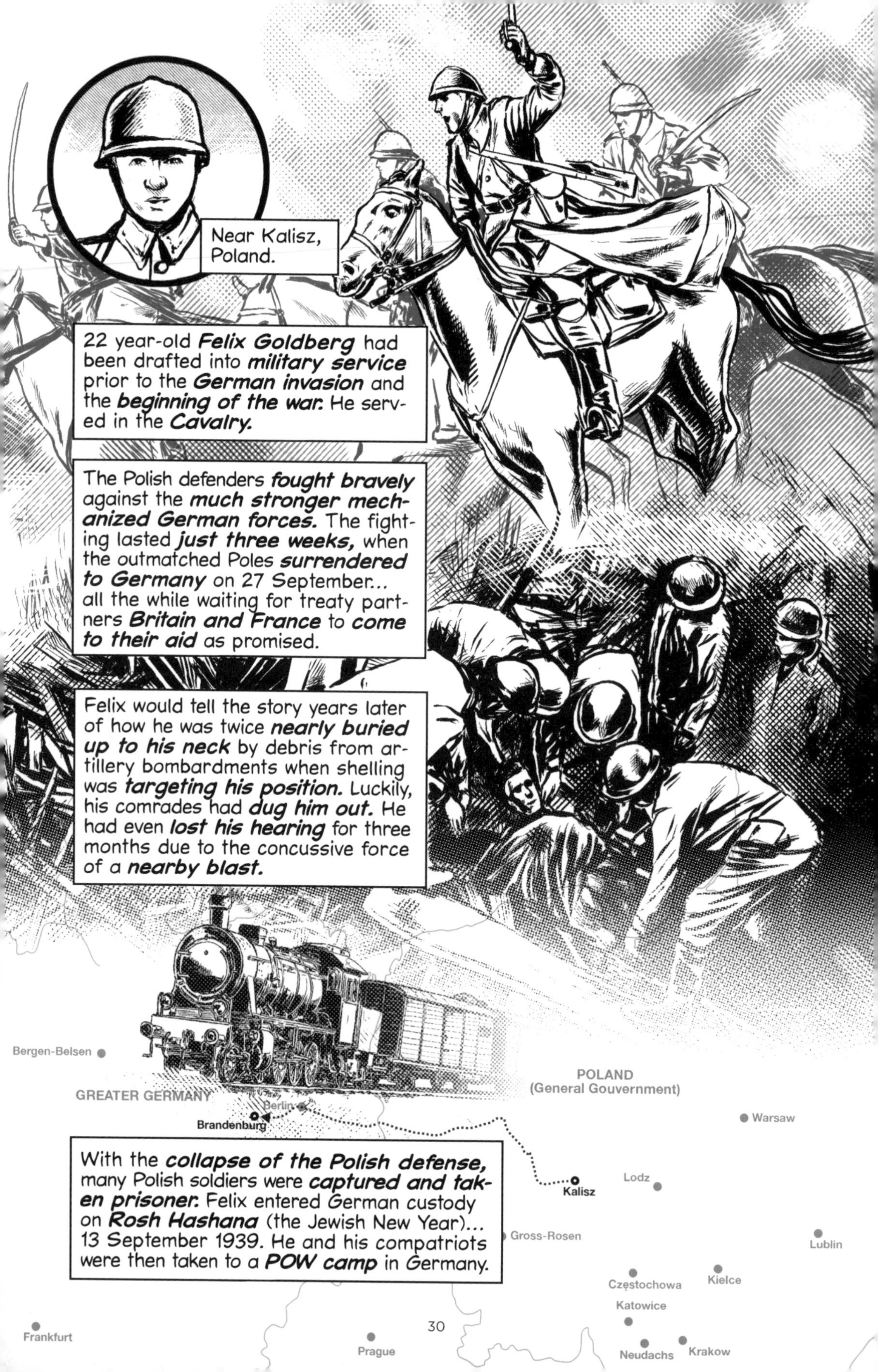
Near Kalisz, Poland.
22 year-old Felix Goldberg had been drafted into military service prior to the German invasion and the beginning of the war. He served in the Cavalry.
The Polish defenders fought bravely against the much stronger mechanized German forces. The fighting lasted just three weeks, when the outmatched Poles surrendered to Germany on 27 September... all the while waiting for treaty partners Britain and France to come to their aid as promised.
Felix would tell the story years later of how he was twice nearly buried up to his neck by debris from artillery bombardments when shelling was targeting his position. Luckily, his comrades had dug him out. He had even lost his hearing for three months due to the concussive force of a nearby blast.
Bergen-Belsen
GREATER GERMANY
Berlin
Brandenburg
POLAND
(General Gouvernment)
Warsaw
Kalisz
Lodz
Gross-Rosen
Lublin
Częstochowa
Kielce
Katowice
Frankfurt
Prague
Neudachs
Krakow
With the collapse of the Polish defense, many Polish soldiers were captured and taken prisoner. Felix entered German custody on Rosh Hashana (the Jewish New Year)... 13 September 1939. He and his compatriots were then taken to a POW camp in Germany.

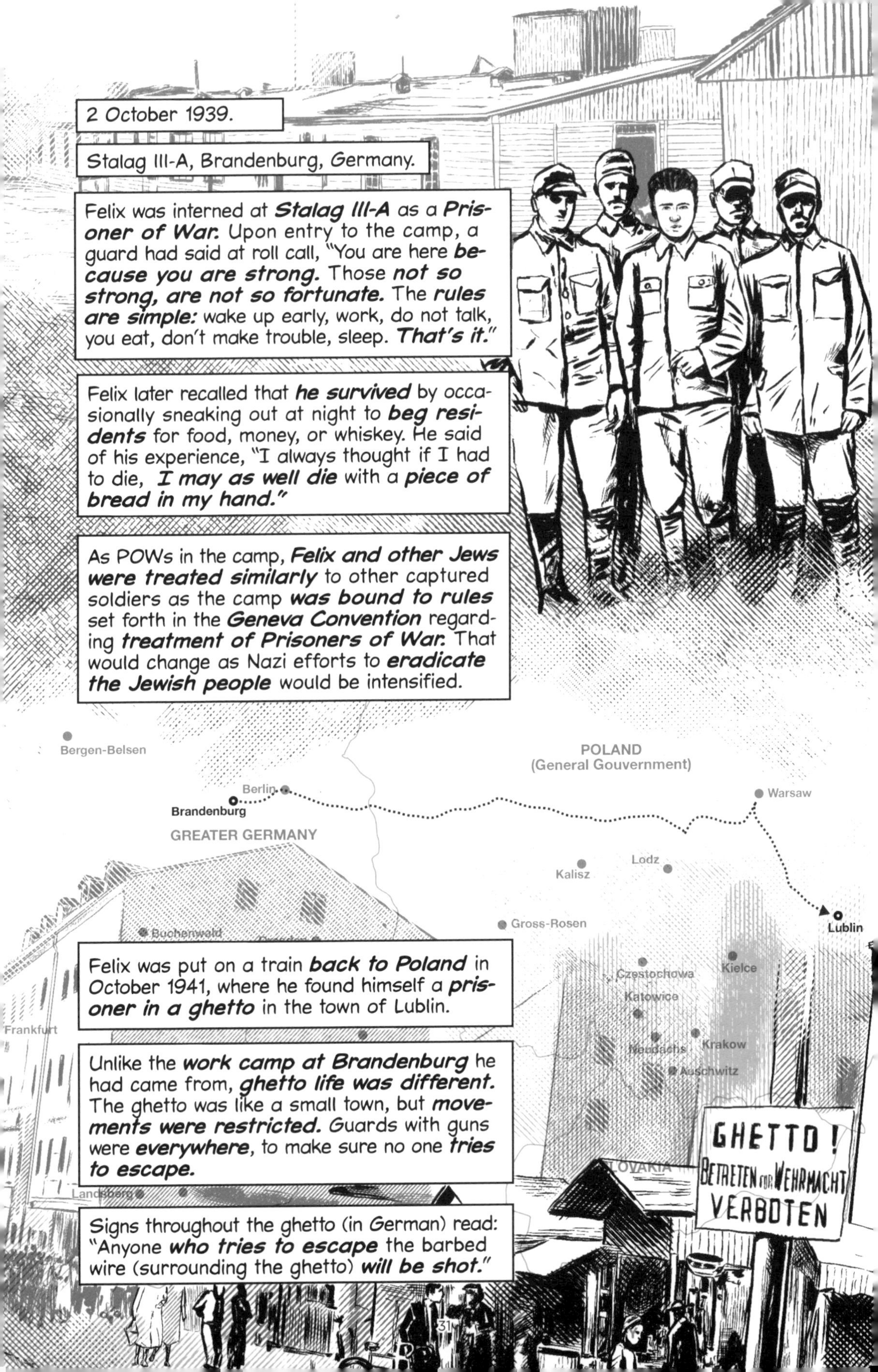
2 October 1939.
Stalag III-A, Brandenburg, Germany.
Felix was interned at ***Stalag III-A*** as a ***Prisoner of War.*** Upon entry to the camp, a guard had said at roll call, "You are here ***because you are strong.*** Those ***not so strong, are not so fortunate.*** The ***rules are simple:*** wake up early, work, do not talk, you eat, don't make trouble, sleep. ***That's it.***"
Felix later recalled that ***he survived*** by occasionally sneaking out at night to ***beg residents*** for food, money, or whiskey. He said of his experience, "I always thought if I had to die, ***I may as well die*** with a ***piece of bread in my hand.***"
As POWs in the camp, ***Felix and other Jews were treated similarly*** to other captured soldiers as the camp ***was bound to rules*** set forth in the ***Geneva Convention*** regarding ***treatment of Prisoners of War.*** That would change as Nazi efforts to ***eradicate the Jewish people*** would be intensified.
Bergen-Belsen
POLAND
(General Gouvernment)
Berlin
Brandenburg
Warsaw
GREATER GERMANY
Kalisz
Lodz
Gross-Rosen
Lublin
Buchenwald
Czestochowa
Kielce
Katowice
Frankfurt
Neudachs
Krakow
Auschwitz
Landsberg
Felix was put on a train ***back to Poland*** in October 1941, where he found himself a ***prisoner in a ghetto*** in the town of Lublin.
Unlike the ***work camp at Brandenburg*** he had came from, ***ghetto life was different.*** The ghetto was like a small town, but ***movements were restricted.*** Guards with guns were ***everywhere***, to make sure no one ***tries to escape.***
GHETTO!
BETRETEN FÜR WEHRMACHT
VERBOTEN
Signs throughout the ghetto (in German) read: "Anyone ***who tries to escape*** the barbed wire (surrounding the ghetto) ***will be shot.***"

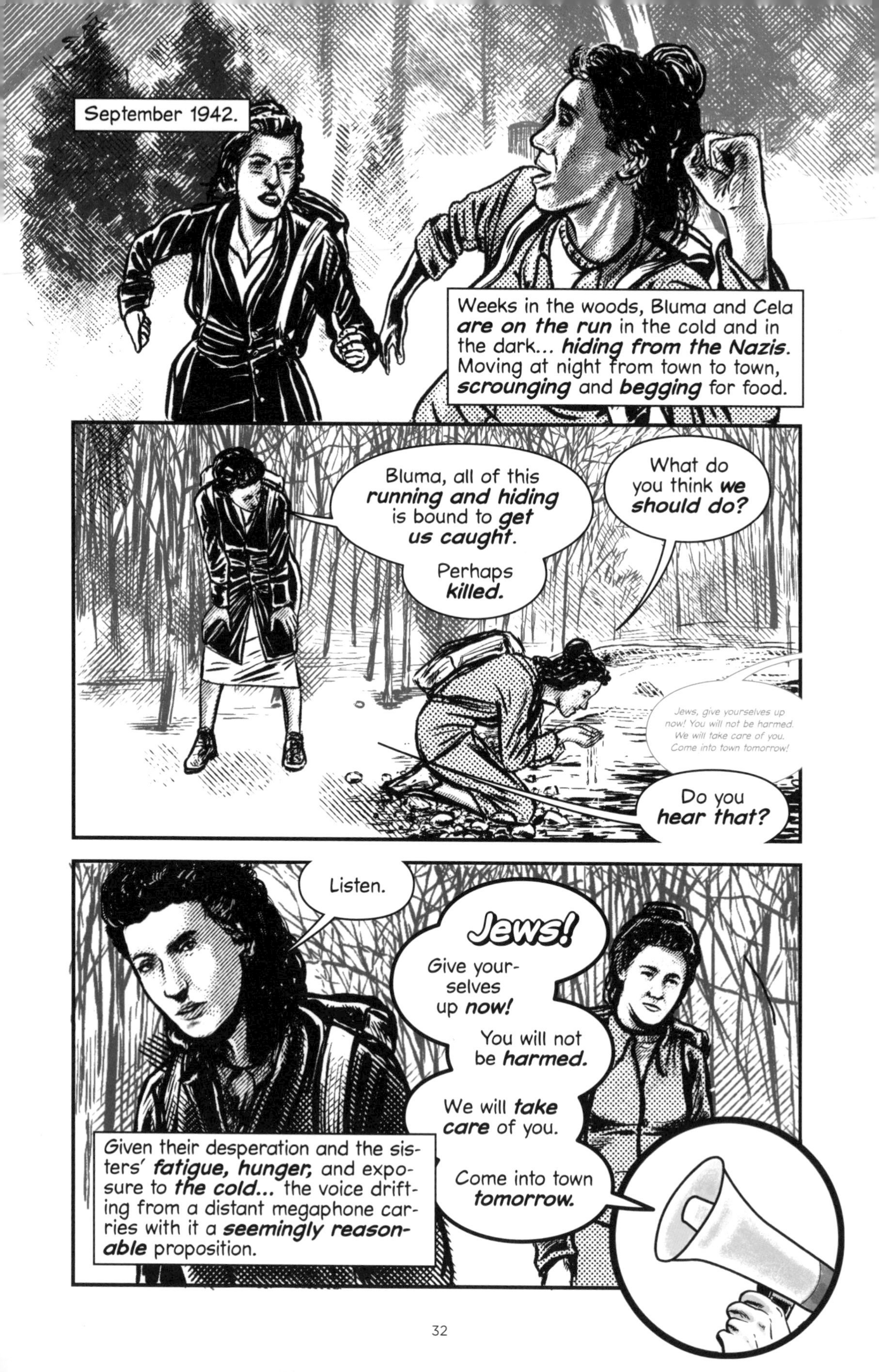
September 1942.
Weeks in the woods, Bluma and Cela are on the run in the cold and in the dark... hiding from the Nazis. Moving at night from town to town, scrounging and begging for food.
Bluma, all of this running and hiding is bound to get us caught.
Perhaps killed.
What do you think we should do?
Jews, give yourselves up now! You will not be harmed. We will take care of you. Come into town tomorrow!
Do you hear that?
Listen.
Jews!
Give yourselves up now!
You will not be harmed.
We will take care of you.
Come into town tomorrow.
Given their desperation and the sisters' fatigue, hunger, and exposure to the cold... the voice drifting from a distant megaphone carries with it a seemingly reasonable proposition.

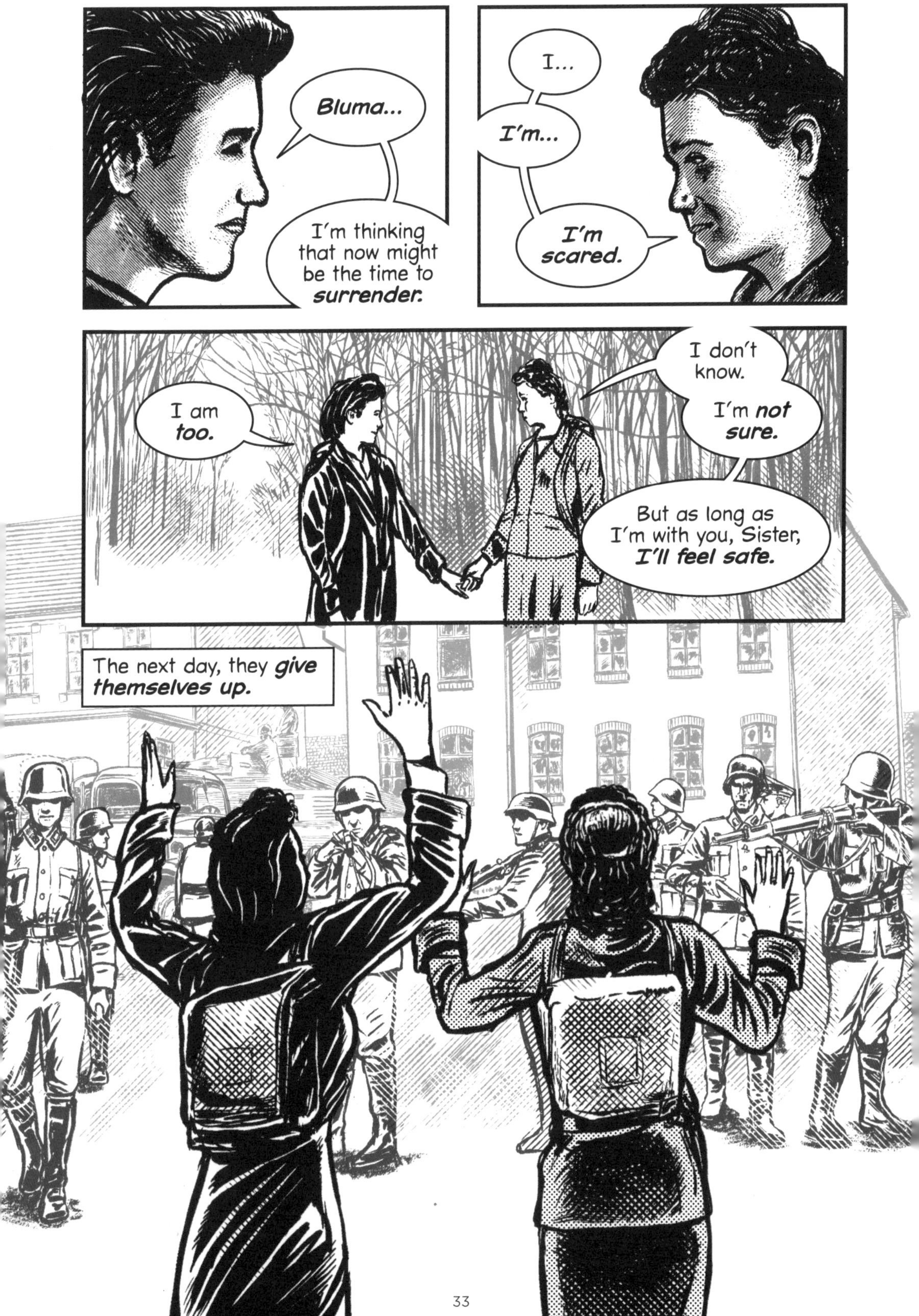
Bluma...
I'm thinking that now might be the time to **surrender.**
I...
I'm...
I'm scared.
I am **too.**
I don't know.
I'm **not sure.**
But as long as I'm with you, Sister, **I'll feel safe.**
The next day, they **give themselves up.**

The Tishgarten sisters were **rounded up** along with other women and herded into **cattle cars**.

Torn away from their families, the 13 year-old Bluma and the 17 year-old Cela are being sent to an **unknown destination** and an **uncertain fate.**

I can **hardly breathe.**

Me either.

The six-hour **journey by rail** would take Bluma and Cela from Pinczow to the **Hasag Slave Labor Camp** in Kielce.

POLAND
(General Gouvernement)

Bergen-Belsen

Cela?

Yes?

Do you think **Mama and Papa...**

I don't know.

I am **so scared.**

I am **so worried...**

Our **sisters and brother...**

Do you think **they're alright?**

I don't know.

Buchenwald   Dresden
GREATER GERMANY

Lub

The sisters were only **there for a month,** after which they were transported to their **next destination** at the **Czestochowa Ghetto.**

Kielce

Czestochowa

Katowice

Pinczow

nkfurt

Neu-Dachs   Krakow

Auschwitz

**PROTECTORATE OF
BOHEMIA & MORAVIA**

Nuremberg

34

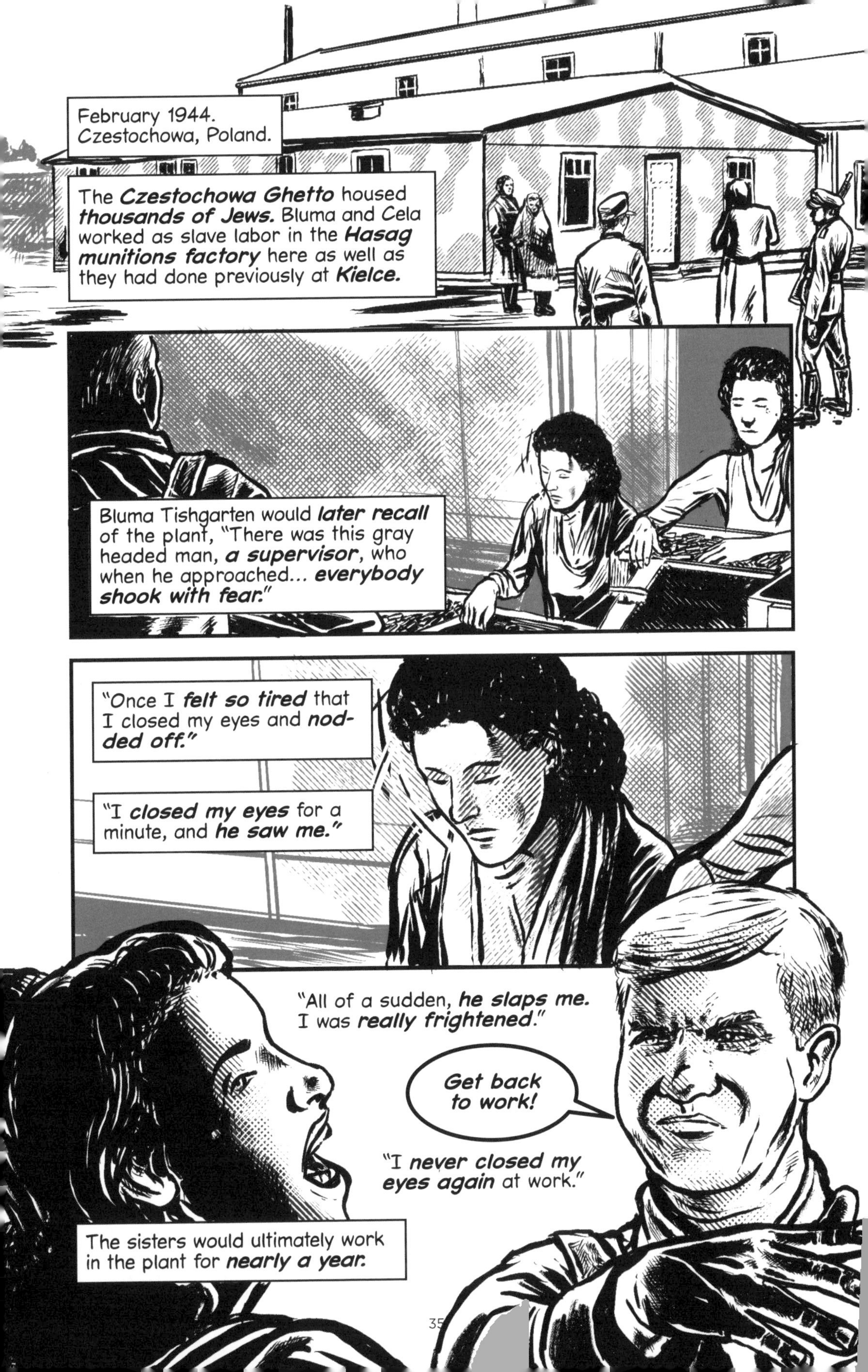

February 1944. Czestochowa, Poland.
The ***Czestochowa Ghetto*** housed ***thousands of Jews.*** Bluma and Cela worked as slave labor in the ***Hasag munitions factory*** here as well as they had done previously at ***Kielce.***
Bluma Tishgarten would ***later recall*** of the plant, "There was this gray headed man, ***a supervisor***, who when he approached... ***everybody shook with fear.***"
"Once I ***felt so tired*** that I closed my eyes and ***nodded off.***"
"I ***closed my eyes*** for a minute, and ***he saw me.***"
"All of a sudden, ***he slaps me.*** I was ***really frightened.***"
Get back to work!
"I ***never closed my eyes again*** at work."
The sisters would ultimately work in the plant for ***nearly a year.***

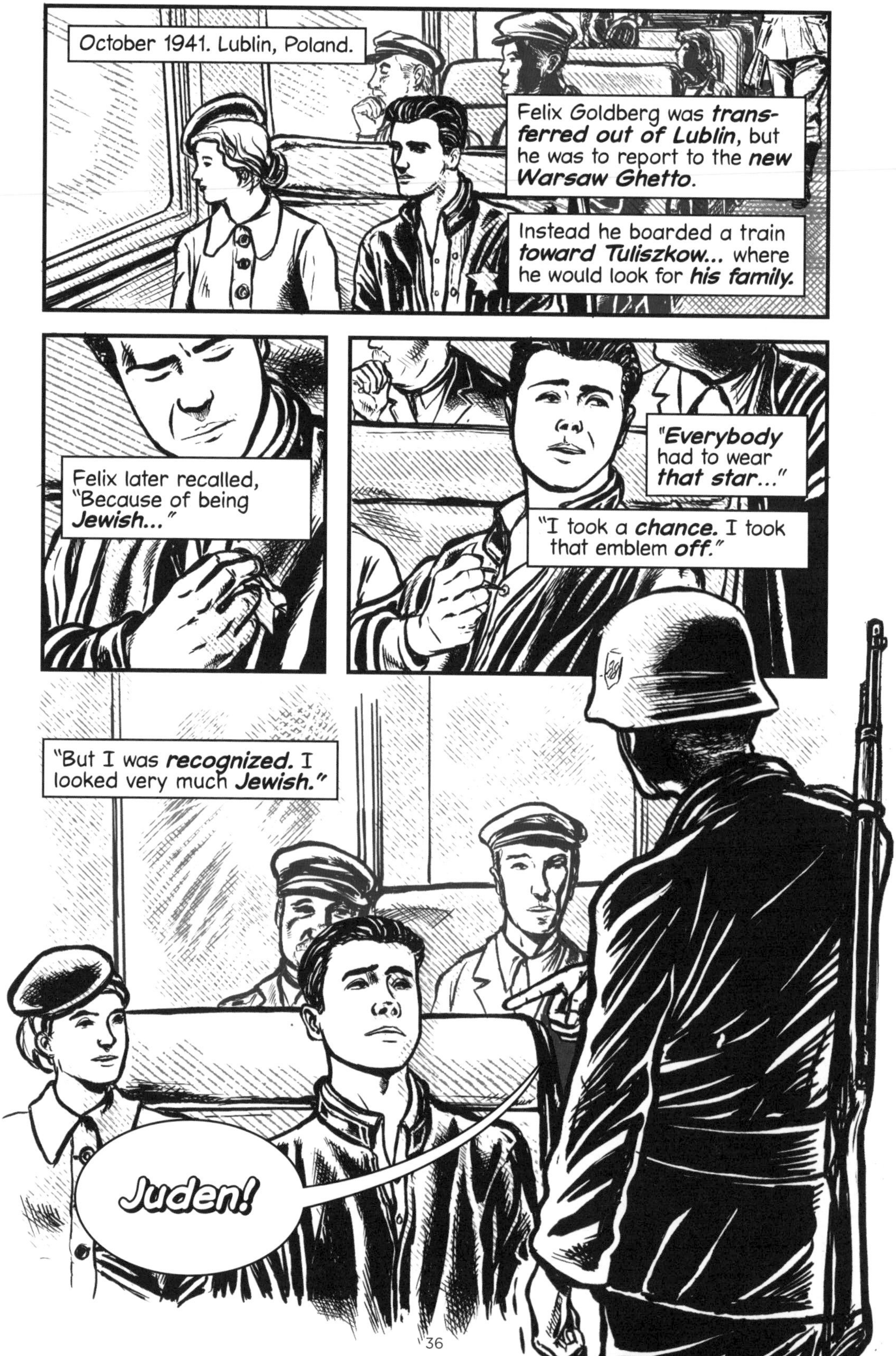
October 1941. Lublin, Poland.
Felix Goldberg was transferred out of Lublin, but he was to report to the new Warsaw Ghetto.
Instead he boarded a train toward Tuliszkow... where he would look for his family.
Felix later recalled, "Because of being Jewish..."
"Everybody had to wear that star..."
"I took a chance. I took that emblem off."
"But I was recognized. I looked very much Jewish."
Juden!

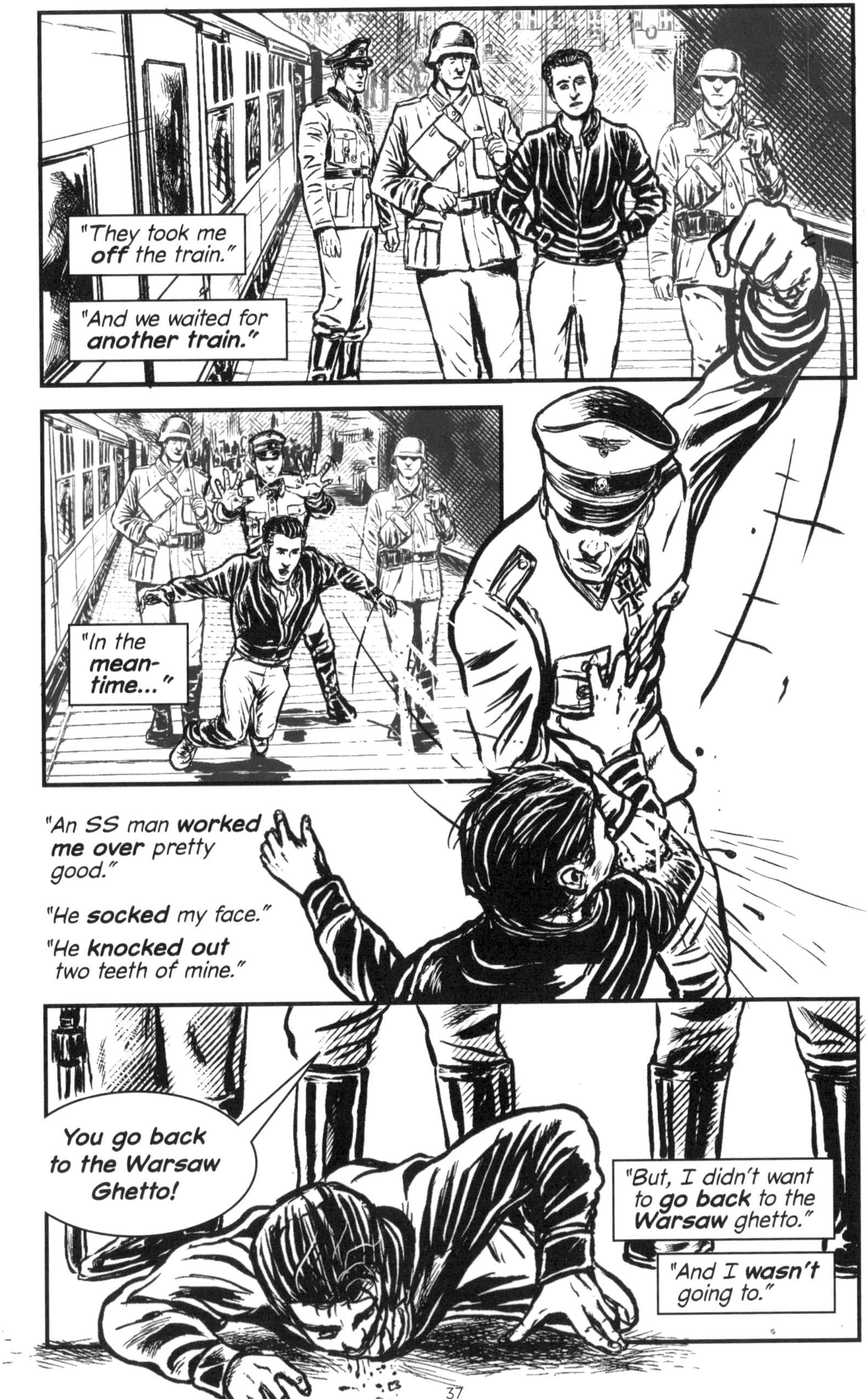
"They took me **off** the train."
"And we waited for **another train.**"
"In the **mean-time...**"
"An SS man **worked me over** pretty good."
"He **socked** my face."
"He **knocked out** two teeth of mine."
You go back to the Warsaw Ghetto!
"But, I didn't want to **go back** to the **Warsaw** ghetto."
"And I **wasn't** going to."

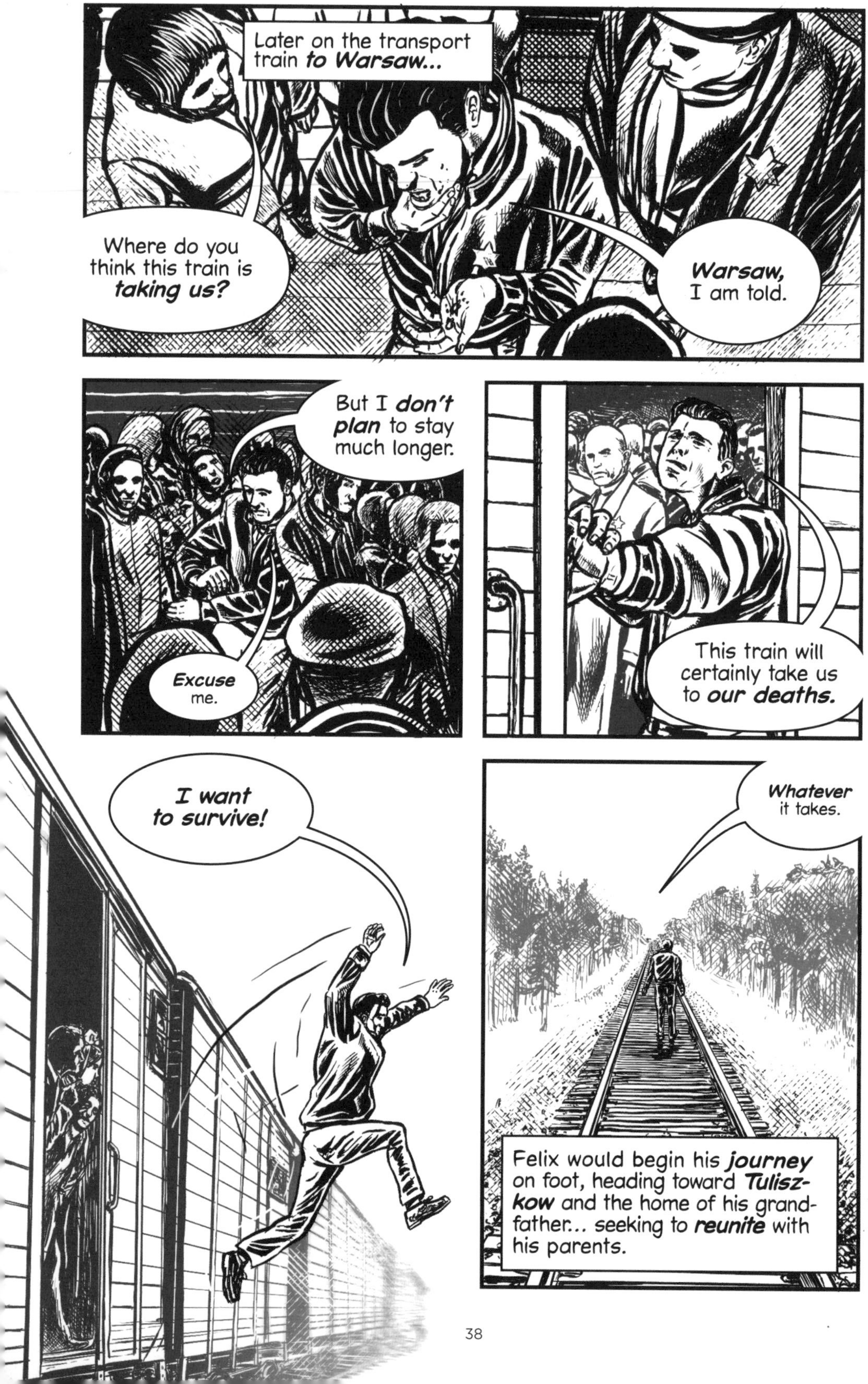

Later on the transport train to Warsaw...
Where do you think this train is taking us?
Warsaw, I am told.
But I don't plan to stay much longer.
Excuse me.
This train will certainly take us to our deaths.
I want to survive!
Whatever it takes.
Felix would begin his journey on foot, heading toward Tuliszkow and the home of his grandfather... seeking to reunite with his parents.

Halt!

October 1942.

Later, Felix was **captured** in a sweep of the vicinity.

People were detained as the Nazis **emptied local ghettos** of Jews. The **German army** along with **local Poles** coordinated this effort.

After several days, they were loaded into **cattle cars.**

2,000 to 3,000 people were **forced** on to the transport with up to **100 or more** packed into each car.

Little light. **Little** air. **No** food.

It took **three days** for the train to cross the Polish countryside after **leaving Rawitsch.**

Bremen
Hanover
Berlin
Wolfsburg
Szczecin
Bydgoszcz
Poland
Poznań
Warsaw
Łódź
Germany
Dresden
Wrocław
Frankfurt
Ratwitsch
Prague
Kraków
Auschwitz
Czechia
Ostrava
Nuremberg
Brno
Mannheim
Karlsruhe
Stuttgart
Slovakia

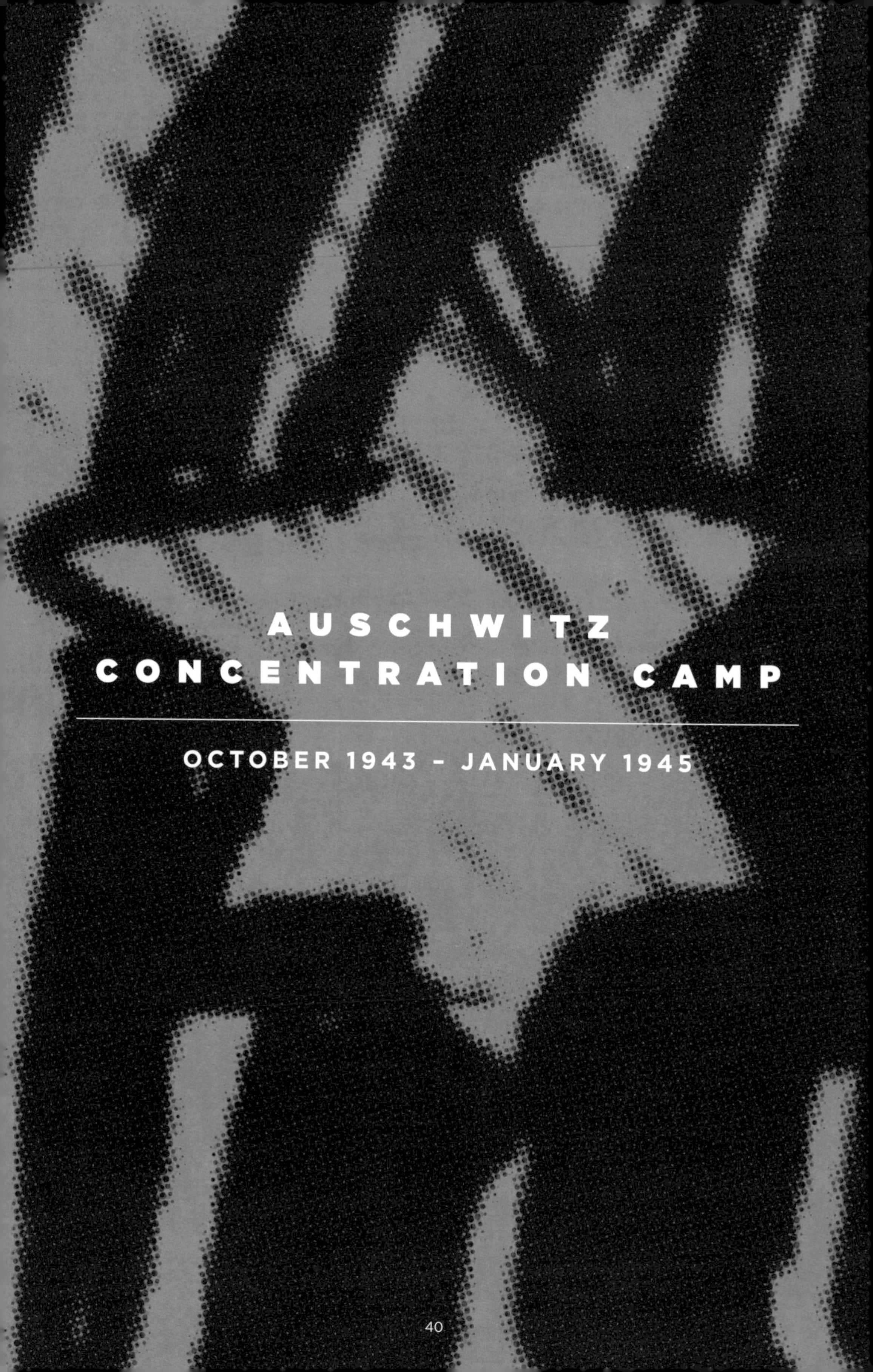

AUSCHWITZ CONCENTRATION CAMP

OCTOBER 1943 – JANUARY 1945

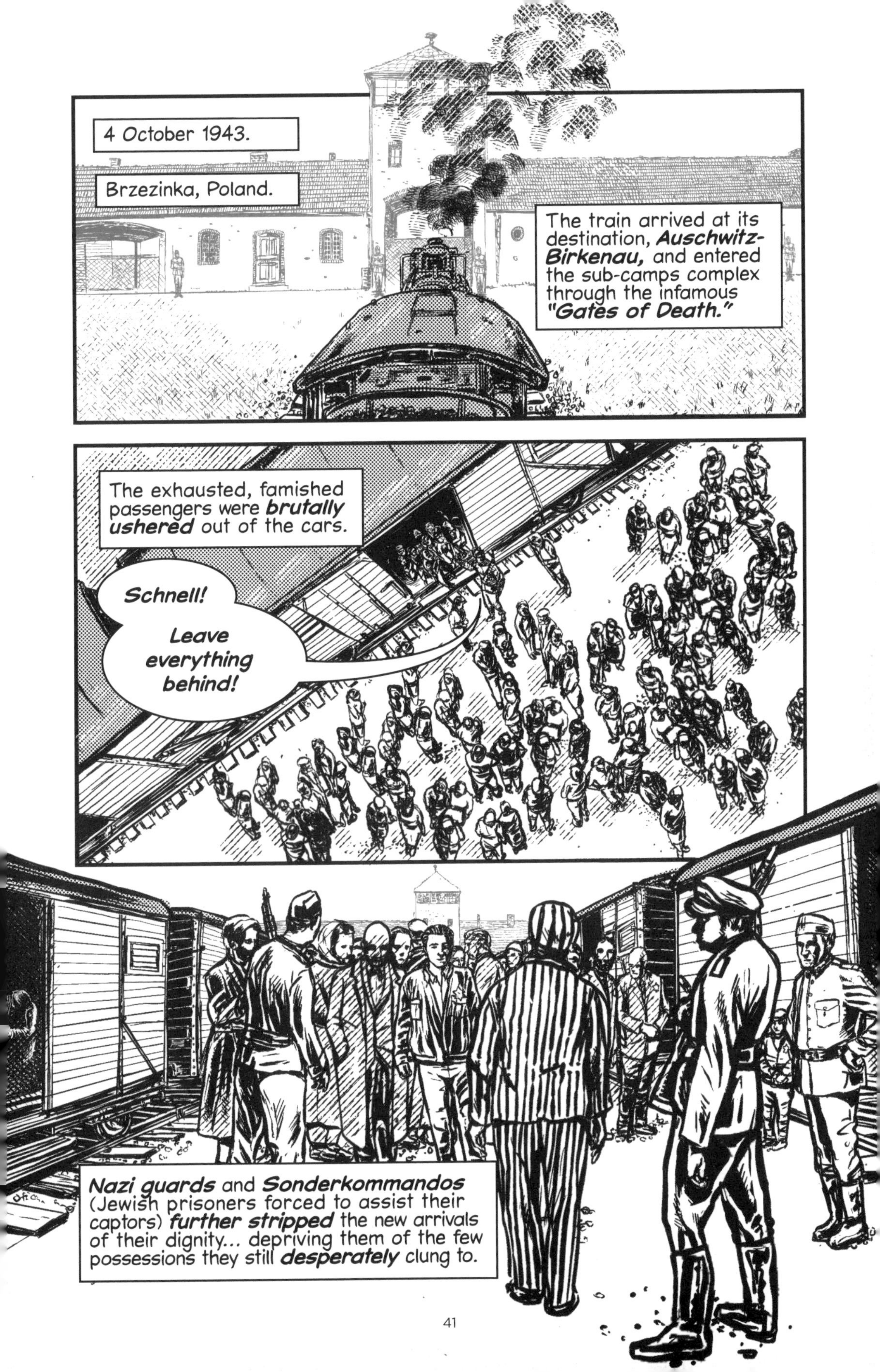
4 October 1943.
Brzezinka, Poland.
The train arrived at its destination, ***Auschwitz-Birkenau,*** and entered the sub-camps complex through the infamous ***"Gates of Death."***
The exhausted, famished passengers were ***brutally ushered*** out of the cars.
Schnell!
Leave everything behind!
Nazi guards and ***Sonderkommandos*** (Jewish prisoners forced to assist their captors) ***further stripped*** the new arrivals of their dignity... depriving them of the few possessions they still ***desperately*** clung to.

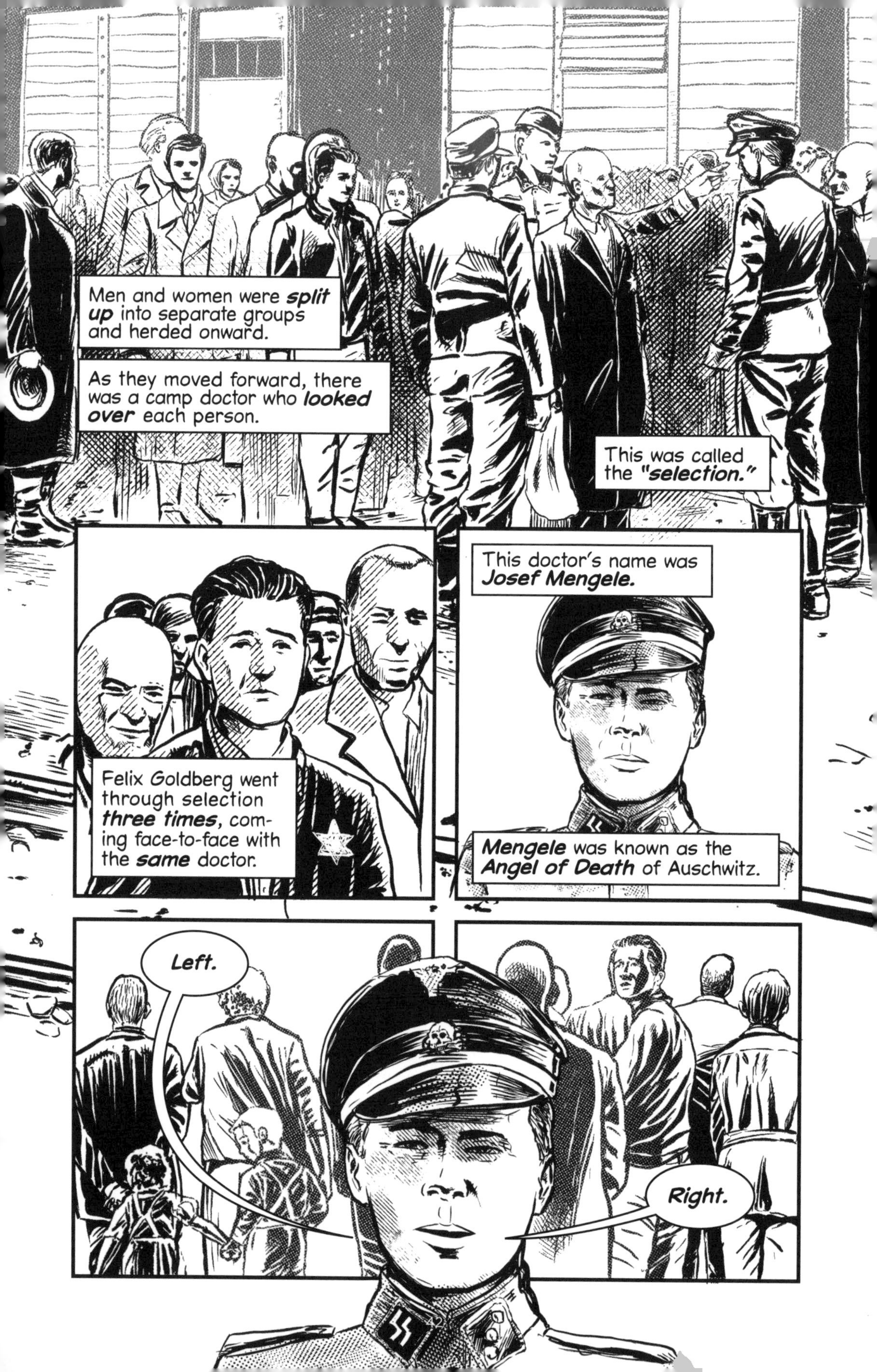
Men and women were ***split up*** into separate groups and herded onward.
As they moved forward, there was a camp doctor who ***looked over*** each person.
This was called the ***"selection."***
Felix Goldberg went through selection ***three times***, coming face-to-face with the ***same*** doctor.
This doctor's name was ***Josef Mengele.***
Mengele was known as the ***Angel of Death*** of Auschwitz.
Left.
Right.

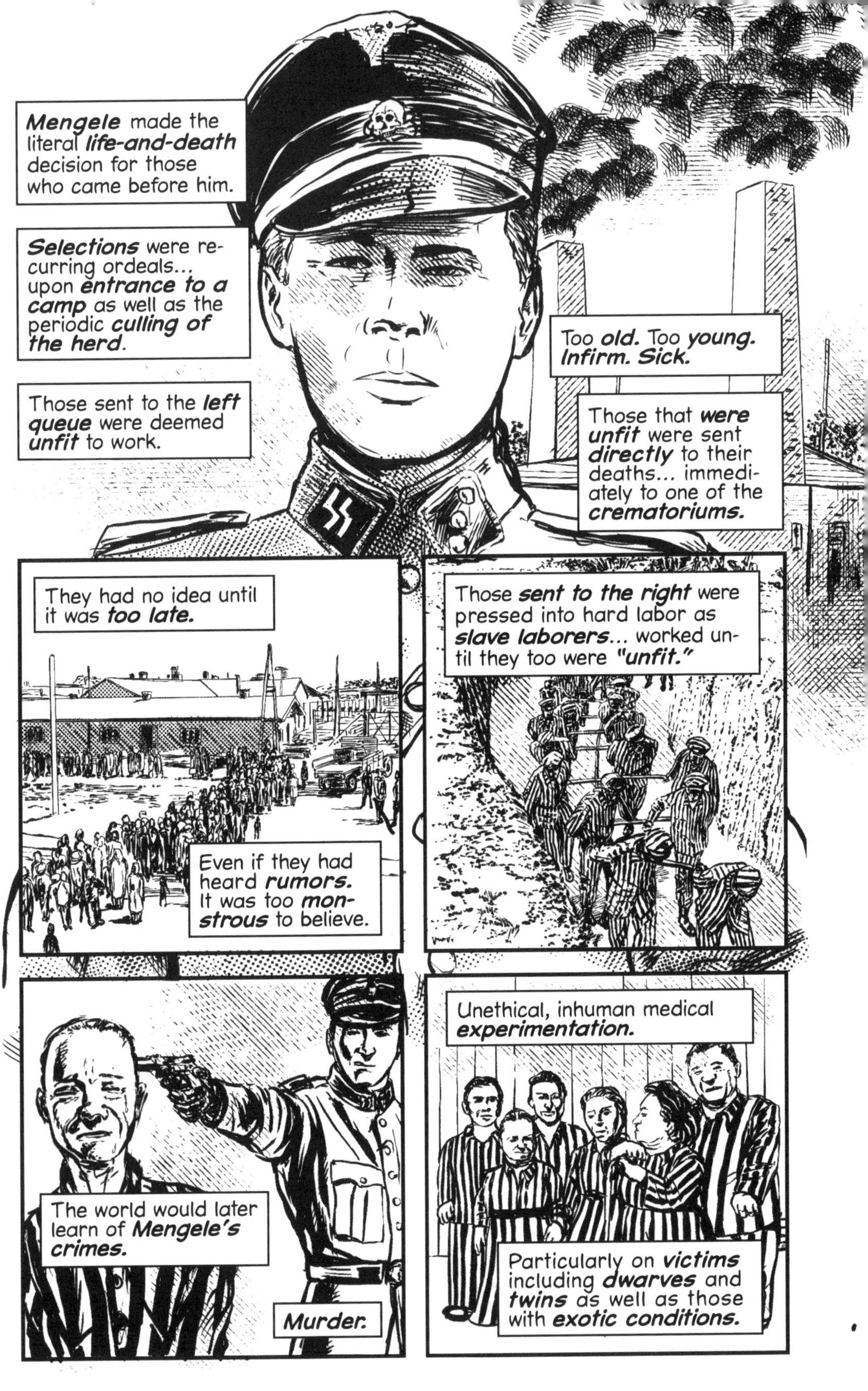
Mengele made the literal life-and-death decision for those who came before him.
Selections were recurring ordeals... upon entrance to a camp as well as the periodic culling of the herd.
Those sent to the left queue were deemed unfit to work.
Too old. Too young. Infirm. Sick.
Those that were unfit were sent directly to their deaths... immediately to one of the crematoriums.
They had no idea until it was too late.
Even if they had heard rumors. It was too monstrous to believe.
Those sent to the right were pressed into hard labor as slave laborers... worked until they too were "unfit."
The world would later learn of Mengele's crimes.
Murder.
Unethical, inhuman medical experimentation.
Particularly on victims including dwarves and twins as well as those with exotic conditions.

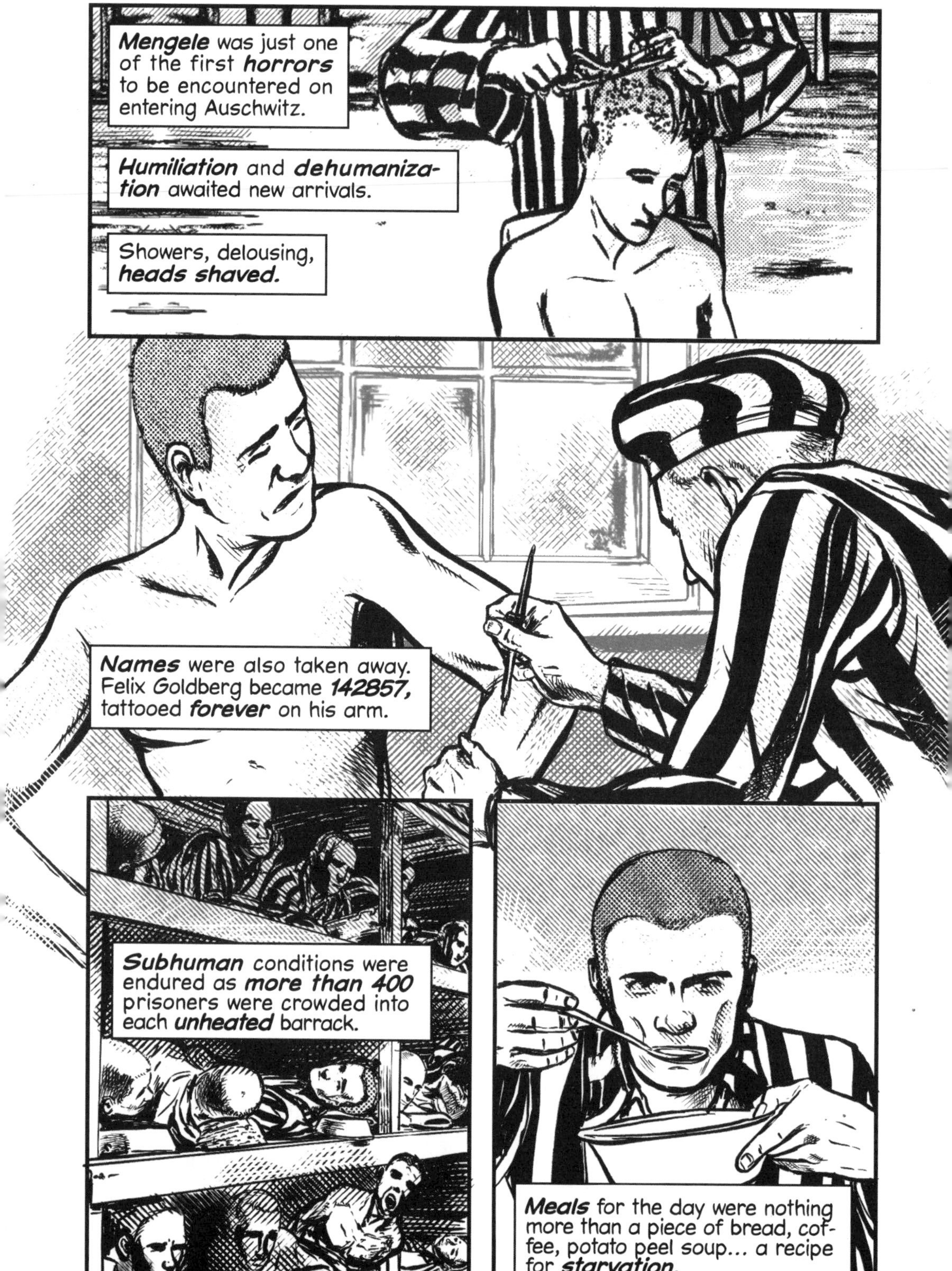
Mengele was just one of the first horrors to be encountered on entering Auschwitz.
Humiliation and dehumanization awaited new arrivals.
Showers, delousing, heads shaved.
Names were also taken away. Felix Goldberg became 142857, tattooed forever on his arm.
Subhuman conditions were endured as more than 400 prisoners were crowded into each unheated barrack.
Meals for the day were nothing more than a piece of bread, coffee, potato peel soup... a recipe for starvation.

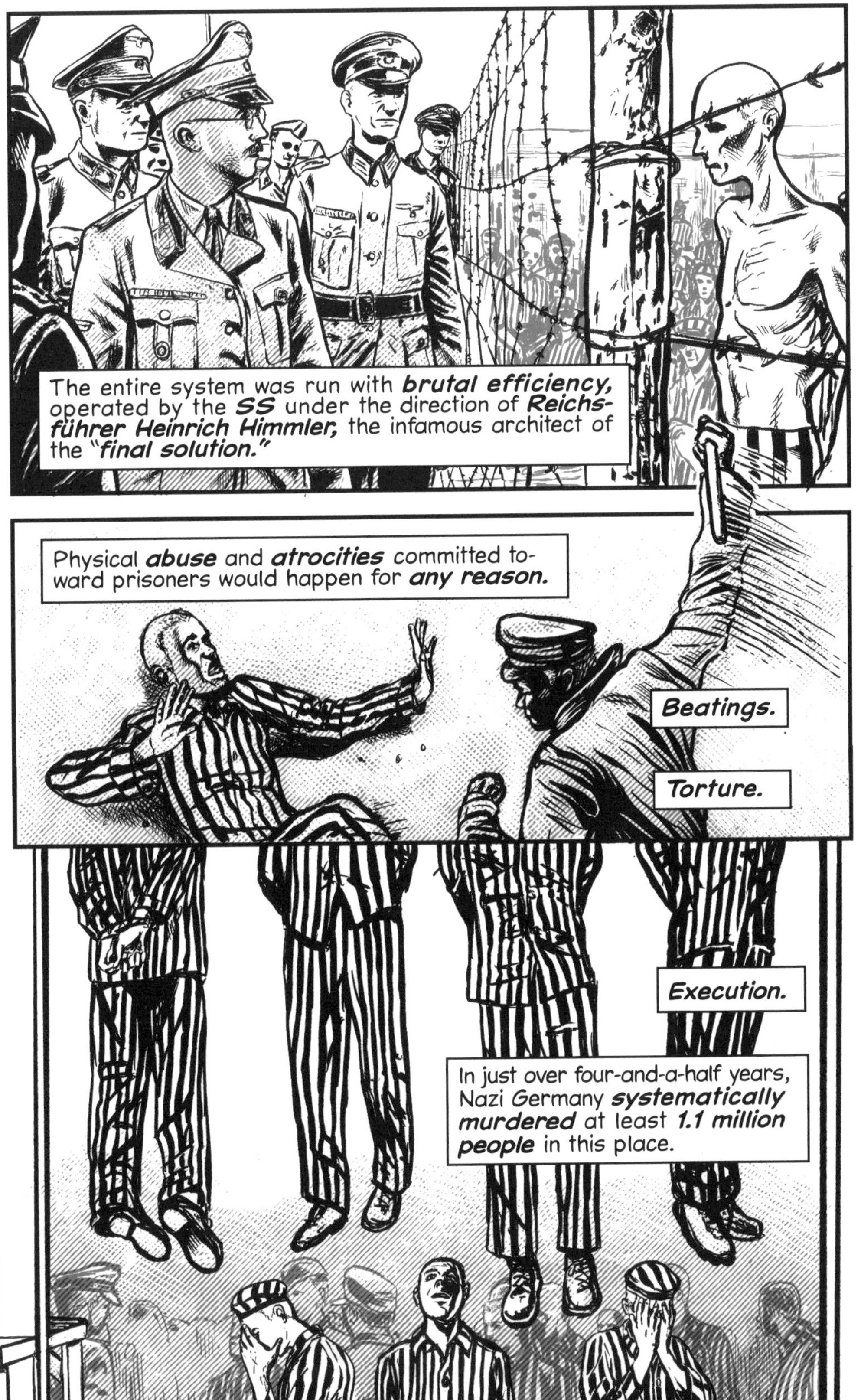
The entire system was run with brutal efficiency, operated by the SS under the direction of Reichsführer Heinrich Himmler, the infamous architect of the "final solution."
Physical abuse and atrocities committed toward prisoners would happen for any reason.
Beatings.
Torture.
Execution.
In just over four-and-a-half years, Nazi Germany systematically murdered at least 1.1 million people in this place.

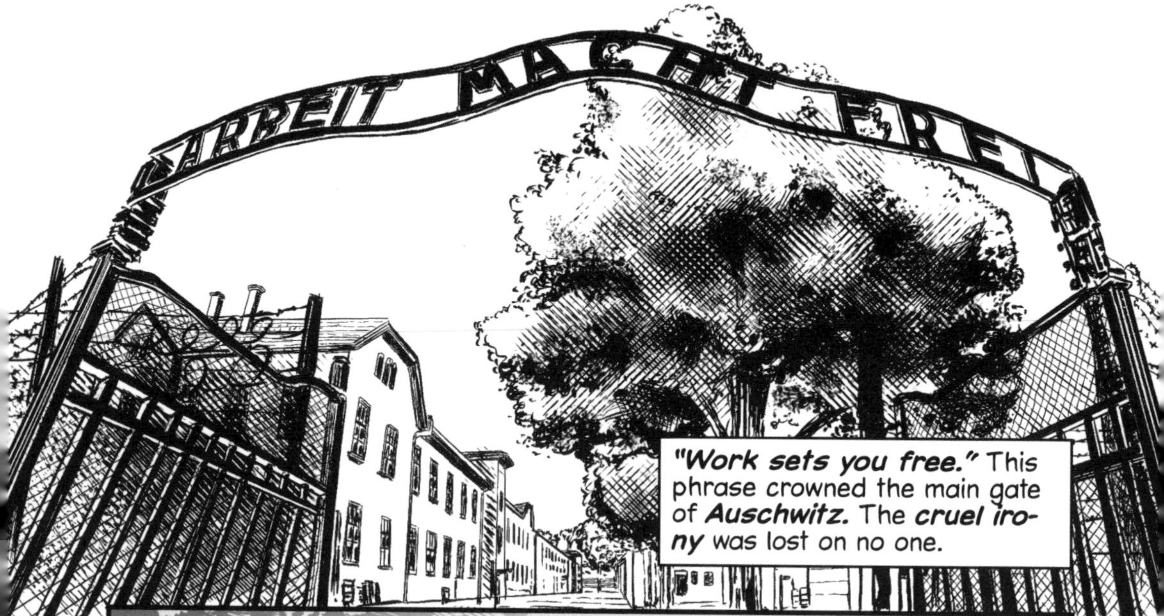
ARBEIT MACHT FREI
"Work sets you free." This phrase crowned the main gate of Auschwitz. The cruel irony was lost on no one.

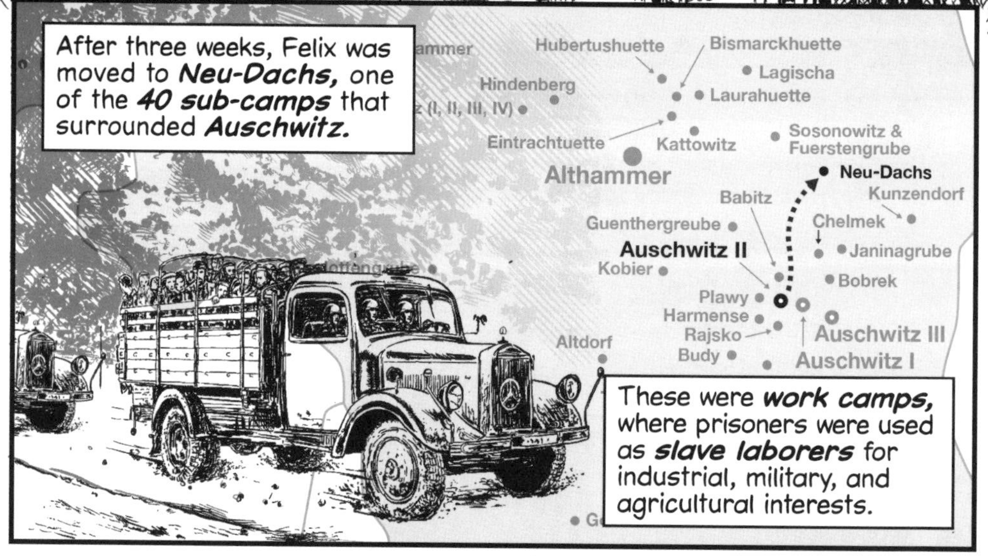
After three weeks, Felix was moved to Neu-Dachs, one of the 40 sub-camps that surrounded Auschwitz.
Hubertushuette
Bismarckhuette
Lagischa
Laurahuette
Hindenberg
Eintrachtuette
Kattowitz
Sosonowitz & Fuerstengrube
Althammer
Neu-Dachs
Babitz
Kunzendorf
Guenthergreube
Chelmek
Auschwitz II
Janinagrube
Kobier
Bobrek
Plawy
Harmense
Rajsko
Auschwitz III
Altdorf
Budy
Auschwitz I
These were work camps, where prisoners were used as slave laborers for industrial, military, and agricultural interests.

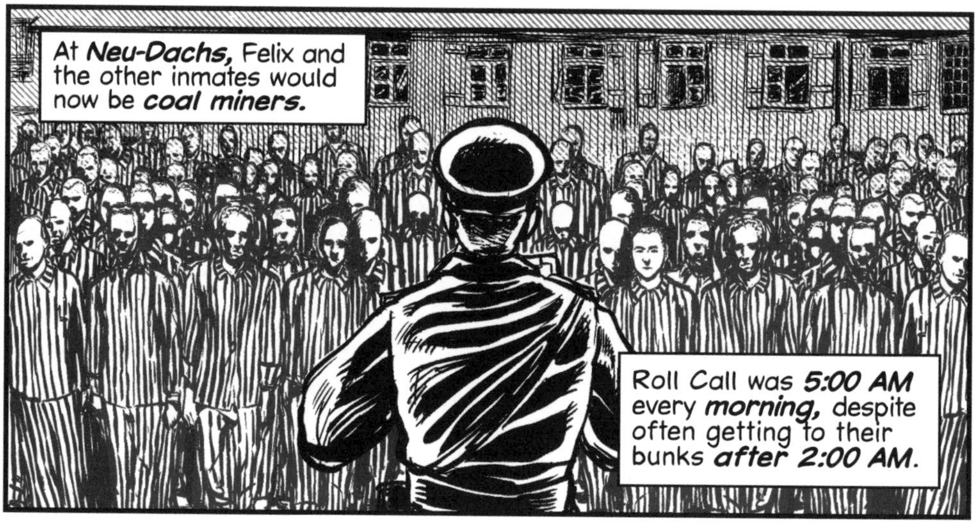
At Neu-Dachs, Felix and the other inmates would now be coal miners.
Roll Call was 5:00 AM every morning, despite often getting to their bunks after 2:00 AM.

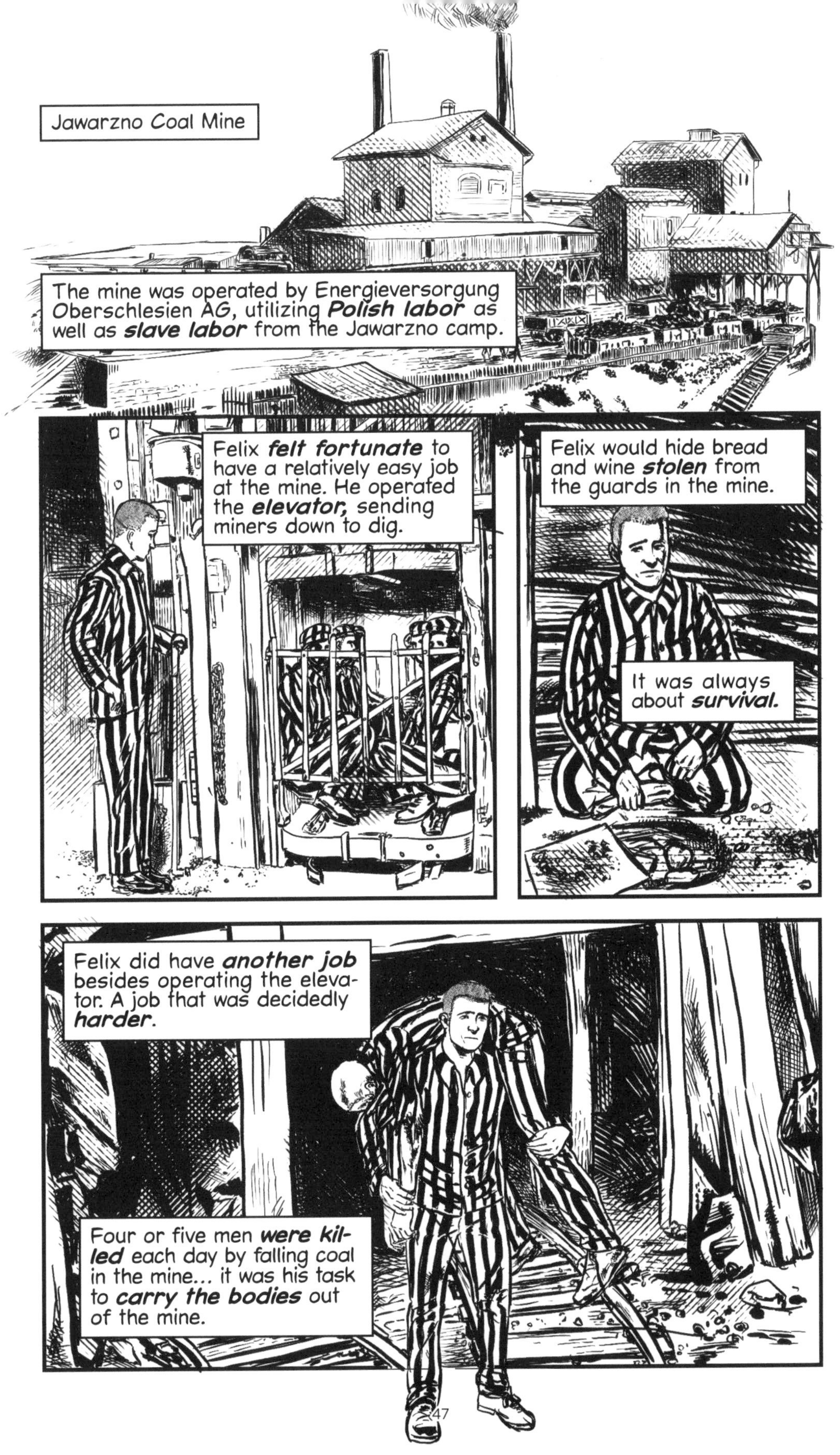
Jawarzno Coal Mine
The mine was operated by Energieversorgung Oberschlesien AG, utilizing **Polish labor** as well as **slave labor** from the Jawarzno camp.
Felix **felt fortunate** to have a relatively easy job at the mine. He operated the **elevator,** sending miners down to dig.
Felix would hide bread and wine **stolen** from the guards in the mine.
It was always about **survival.**
Felix did have **another job** besides operating the elevator. A job that was decidedly **harder**.
Four or five men **were killed** each day by falling coal in the mine... it was his task to **carry the bodies** out of the mine.

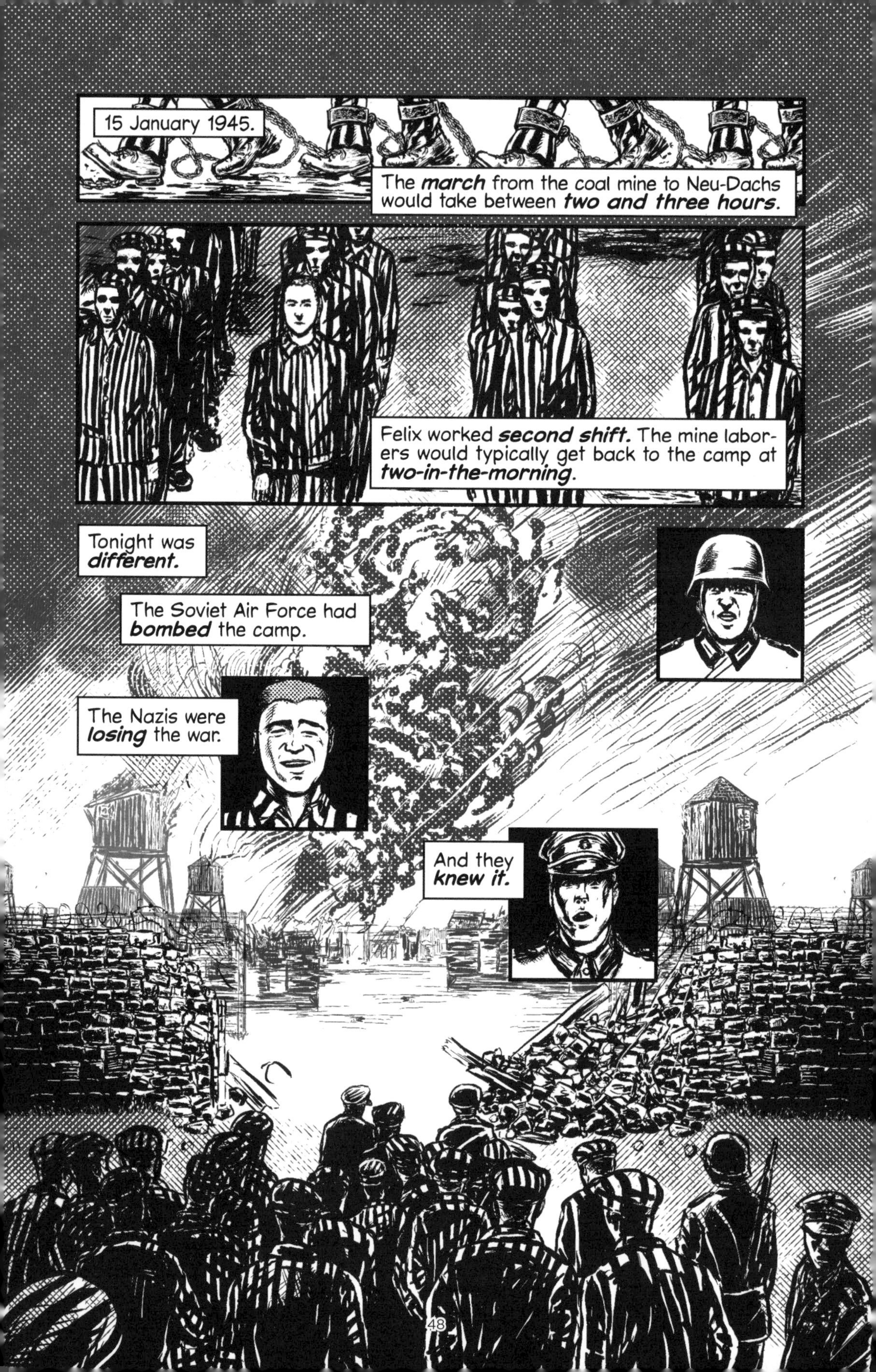
15 January 1945.
The **march** from the coal mine to Neu-Dachs would take between **two and three hours**.
Felix worked **second shift.** The mine laborers would typically get back to the camp at **two-in-the-morning**.
Tonight was **different.**
The Soviet Air Force had **bombed** the camp.
The Nazis were **losing** the war.
And they **knew it.**

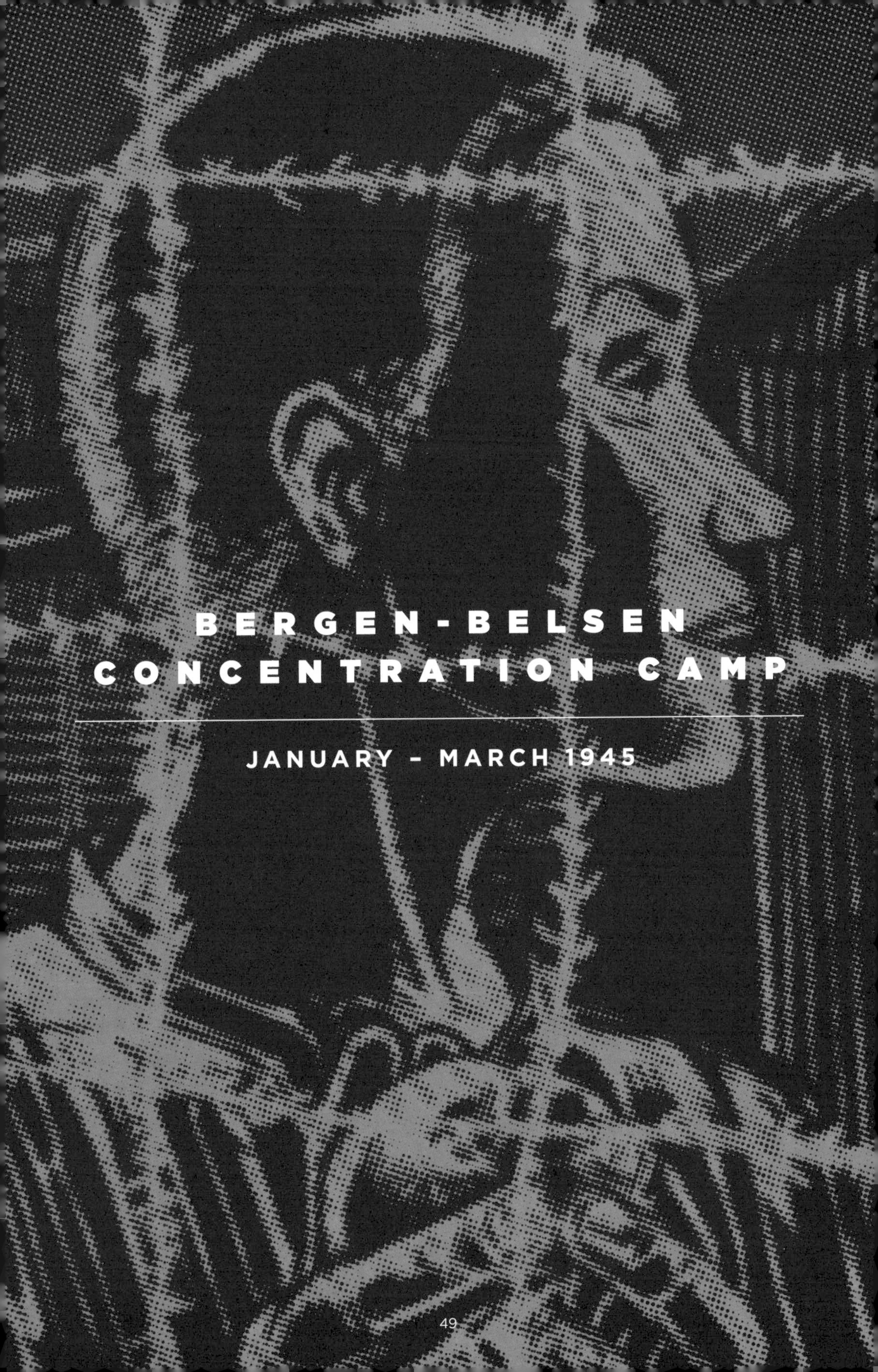

BERGEN-BELSEN CONCENTRATION CAMP

JANUARY – MARCH 1945

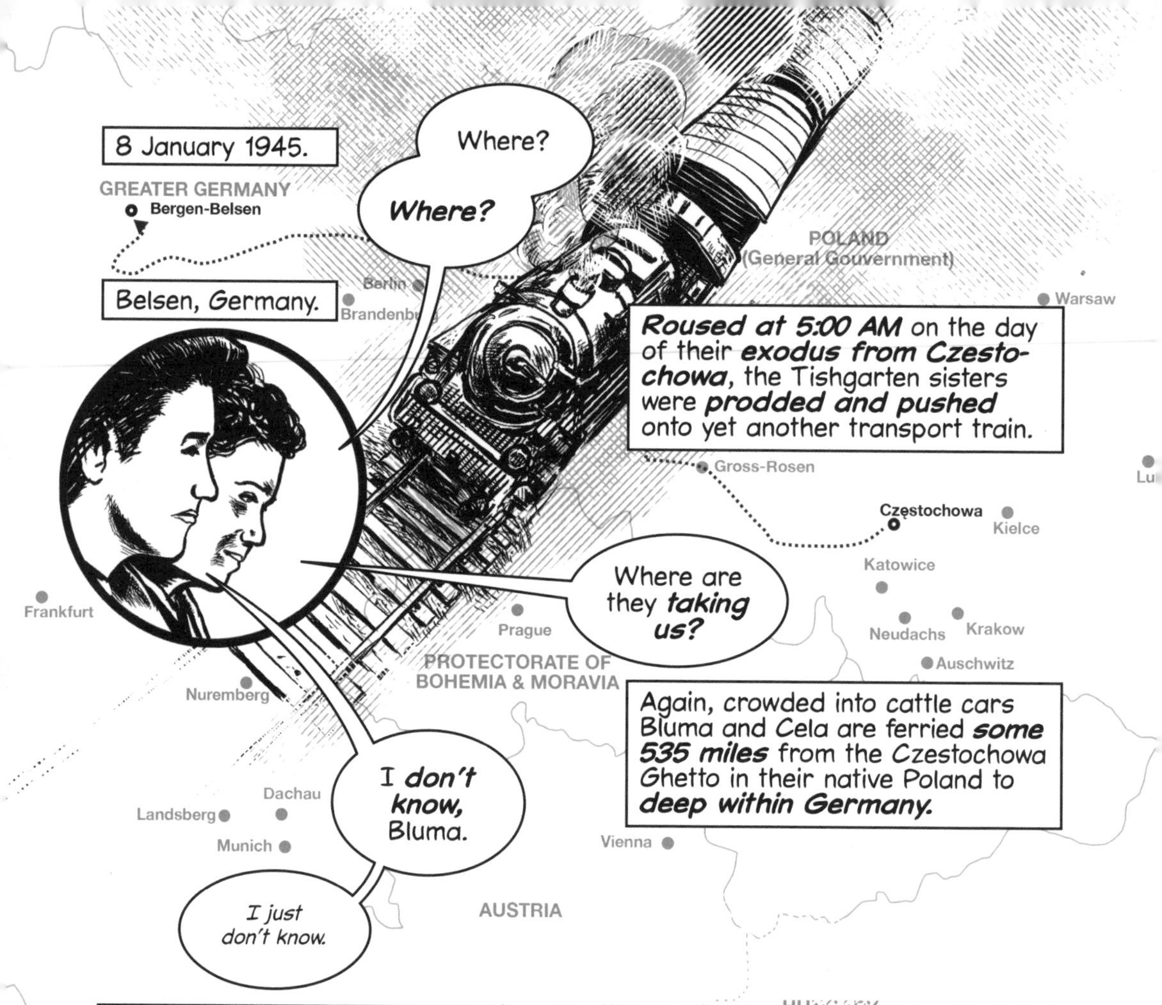
8 January 1945.
Belsen, Germany.
GREATER GERMANY
Bergen-Belsen
Berlin
Brandenb
POLAND
(General Gouvernment)
Warsaw
Where?
Where?
Roused at 5:00 AM on the day of their exodus from Czestochowa, the Tishgarten sisters were prodded and pushed onto yet another transport train.
Gross-Rosen
Częstochowa
Kielce
Katowice
Neudachs
Krakow
Auschwitz
Frankfurt
Prague
PROTECTORATE OF BOHEMIA & MORAVIA
Nuremberg
Where are they taking us?
Again, crowded into cattle cars Bluma and Cela are ferried some 535 miles from the Czestochowa Ghetto in their native Poland to deep within Germany.
I don't know, Bluma.
I just don't know.
Dachau
Landsberg
Munich
Vienna
AUSTRIA

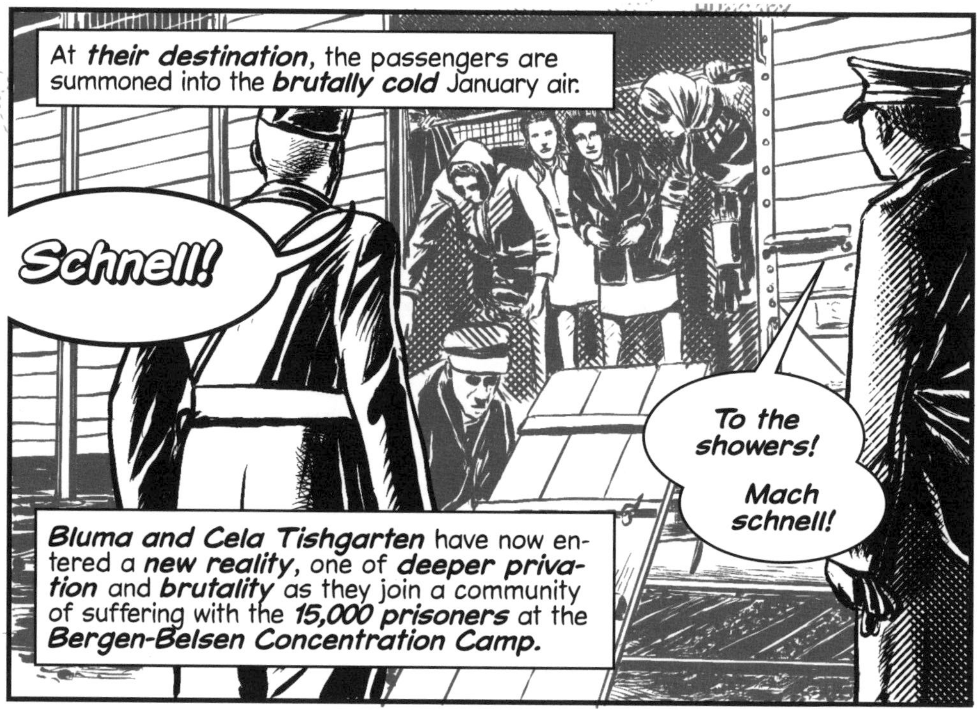
At their destination, the passengers are summoned into the brutally cold January air.
Schnell!
To the showers!
Mach schnell!
Bluma and Cela Tishgarten have now entered a new reality, one of deeper privation and brutality as they join a community of suffering with the 15,000 prisoners at the Bergen-Belsen Concentration Camp.

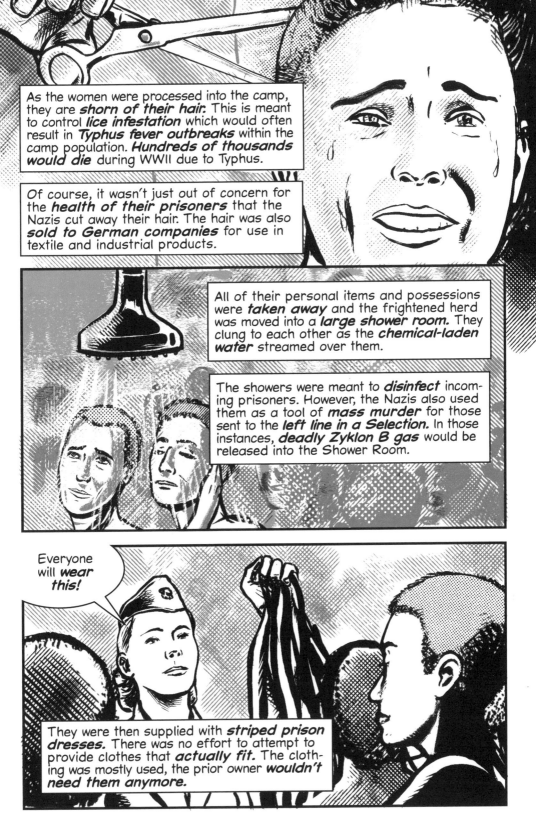

As the women were processed into the camp, they are **shorn of their hair.** This is meant to control **lice infestation** which would often result in **Typhus fever outbreaks** within the camp population. **Hundreds of thousands would die** during WWII due to Typhus.

Of course, it wasn't just out of concern for the **health of their prisoners** that the Nazis cut away their hair. The hair was also **sold to German companies** for use in textile and industrial products.

All of their personal items and possessions were **taken away** and the frightened herd was moved into a **large shower room.** They clung to each other as the **chemical-laden water** streamed over them.

The showers were meant to **disinfect** incoming prisoners. However, the Nazis also used them as a tool of **mass murder** for those sent to the **left line in a Selection.** In those instances, **deadly Zyklon B gas** would be released into the Shower Room.

Everyone will **wear this!**

They were then supplied with **striped prison dresses.** There was no effort to attempt to provide clothes that **actually fit.** The clothing was mostly used, the prior owner **wouldn't need them anymore.**

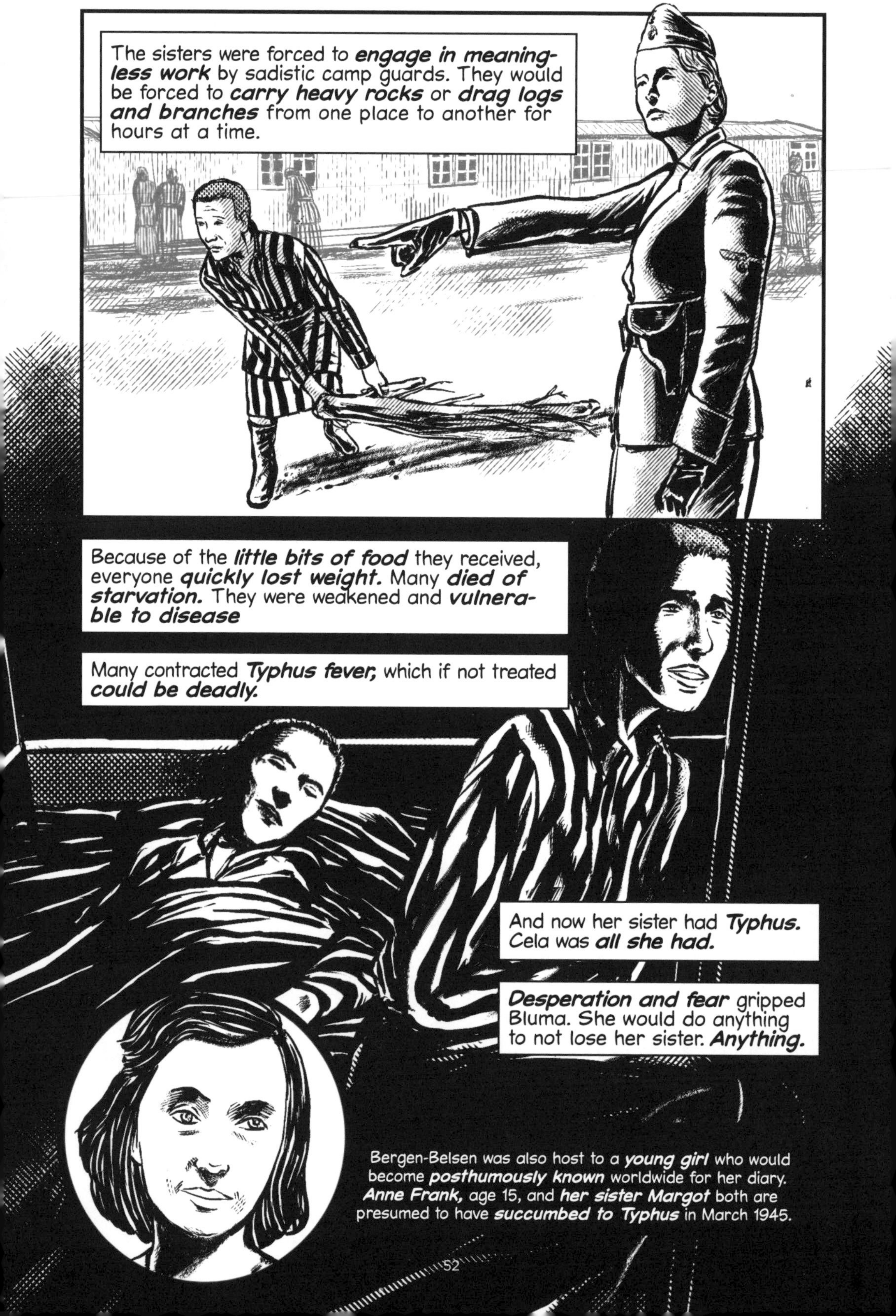
The sisters were forced to ***engage in meaningless work*** by sadistic camp guards. They would be forced to ***carry heavy rocks*** or ***drag logs and branches*** from one place to another for hours at a time.
Because of the ***little bits of food*** they received, everyone ***quickly lost weight.*** Many ***died of starvation.*** They were weakened and ***vulnerable to disease***
Many contracted ***Typhus fever,*** which if not treated ***could be deadly.***
And now her sister had ***Typhus.*** Cela was ***all she had.***
Desperation and fear gripped Bluma. She would do anything to not lose her sister. ***Anything.***
Bergen-Belsen was also host to a ***young girl*** who would become ***posthumously known*** worldwide for her diary. ***Anne Frank,*** age 15, and ***her sister Margot*** both are presumed to have ***succumbed to Typhus*** in March 1945.

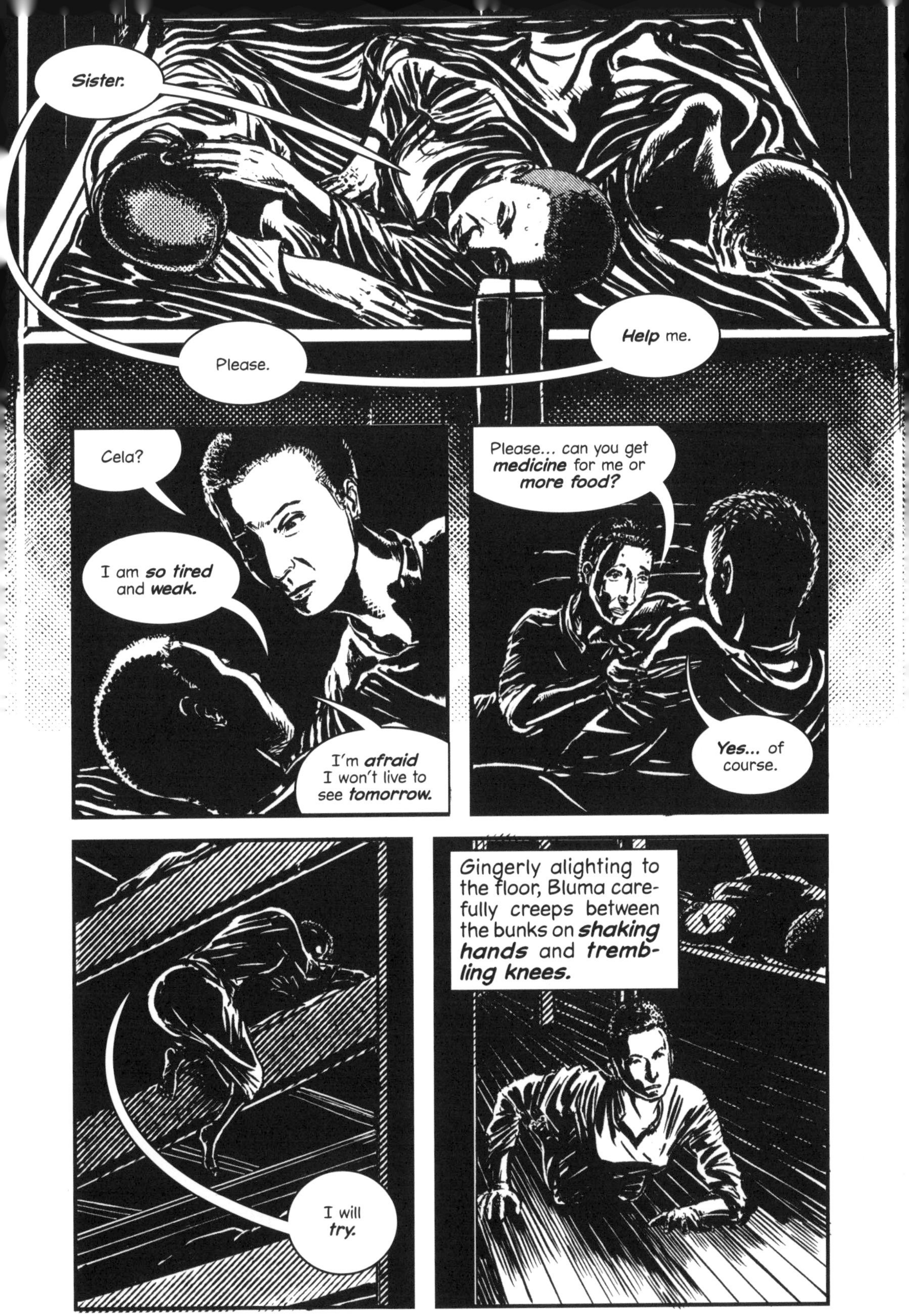
Sister.
Please.
Help me.
Cela?
I am so tired and weak.
I'm afraid I won't live to see tomorrow.
Please... can you get medicine for me or more food?
Yes... of course.
I will try.
Gingerly alighting to the floor, Bluma carefully creeps between the bunks on shaking hands and trembling knees.

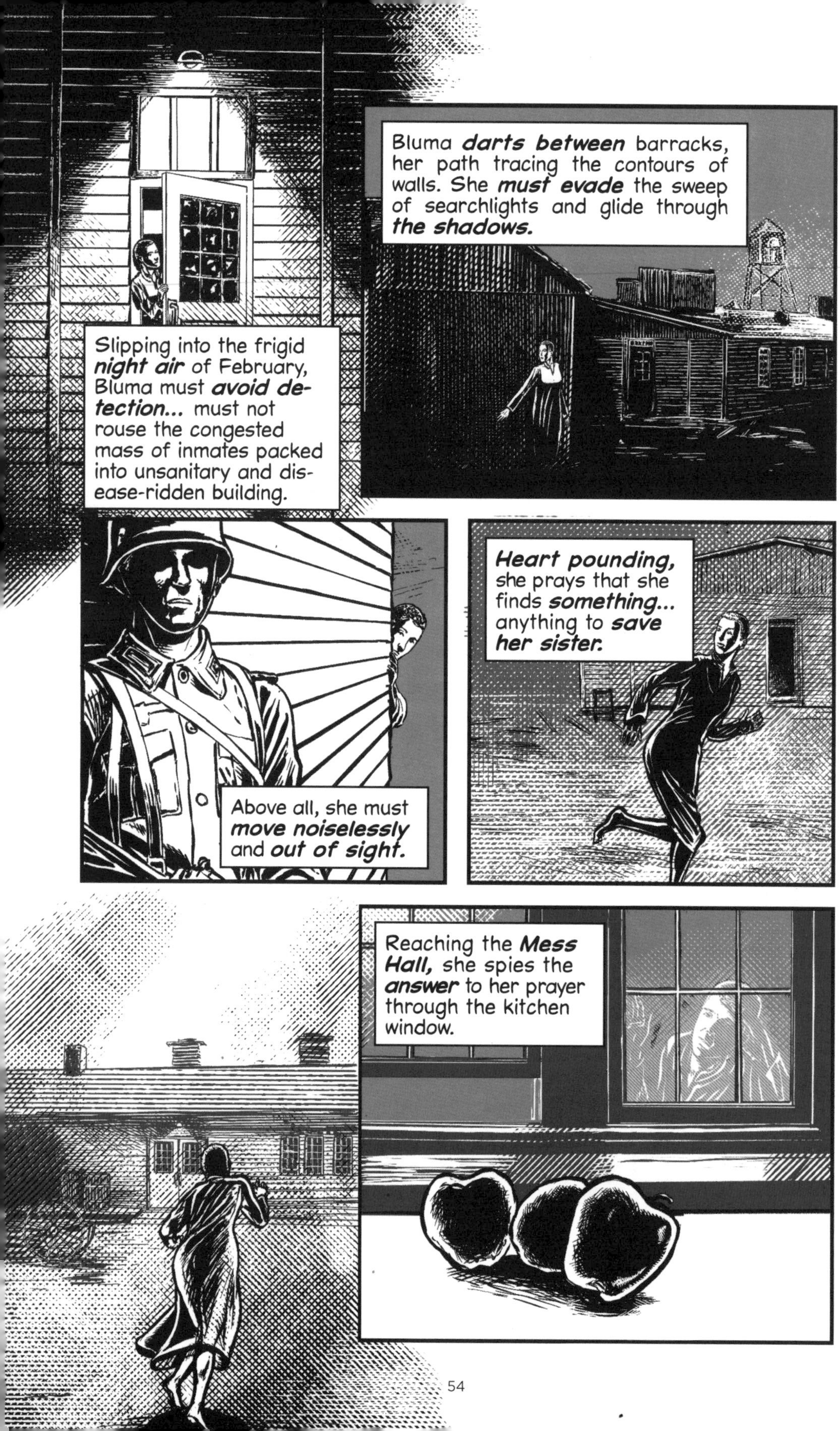
Slipping into the frigid night air of February, Bluma must avoid detection... must not rouse the congested mass of inmates packed into unsanitary and disease-ridden building.
Bluma darts between barracks, her path tracing the contours of walls. She must evade the sweep of searchlights and glide through the shadows.
Above all, she must move noiselessly and out of sight.
Heart pounding, she prays that she finds something... anything to save her sister.
Reaching the Mess Hall, she spies the answer to her prayer through the kitchen window.

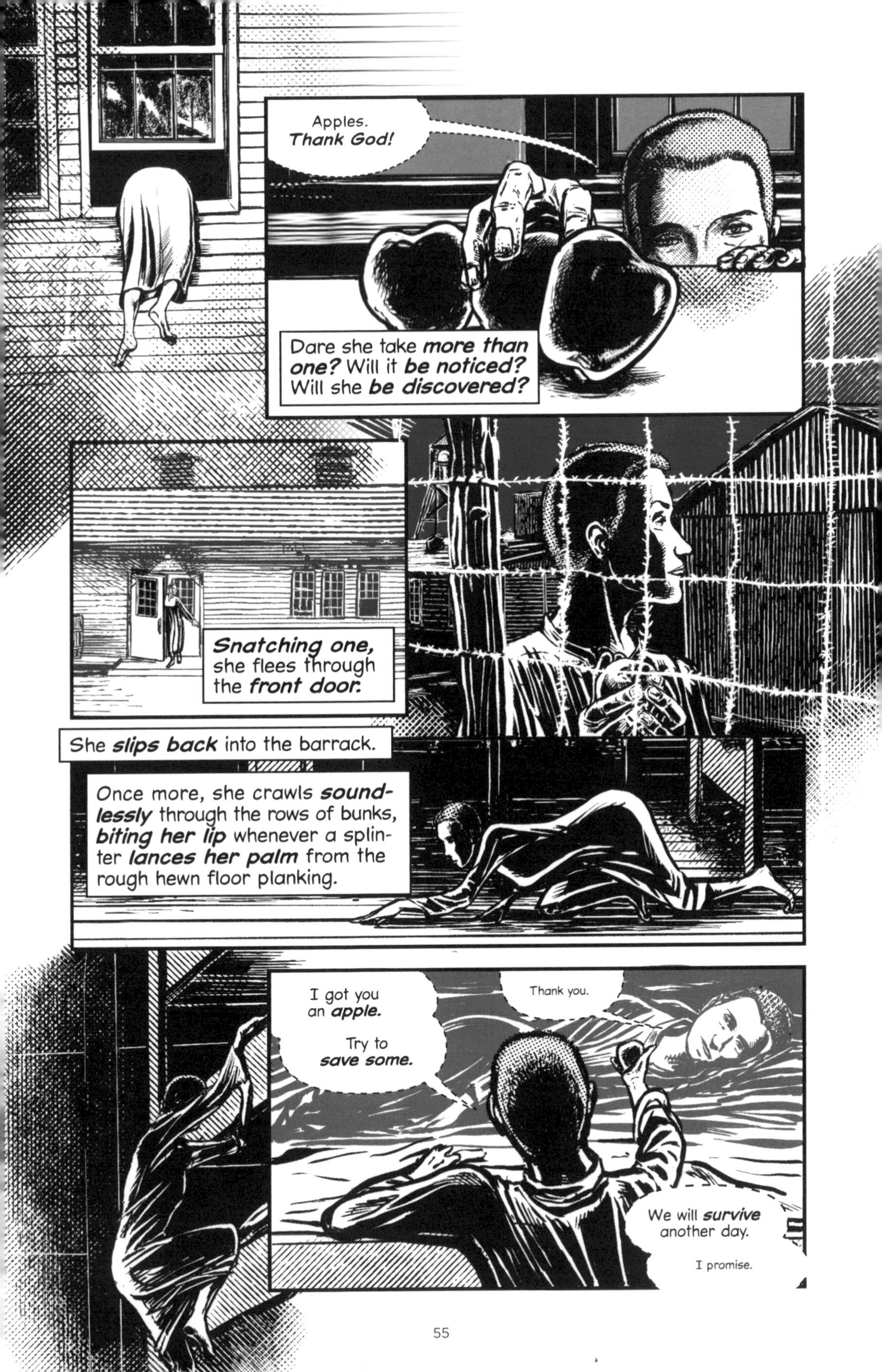

Apples.
Thank God!
Dare she take more than one? Will it be noticed? Will she be discovered?
Snatching one, she flees through the front door.
She slips back into the barrack.
Once more, she crawls soundlessly through the rows of bunks, biting her lip whenever a splinter lances her palm from the rough hewn floor planking.
I got you an apple.
Try to save some.
Thank you.
We will survive another day.
I promise.

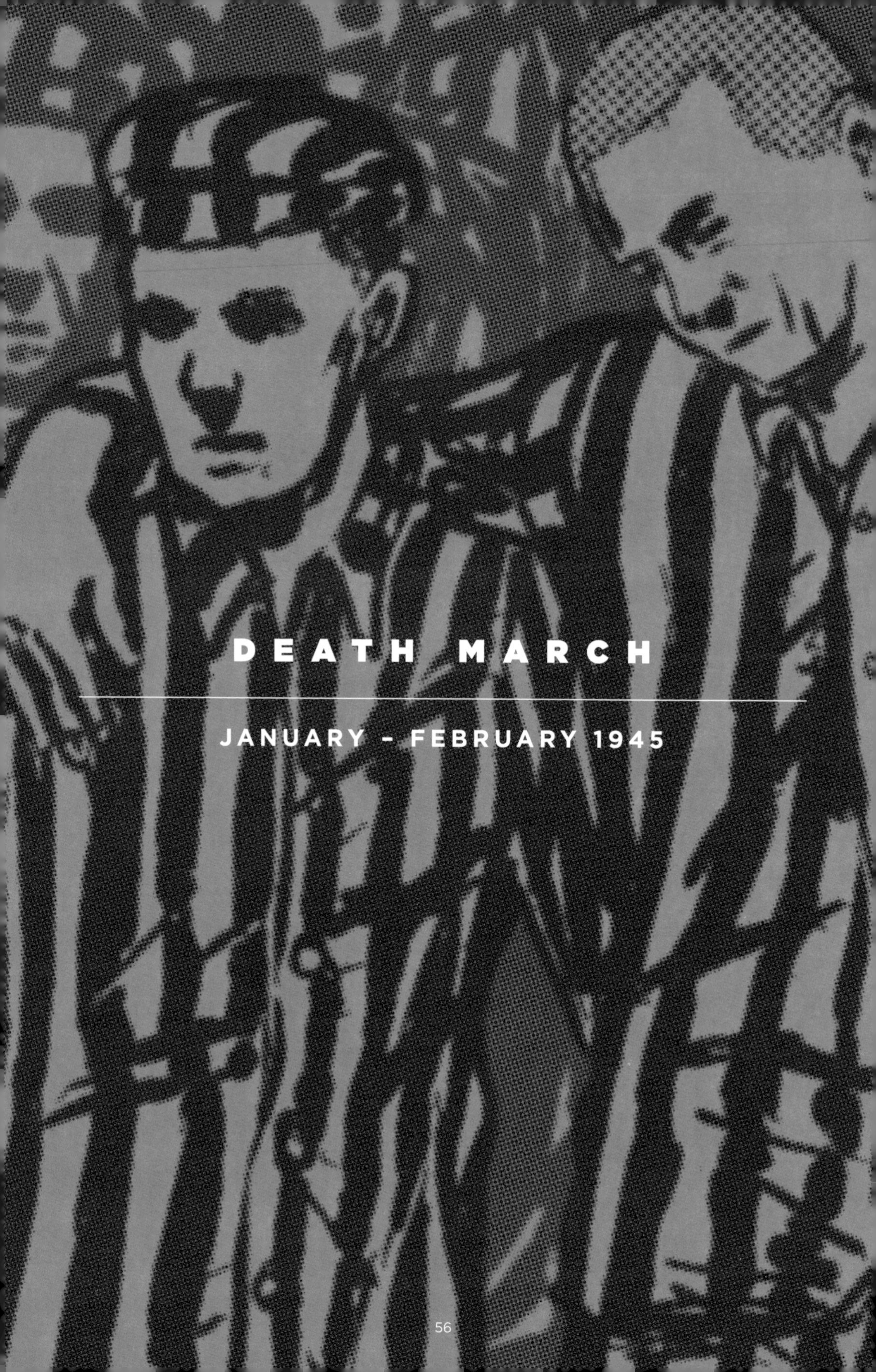

DEATH MARCH

JANUARY – FEBRUARY 1945

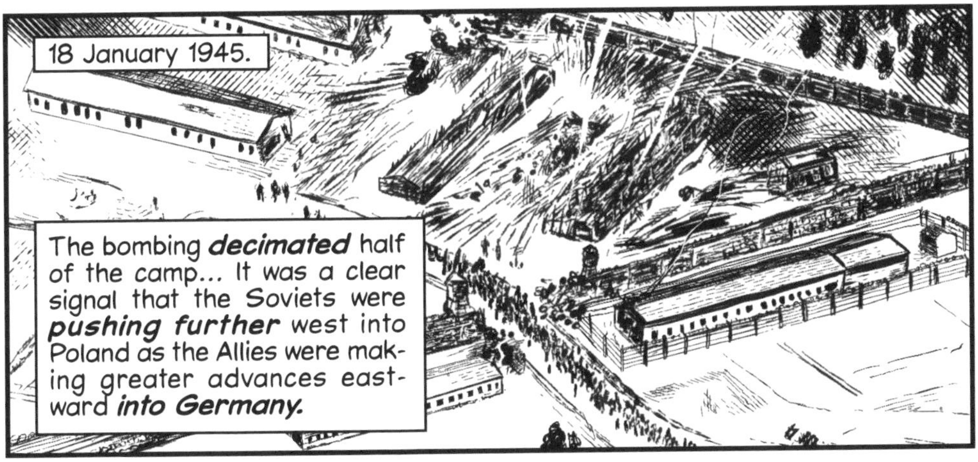
18 January 1945.
The bombing *decimated* half of the camp... It was a clear signal that the Soviets were *pushing further* west into Poland as the Allies were making greater advances eastward *into Germany.*

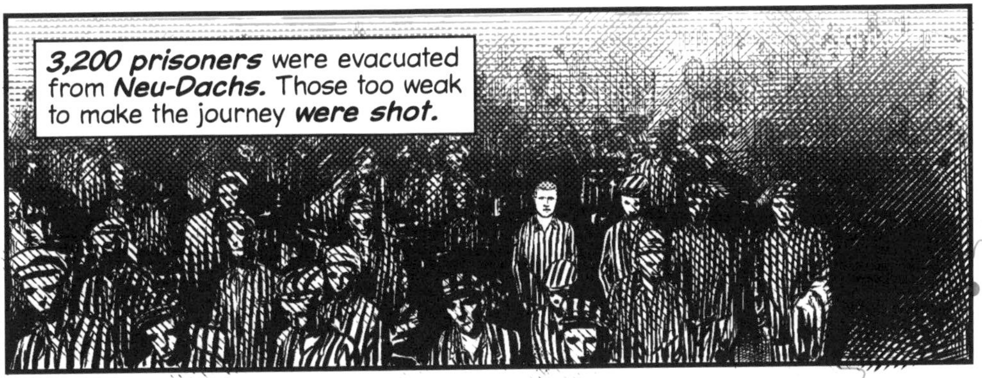
3,200 prisoners were evacuated from *Neu-Dachs.* Those too weak to make the journey *were shot.*

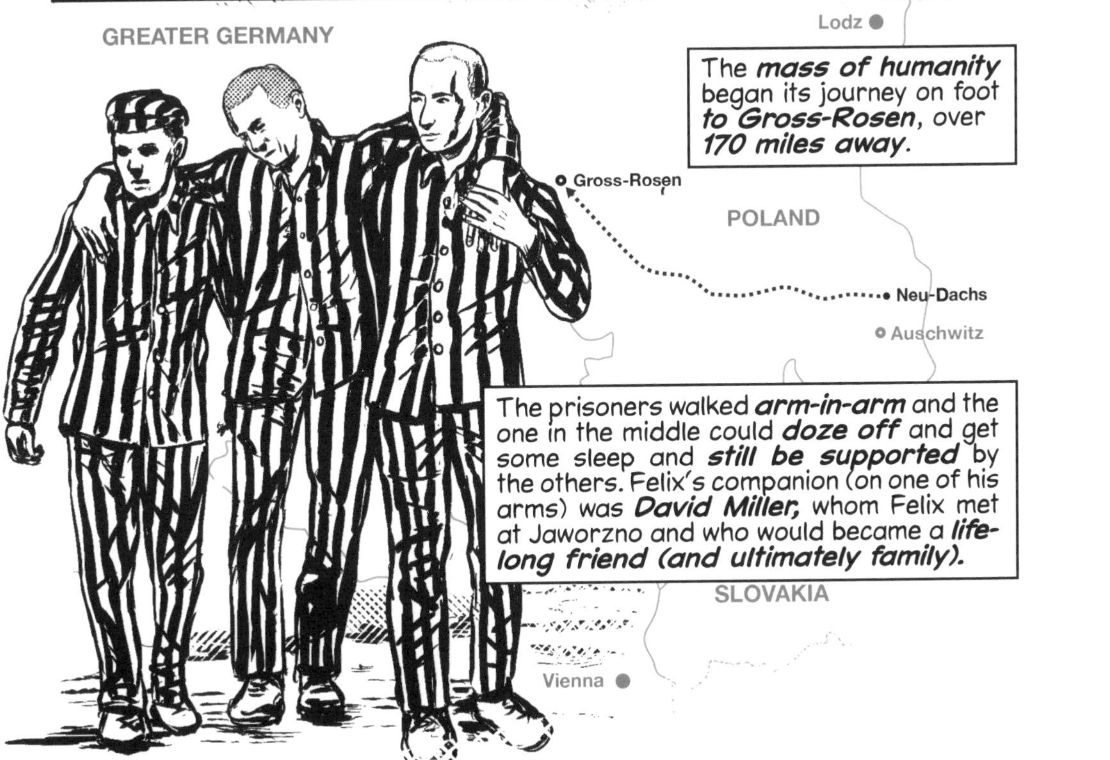
Warsaw
Lodz
GREATER GERMANY
The *mass of humanity* began its journey on foot *to Gross-Rosen*, over *170 miles away*.
Gross-Rosen
POLAND
Neu-Dachs
Auschwitz
The prisoners walked *arm-in-arm* and the one in the middle could *doze off* and get some sleep and *still be supported* by the others. Felix's companion (on one of his arms) was *David Miller,* whom Felix met at Jaworzno and who would became a *lifelong friend (and ultimately family).*
SLOVAKIA
Vienna

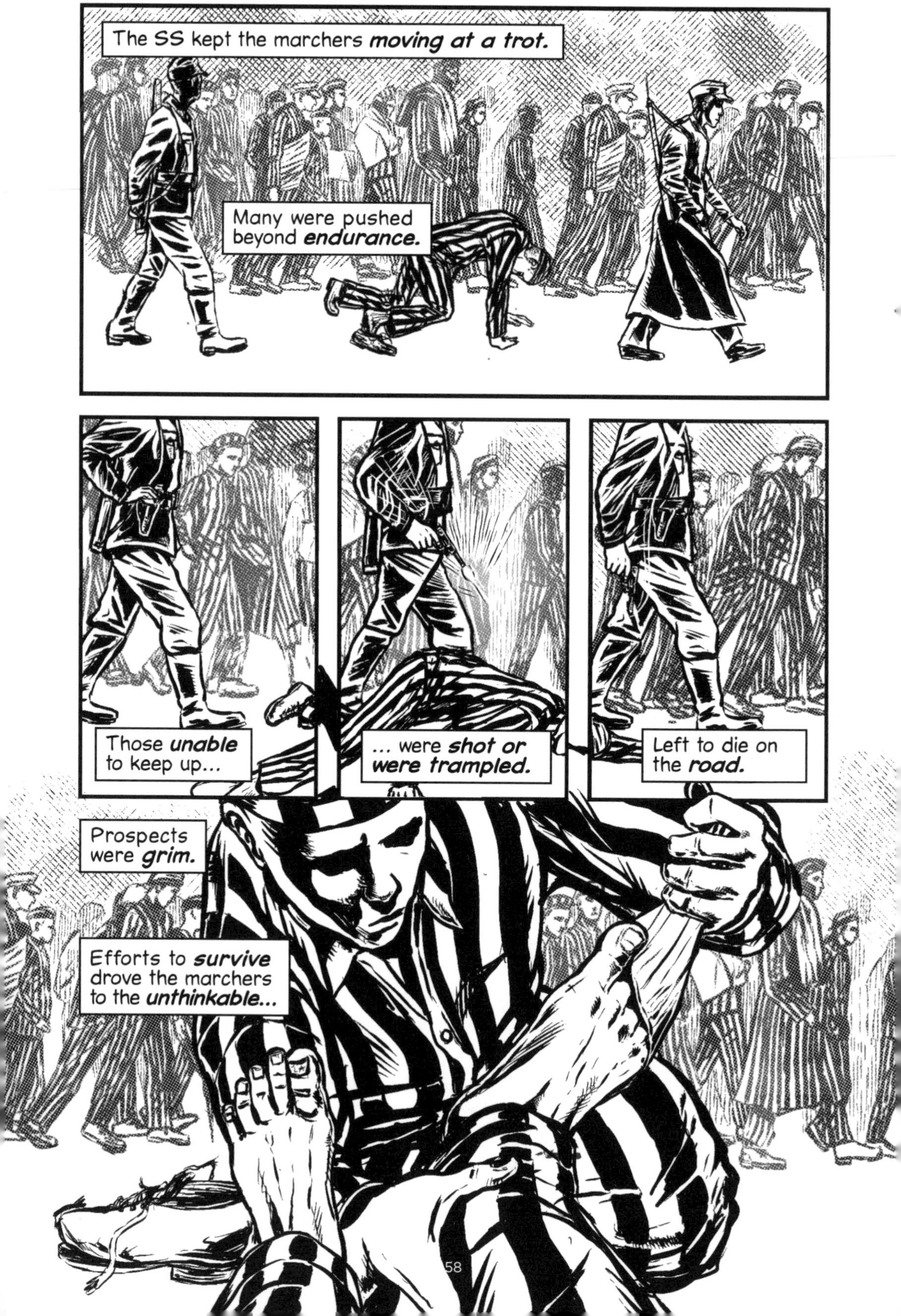

The SS kept the marchers moving at a trot.
Many were pushed beyond endurance.
Those unable to keep up...
... were shot or were trampled.
Left to die on the road.
Prospects were grim.
Efforts to survive drove the marchers to the unthinkable...

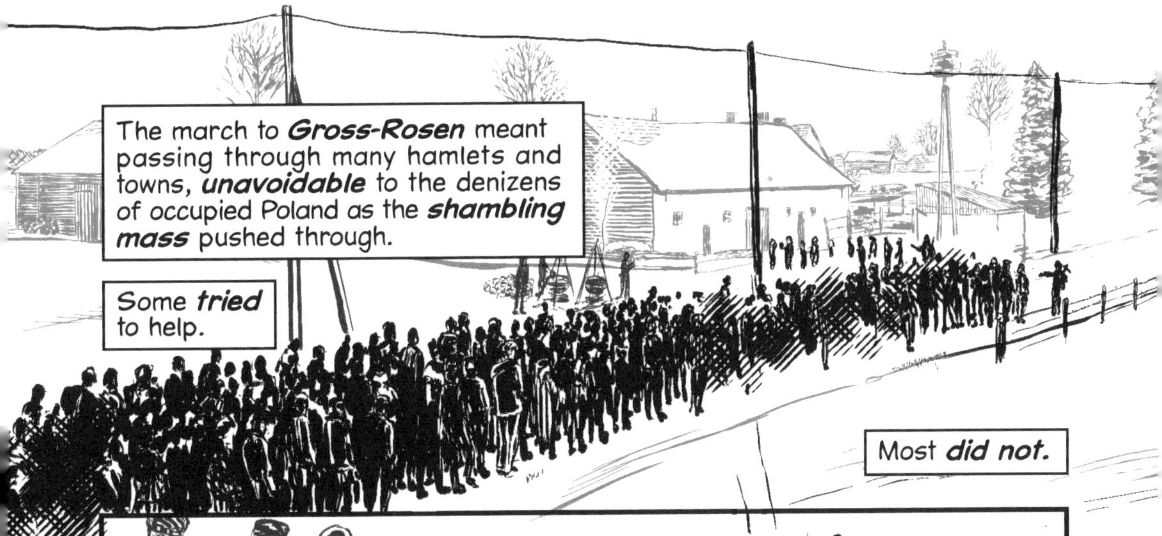
The march to Gross-Rosen meant passing through many hamlets and towns, unavoidable to the denizens of occupied Poland as the shambling mass pushed through.
Some tried to help.
Most did not.

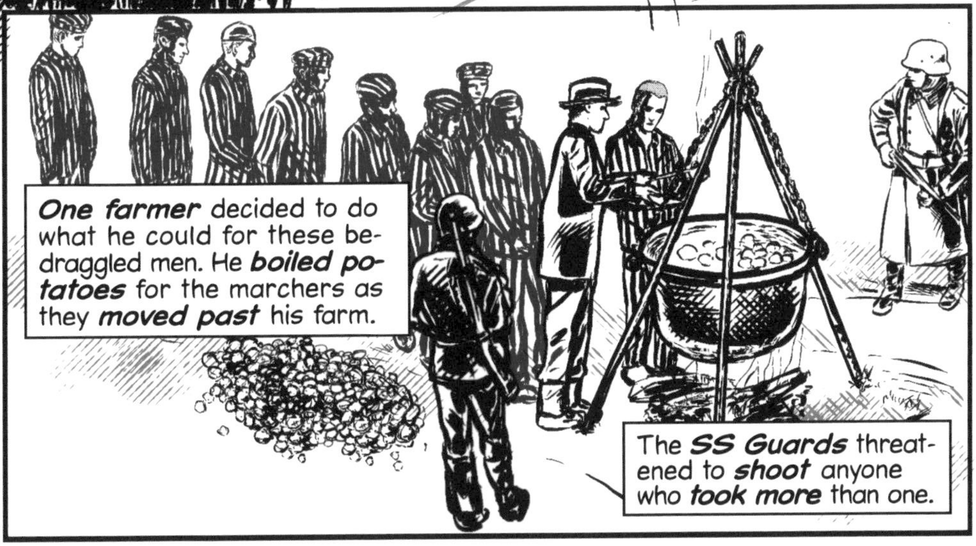
One farmer decided to do what he could for these bedraggled men. He boiled potatoes for the marchers as they moved past his farm.
The SS Guards threatened to shoot anyone who took more than one.

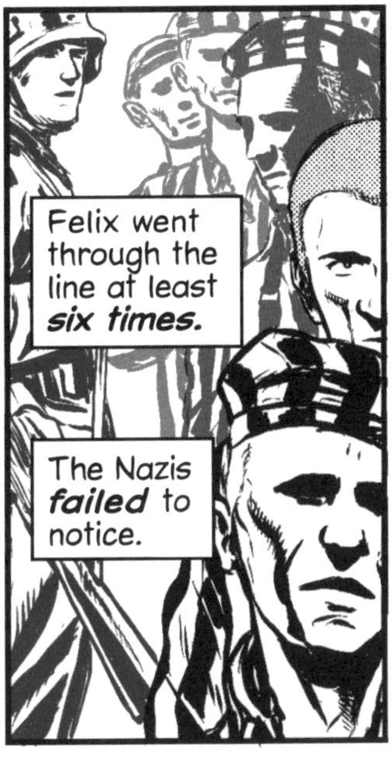
Felix went through the line at least six times.
The Nazis failed to notice.

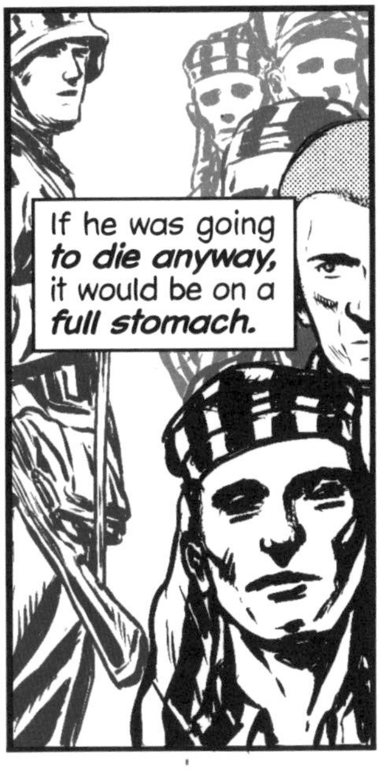
If he was going to die anyway, it would be on a full stomach.

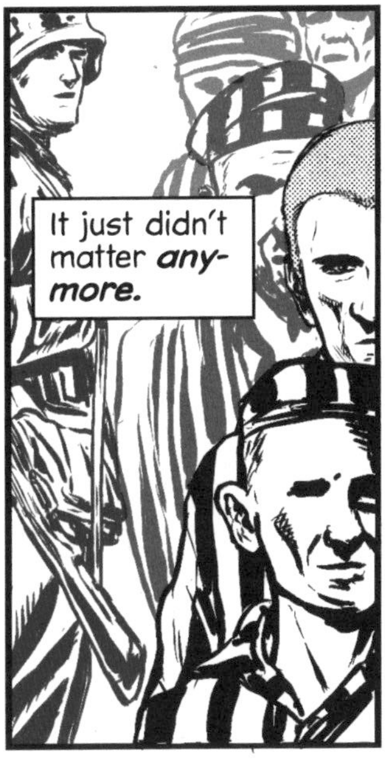
It just didn't matter anymore.

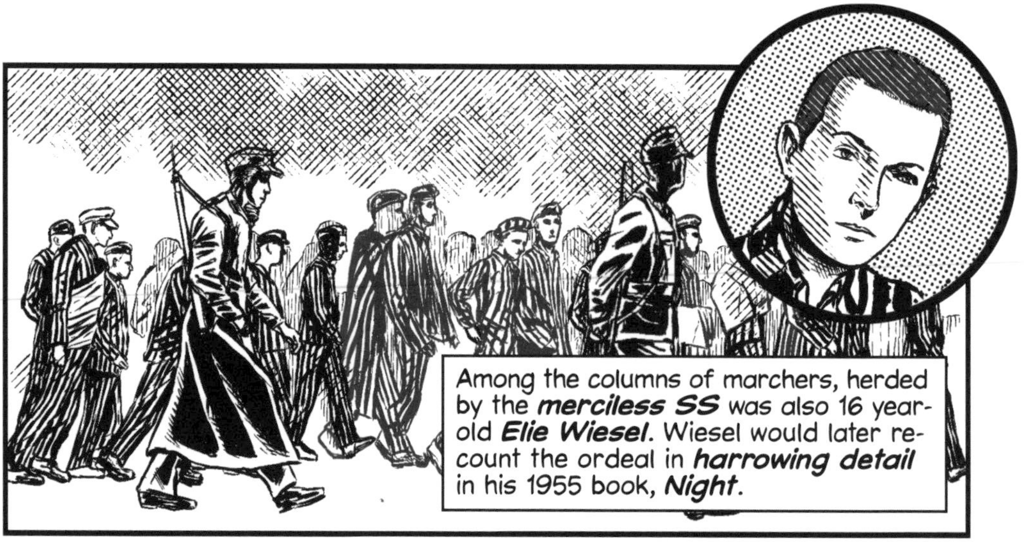
Among the columns of marchers, herded by the ***merciless SS*** was also 16 year-old ***Elie Wiesel***. Wiesel would later recount the ordeal in ***harrowing detail*** in his 1955 book, ***Night***.

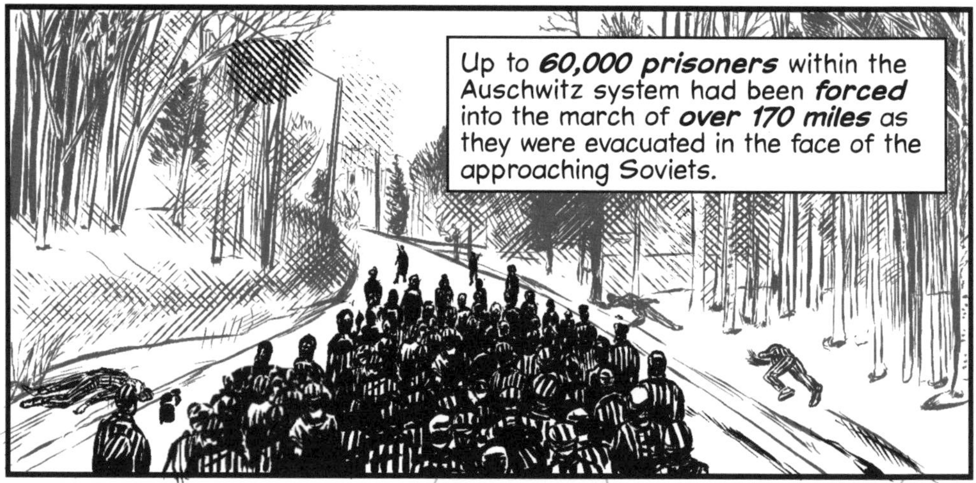
Up to ***60,000 prisoners*** within the Auschwitz system had been ***forced*** into the march of ***over 170 miles*** as they were evacuated in the face of the approaching Soviets.

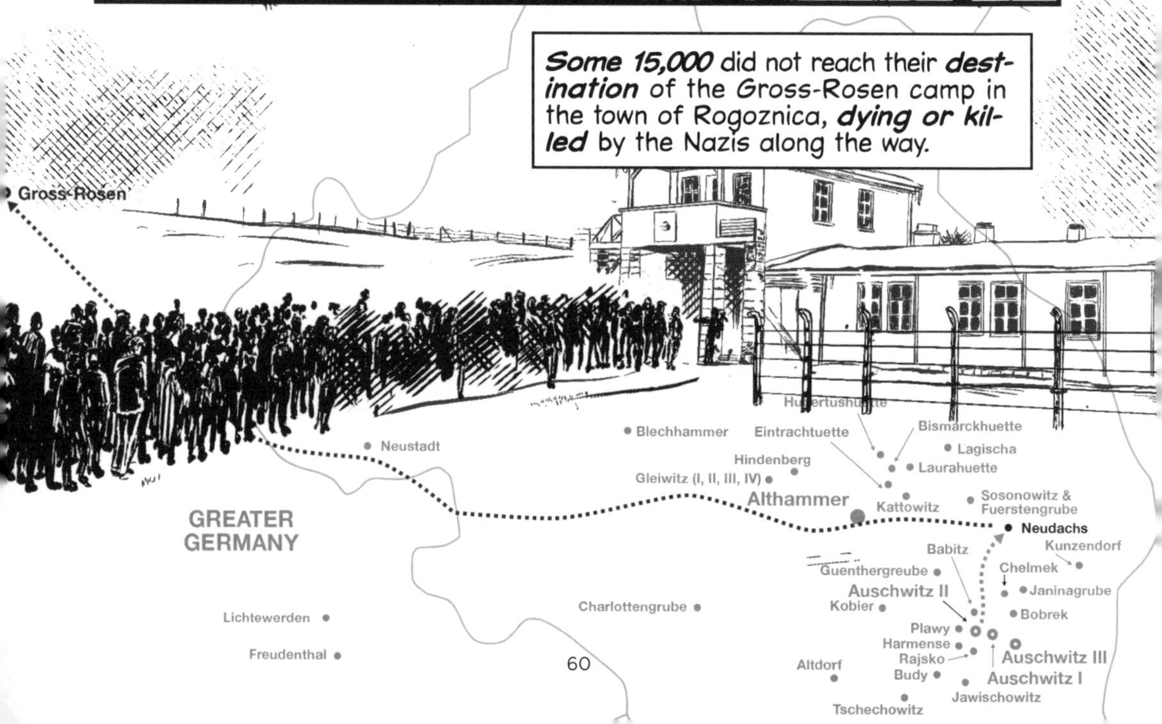
Some 15,000 did not reach their ***destination*** of the Gross-Rosen camp in the town of Rogoznica, ***dying or killed*** by the Nazis along the way.
Gross-Rosen
Blechhammer
Eintrachtuette
Bismarckhuette
Lagischa
Laurahuette
Neustadt
Hindenberg
Gleiwitz (I, II, III, IV)
Althammer
Kattowitz
Sosonowitz & Fuerstengrube
Neudachs
GREATER GERMANY
Babitz
Kunzendorf
Guenthergreube
Chelmek
Auschwitz II
Janinagrube
Kobier
Bobrek
Lichtewerden
Charlottengrube
Plawy
Harmense
Rajsko
Auschwitz III
Freudenthal
Altdorf
Budy
Auschwitz I
Jawischowitz
Tschechowitz

From *Gross-Rosen*, the *marchers* were then placed on a *transport* and moved to their *next destination*.

GREATER GERMANY

Dresden ●
Buchenwald ○◀ · ● Gross-Rosen
· ● Neudachs
Frankfurt · ○ Auschwitz

All told, *hundreds of thousands* were forced into the *Death Marches* as the Nazis liquidated camps across Germany and its occupied territories. *Tens of thousands* were killed.

BOHEMIA & MORAVIA

10 February 1945.

The train had come to its *final stop*.

Felix Goldberg had arrived at *Buchenwald*.

61

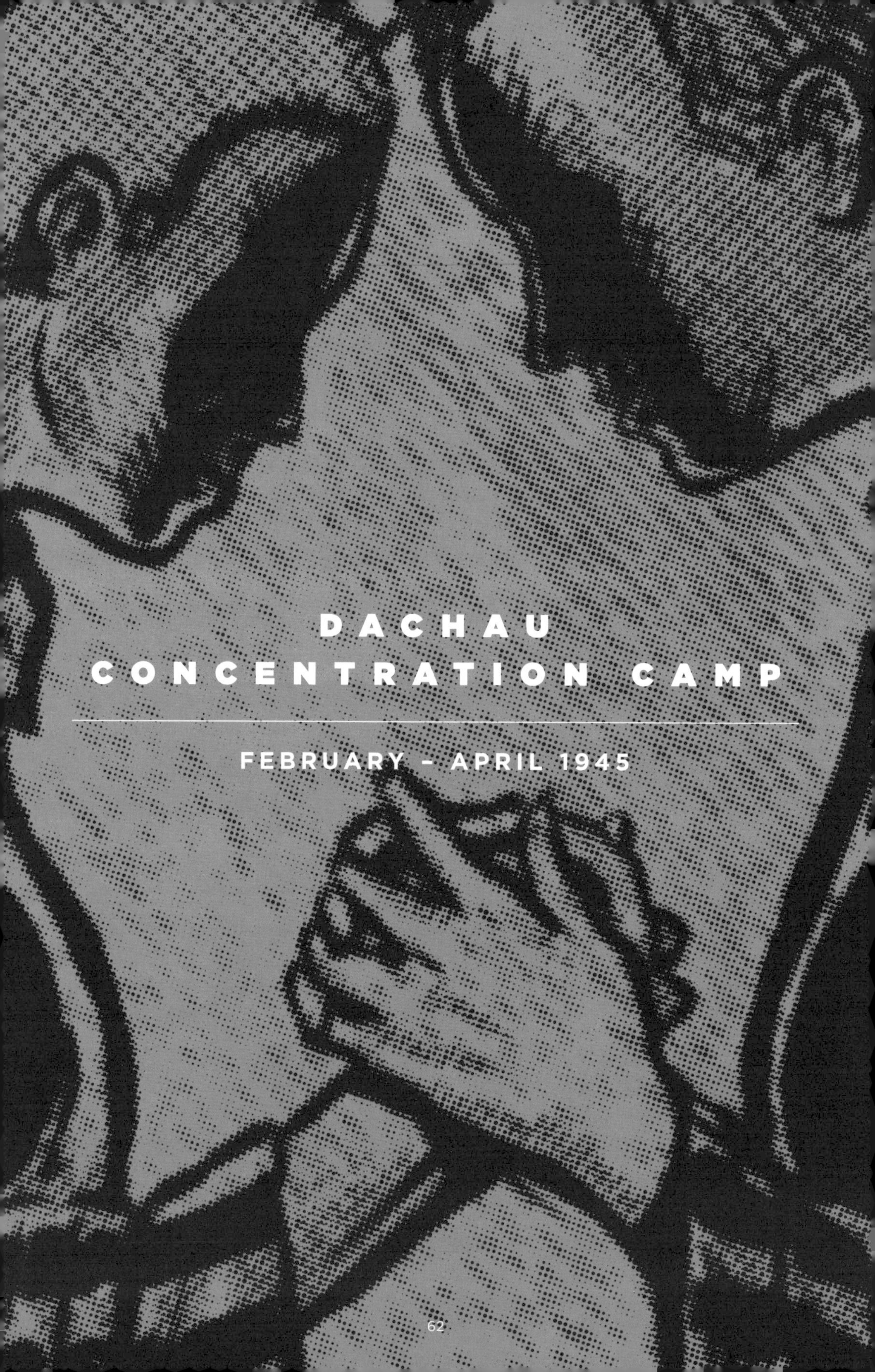

DACHAU CONCENTRATION CAMP

FEBRUARY – APRIL 1945

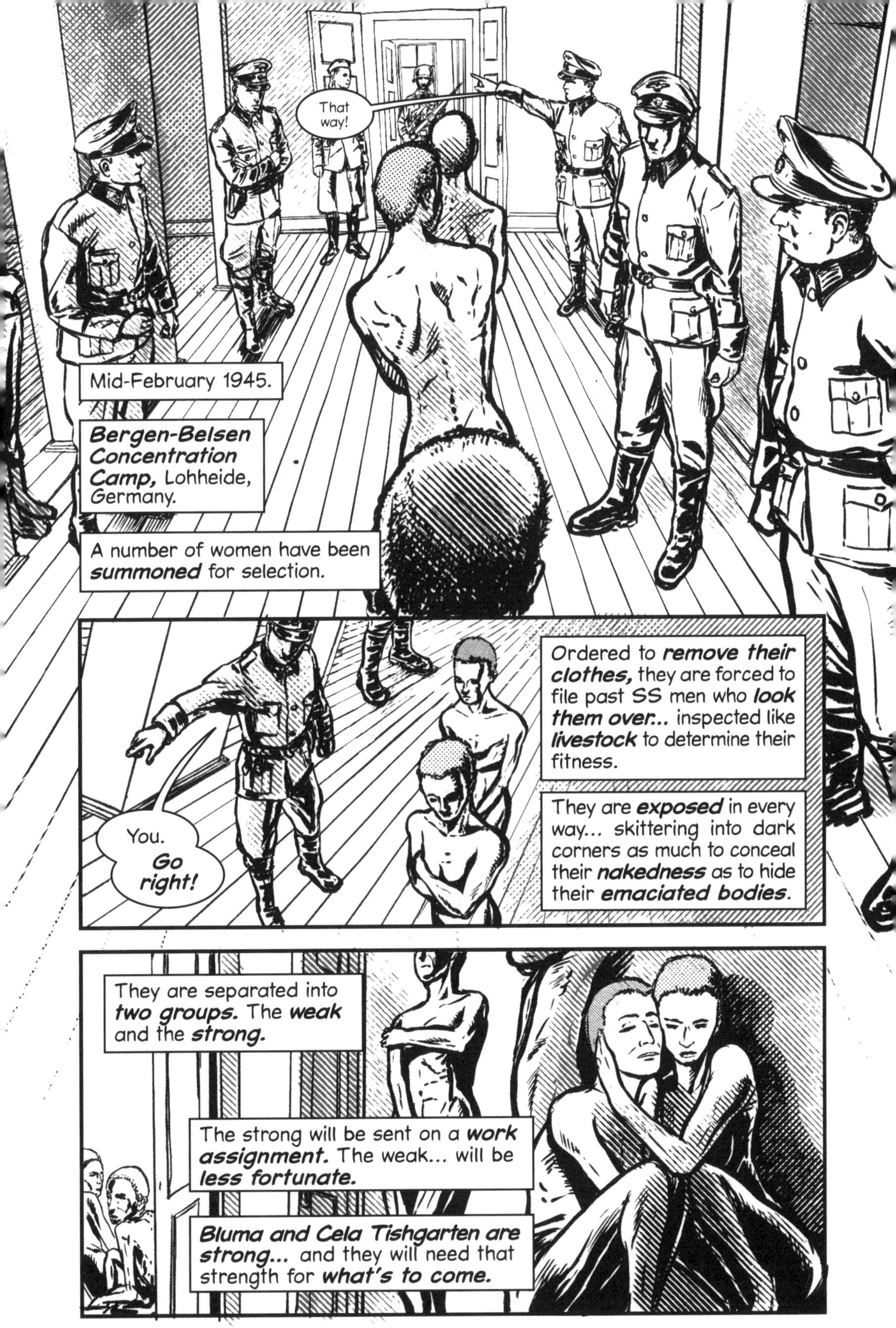
That way!
Mid-February 1945.
Bergen-Belsen Concentration Camp, Lohheide, Germany.
A number of women have been summoned for selection.
Ordered to remove their clothes, they are forced to file past SS men who look them over... inspected like livestock to determine their fitness.
They are exposed in every way... skittering into dark corners as much to conceal their nakedness as to hide their emaciated bodies.
You. Go right!
They are separated into two groups. The weak and the strong.
The strong will be sent on a work assignment. The weak... will be less fortunate.
Bluma and Cela Tishgarten are strong... and they will need that strength for what's to come.

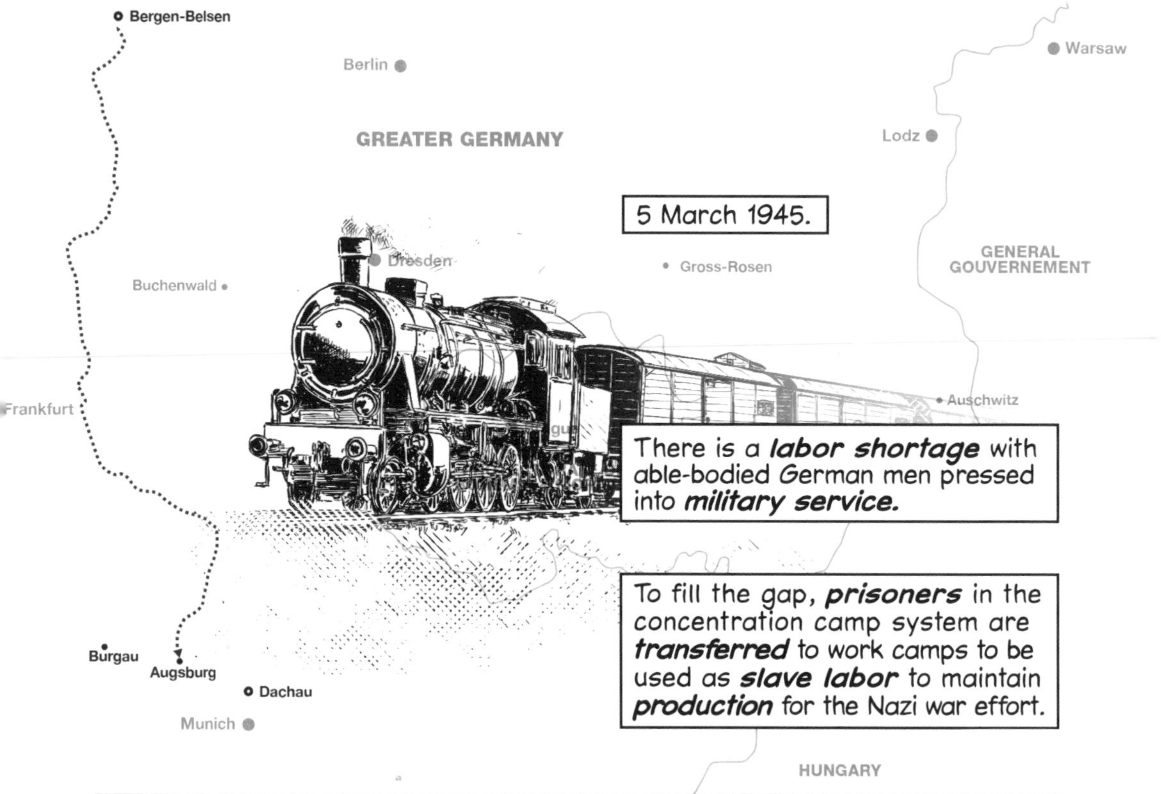
Bergen-Belsen
Berlin
Warsaw
GREATER GERMANY
Lodz
5 March 1945.
Dresden
Gross-Rosen
GENERAL GOUVERNEMENT
Buchenwald
Auschwitz
Frankfurt
There is a *labor shortage* with able-bodied German men pressed into *military service.*
To fill the gap, *prisoners* in the concentration camp system are *transferred* to work camps to be used as *slave labor* to maintain *production* for the Nazi war effort.
Burgau
Augsburg
Dachau
Munich
HUNGARY

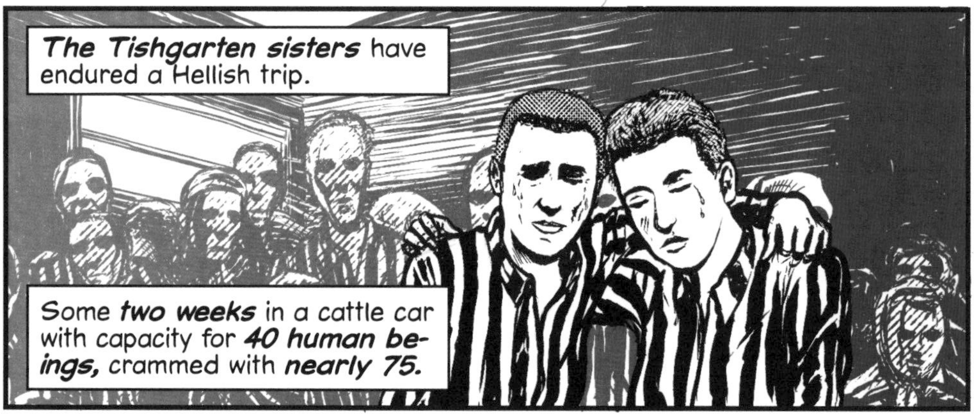
The Tishgarten sisters have endured a Hellish trip.
Some *two weeks* in a cattle car with capacity for *40 human beings,* crammed with *nearly 75.*

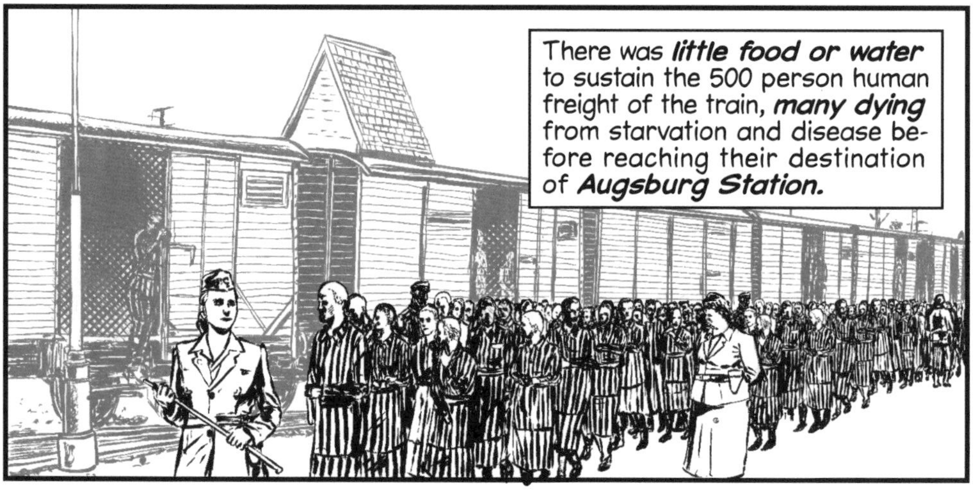
There was *little food or water* to sustain the 500 person human freight of the train, *many dying* from starvation and disease before reaching their destination of *Augsburg Station.*

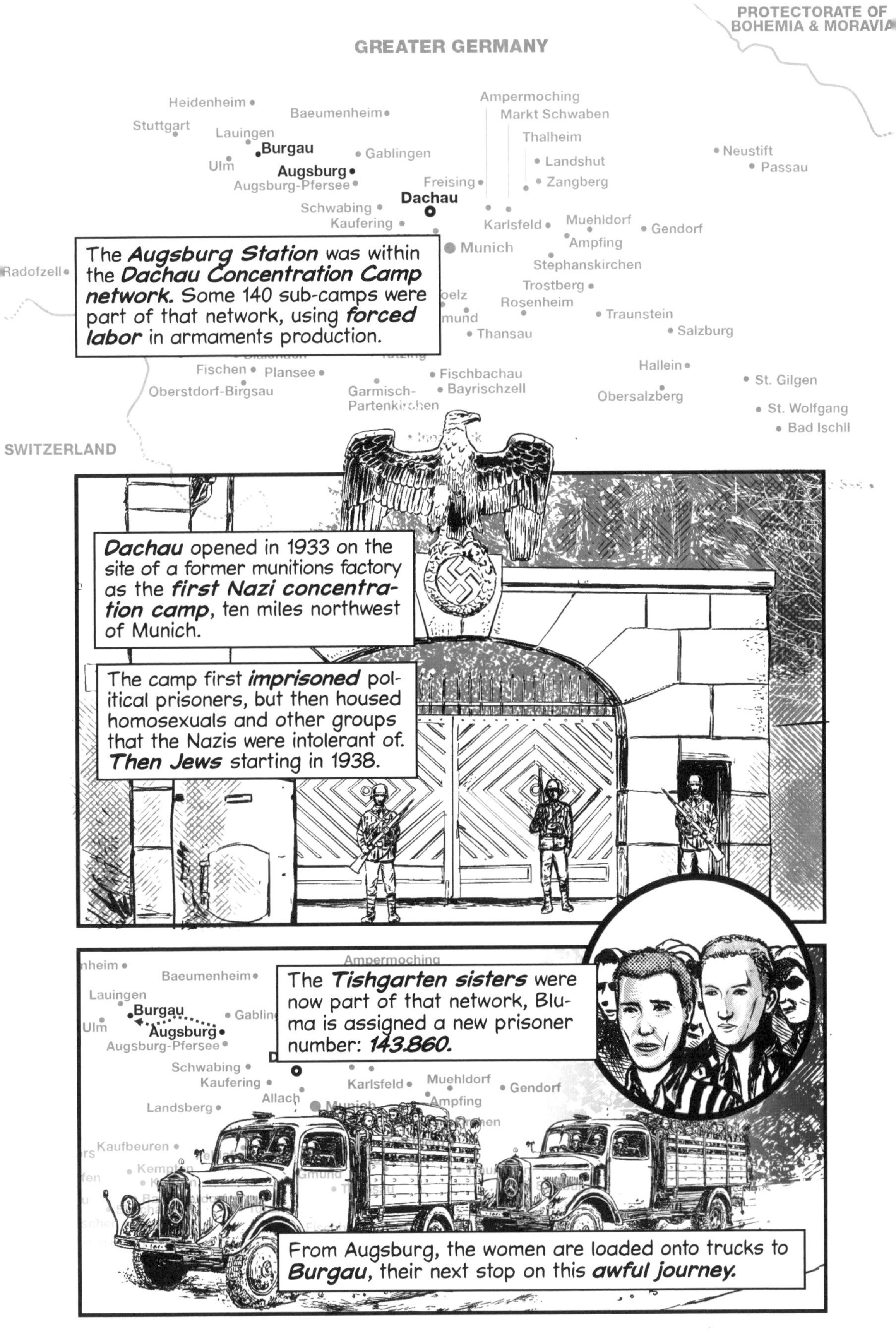
PROTECTORATE OF BOHEMIA & MORAVIA
GREATER GERMANY
Heidenheim
Baeumenheim
Stuttgart
Lauingen
Burgau
Ulm
Augsburg
Augsburg-Pfersee
Gablingen
Ampermoching
Markt Schwaben
Thalheim
Landshut
Zangberg
Freising
Dachau
Neustift
Passau
Schwabing
Kaufering
Karlsfeld
Muehldorf
Gendorf
Ampfing
Munich
Stephanskirchen
Radofzell
Trostberg
Rosenheim
Traunstein
Salzburg
Thansau
The Augsburg Station was within the Dachau Concentration Camp network. Some 140 sub-camps were part of that network, using forced labor in armaments production.
Fischen
Plansee
Oberstdorf-Birgsau
Garmisch-Partenkirchen
Fischbachau
Bayrischzell
Hallein
Obersalzberg
St. Gilgen
St. Wolfgang
Bad Ischll
SWITZERLAND
Dachau opened in 1933 on the site of a former munitions factory as the first Nazi concentration camp, ten miles northwest of Munich.
The camp first imprisoned political prisoners, but then housed homosexuals and other groups that the Nazis were intolerant of. Then Jews starting in 1938.
Baeumenheim
Lauingen
Burgau
Ulm
Augsburg
Augsburg-Pfersee
Schwabing
Kaufering
Allach
Landsberg
Karlsfeld
Muehldorf
Gendorf
Ampfing
Kaufbeuren
The Tishgarten sisters were now part of that network, Bluma is assigned a new prisoner number: 143.860.
From Augsburg, the women are loaded onto trucks to Burgau, their next stop on this awful journey.

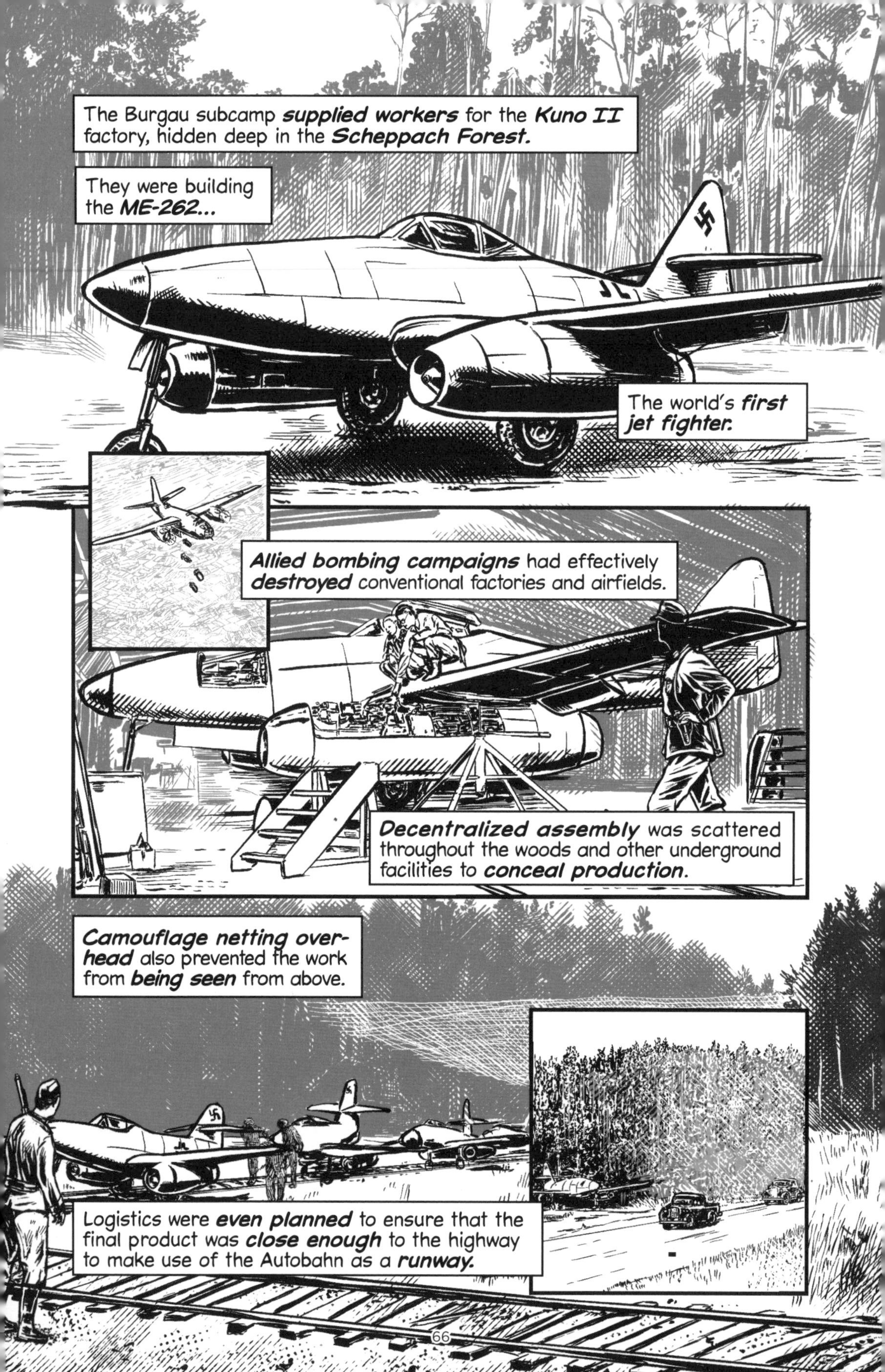
The Burgau subcamp supplied workers for the Kuno II factory, hidden deep in the Scheppach Forest.
They were building the ME-262...
The world's first jet fighter.
Allied bombing campaigns had effectively destroyed conventional factories and airfields.
Decentralized assembly was scattered throughout the woods and other underground facilities to conceal production.
Camouflage netting overhead also prevented the work from being seen from above.
Logistics were even planned to ensure that the final product was close enough to the highway to make use of the Autobahn as a runway.

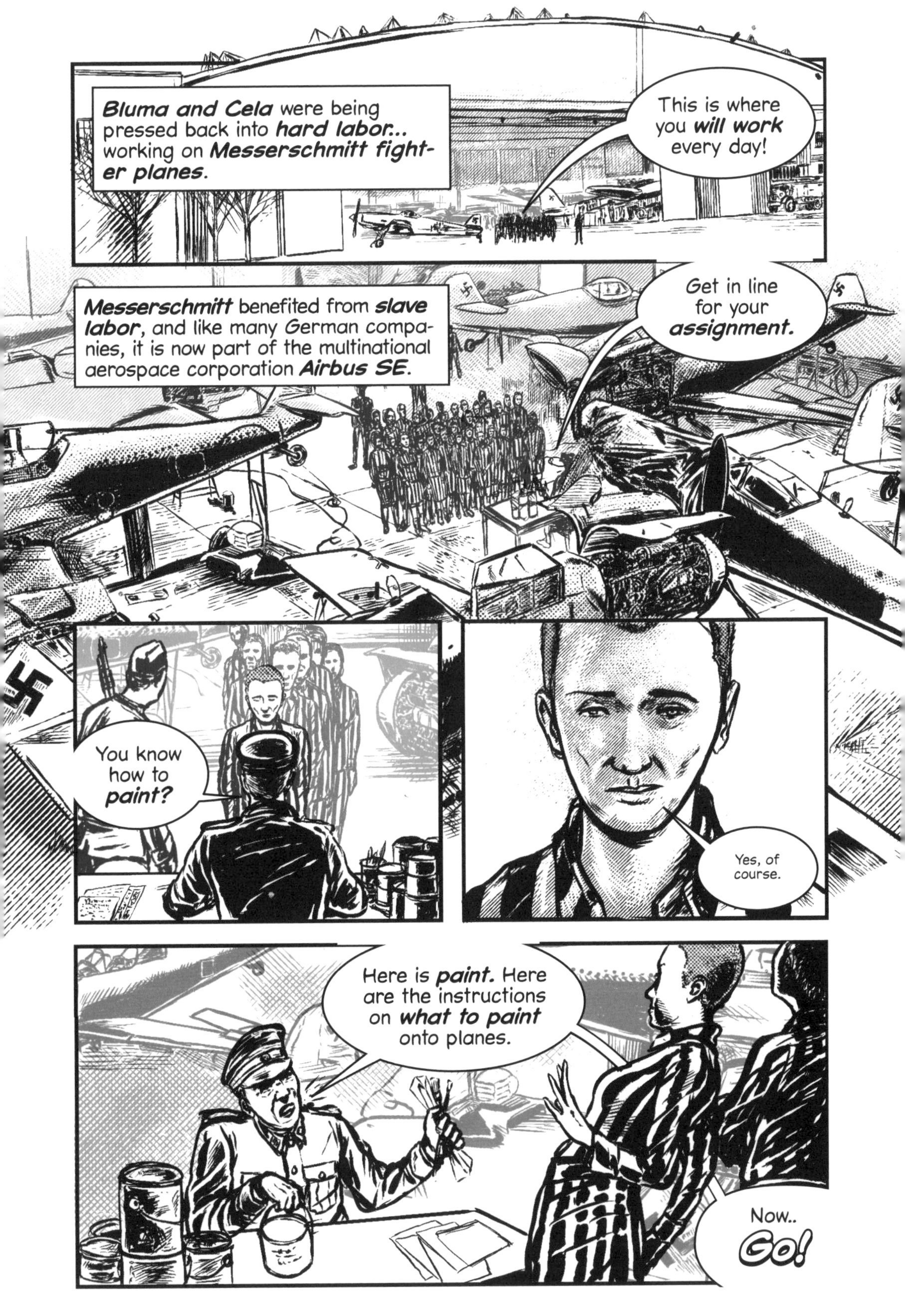

Bluma and Cela were being pressed back into hard labor... working on Messerschmitt fighter planes.
This is where you will work every day!
Messerschmitt benefited from slave labor, and like many German companies, it is now part of the multinational aerospace corporation Airbus SE.
Get in line for your assignment.
You know how to paint?
Yes, of course.
Here is paint. Here are the instructions on what to paint onto planes.
Now.. Go!

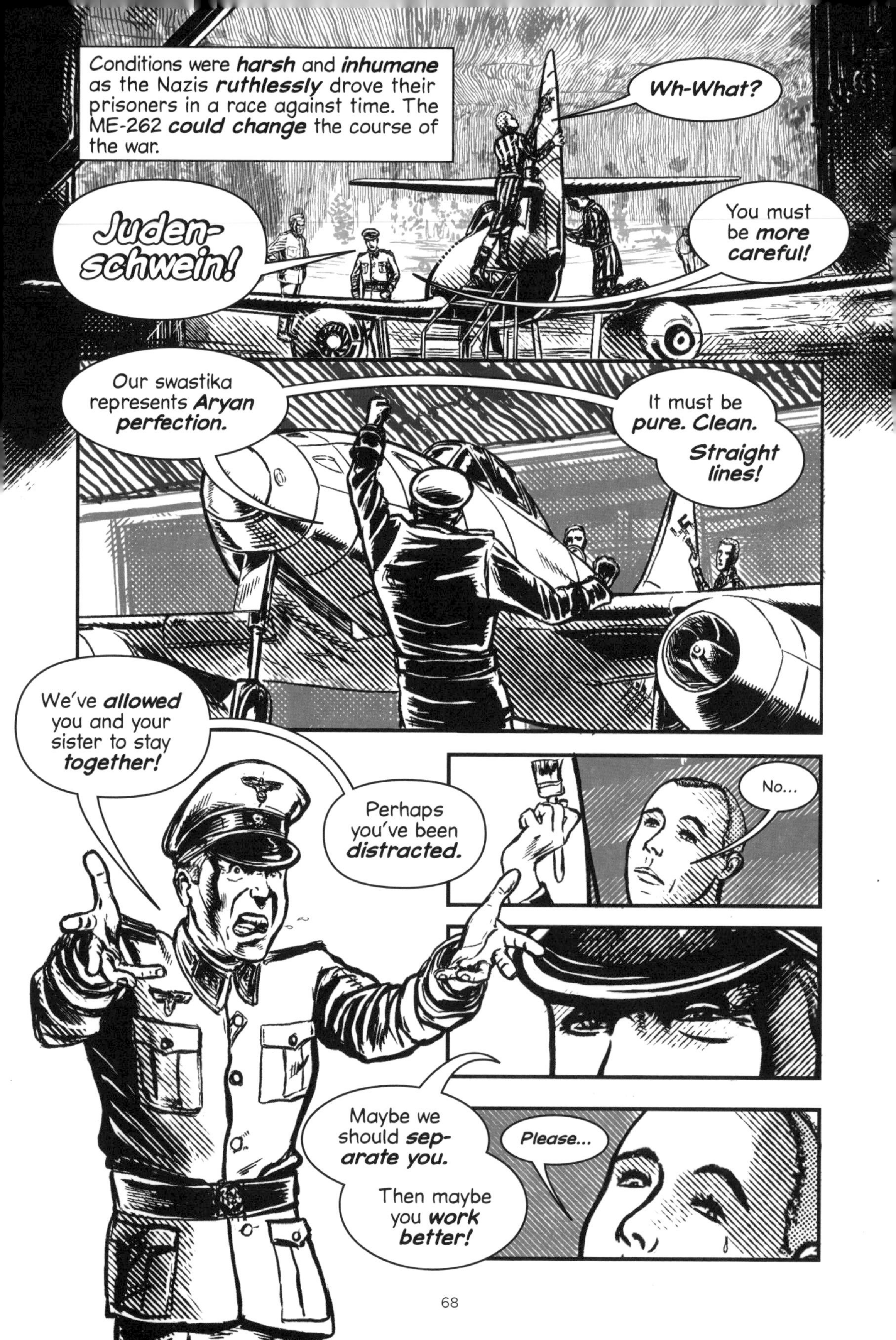
Conditions were **harsh** and **inhumane** as the Nazis **ruthlessly** drove their prisoners in a race against time. The ME-262 **could change** the course of the war.
Wh-What?
Juden-schwein!
You must be **more careful!**
Our swastika represents **Aryan perfection.**
It must be **pure. Clean.**
Straight lines!
We've **allowed** you and your sister to stay **together!**
Perhaps you've been **distracted.**
No...
Maybe we should **sep-arate you.**
Then maybe you **work better!**
Please...

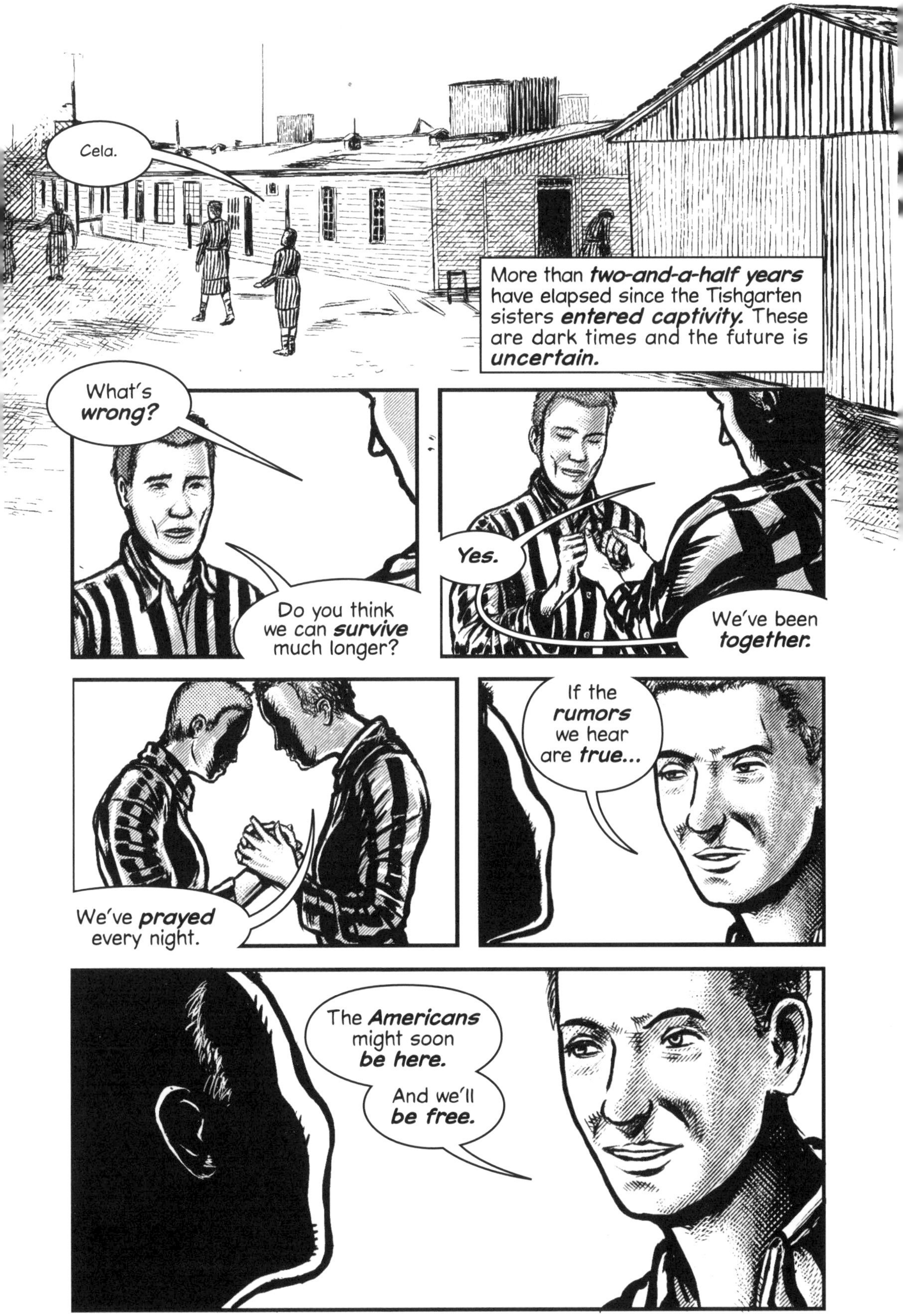
Cela.
More than **two-and-a-half years** have elapsed since the Tishgarten sisters **entered captivity.** These are dark times and the future is **uncertain.**
What's **wrong?**
Do you think we can **survive** much longer?
Yes.
We've been **together.**
We've **prayed** every night.
If the **rumors** we hear are **true...**
The **Americans** might soon **be here.**
And we'll **be free.**

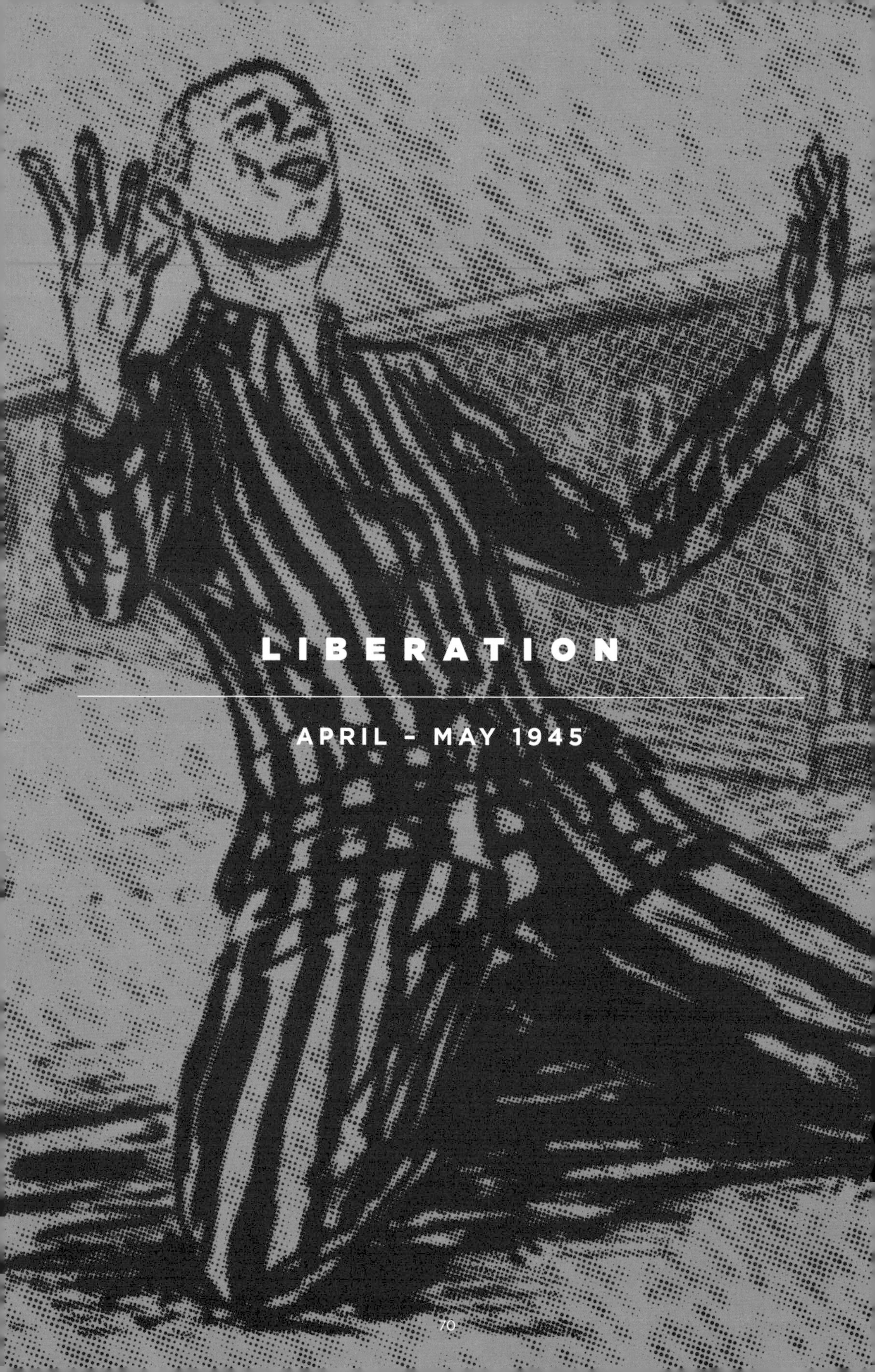

LIBERATION

APRIL – MAY 1945

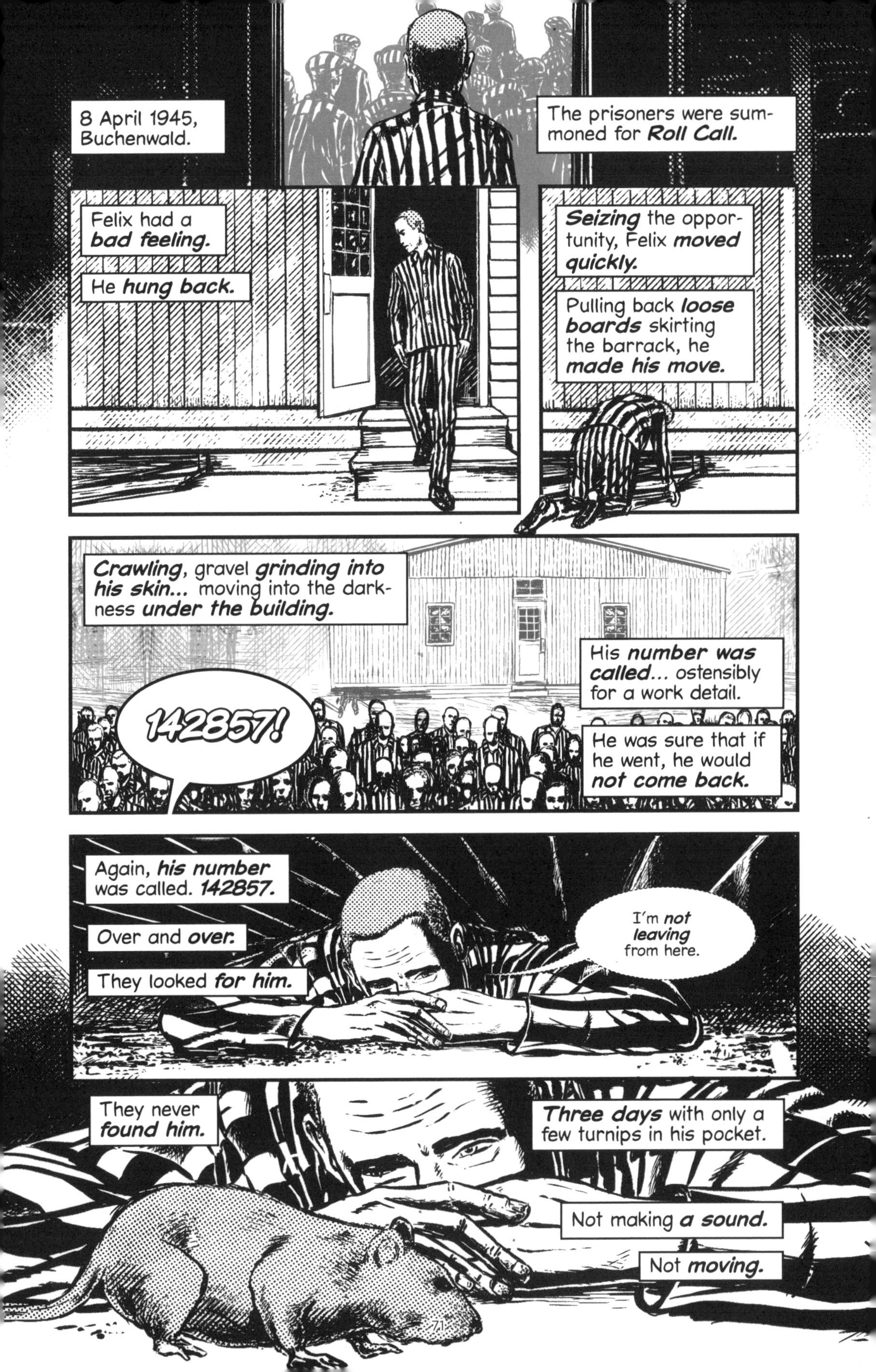
8 April 1945, Buchenwald.
The prisoners were summoned for *Roll Call.*
Felix had a *bad feeling.*
He *hung back.*
Seizing the opportunity, Felix *moved quickly.*
Pulling back *loose boards* skirting the barrack, he *made his move.*
Crawling, gravel *grinding into his skin...* moving into the darkness *under the building.*
142857!
His *number was called...* ostensibly for a work detail.
He was sure that if he went, he would *not come back.*
Again, *his number* was called. *142857.*
Over and *over.*
They looked *for him.*
I'm *not leaving* from here.
They never *found him.*
Three days with only a few turnips in his pocket.
Not making *a sound.*
Not *moving.*

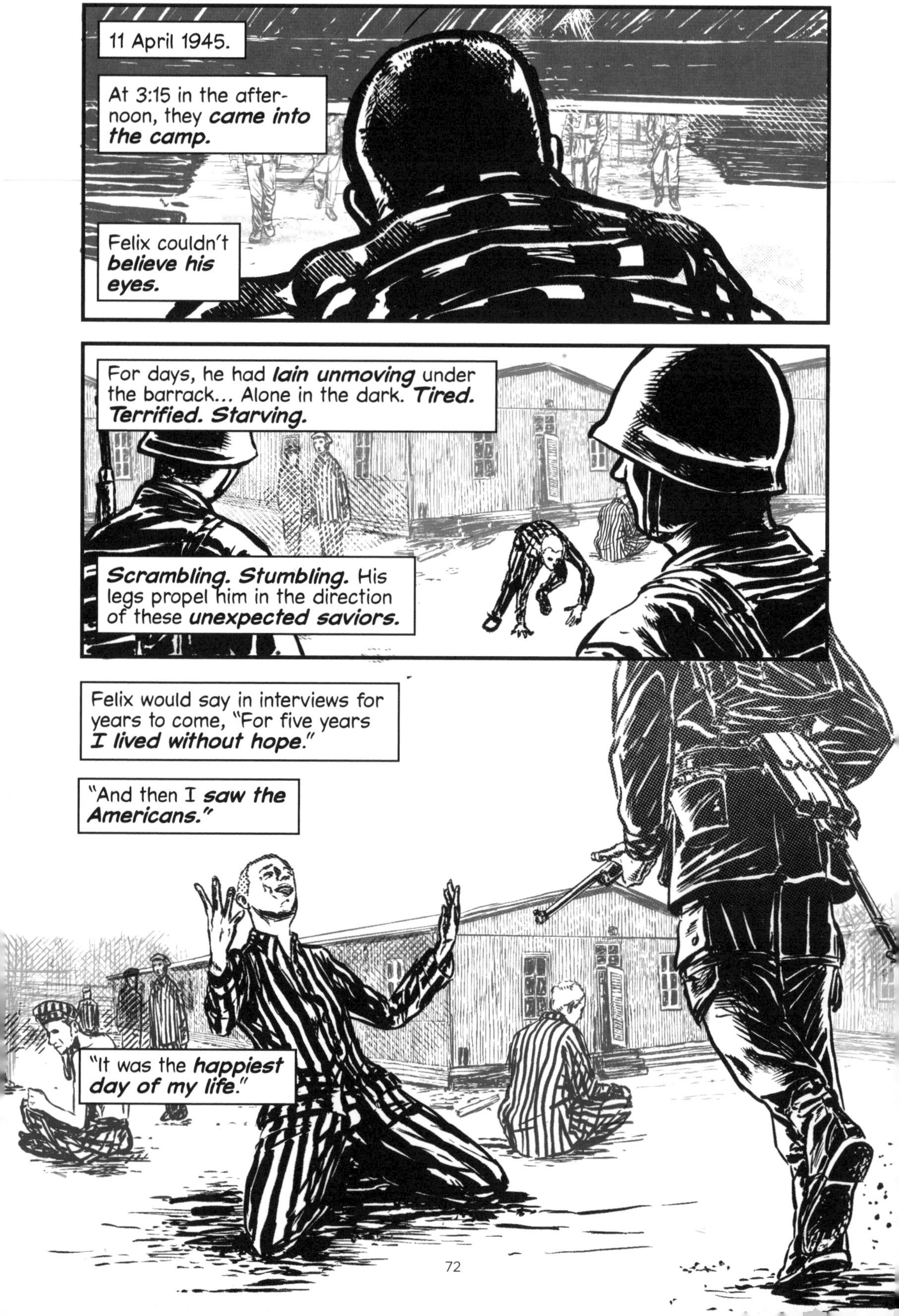
11 April 1945.
At 3:15 in the afternoon, they *came into the camp.*
Felix couldn't *believe his eyes.*
For days, he had *lain unmoving* under the barrack... Alone in the dark. *Tired. Terrified. Starving.*
Scrambling. Stumbling. His legs propel him in the direction of these *unexpected saviors.*
Felix would say in interviews for years to come, "For five years *I lived without hope.*"
"And then I *saw the Americans.*"
"It was the *happiest day of my life.*"

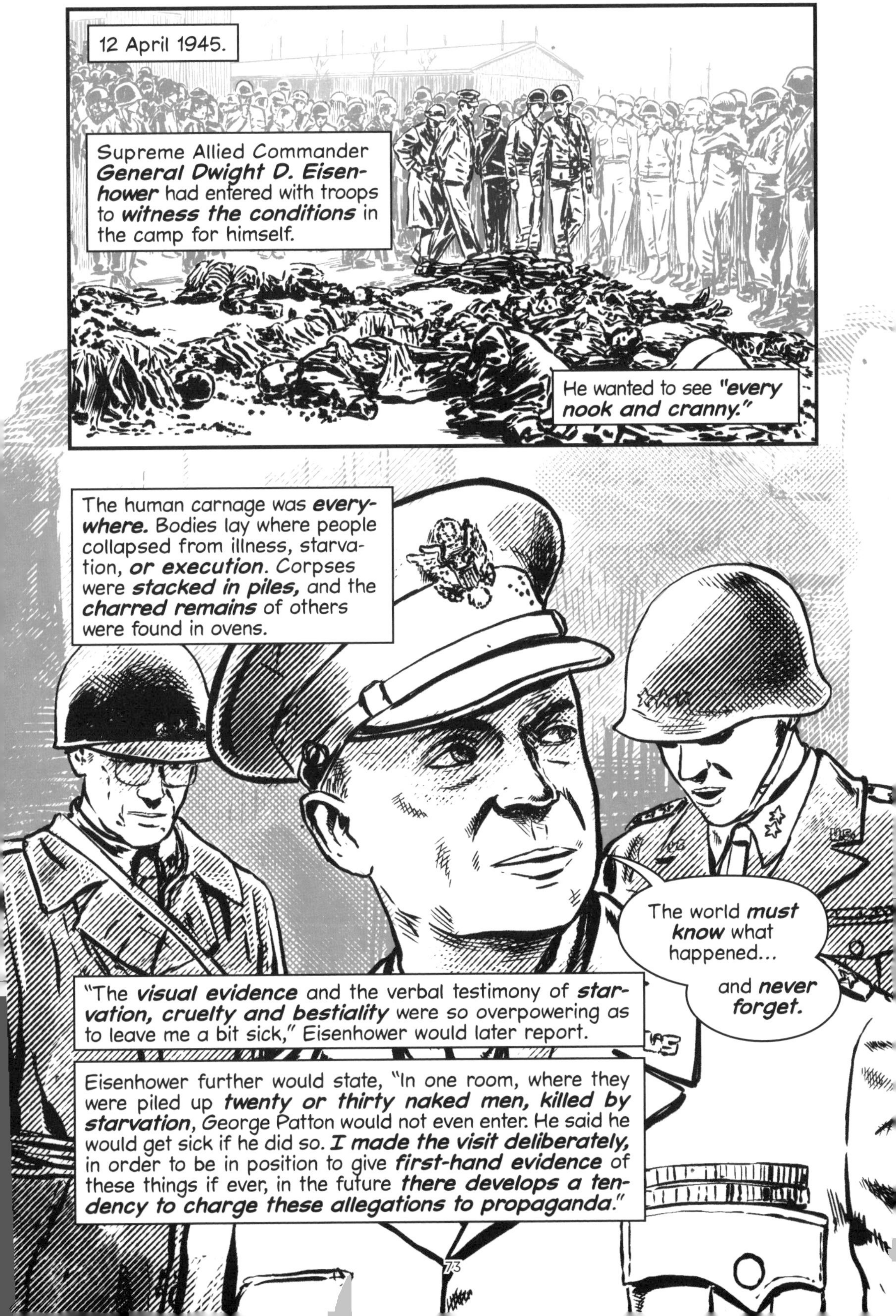
12 April 1945.
Supreme Allied Commander **General Dwight D. Eisenhower** had entered with troops to **witness the conditions** in the camp for himself.
He wanted to see **"every nook and cranny."**
The human carnage was **everywhere.** Bodies lay where people collapsed from illness, starvation, **or execution**. Corpses were **stacked in piles,** and the **charred remains** of others were found in ovens.
The world **must know** what happened...
and **never forget.**
"The **visual evidence** and the verbal testimony of **starvation, cruelty and bestiality** were so overpowering as to leave me a bit sick," Eisenhower would later report.
Eisenhower further would state, "In one room, where they were piled up **twenty or thirty naked men, killed by starvation**, George Patton would not even enter. He said he would get sick if he did so. **I made the visit deliberately,** in order to be in position to give **first-hand evidence** of these things if ever, in the future **there develops a tendency to charge these allegations to propaganda.**"

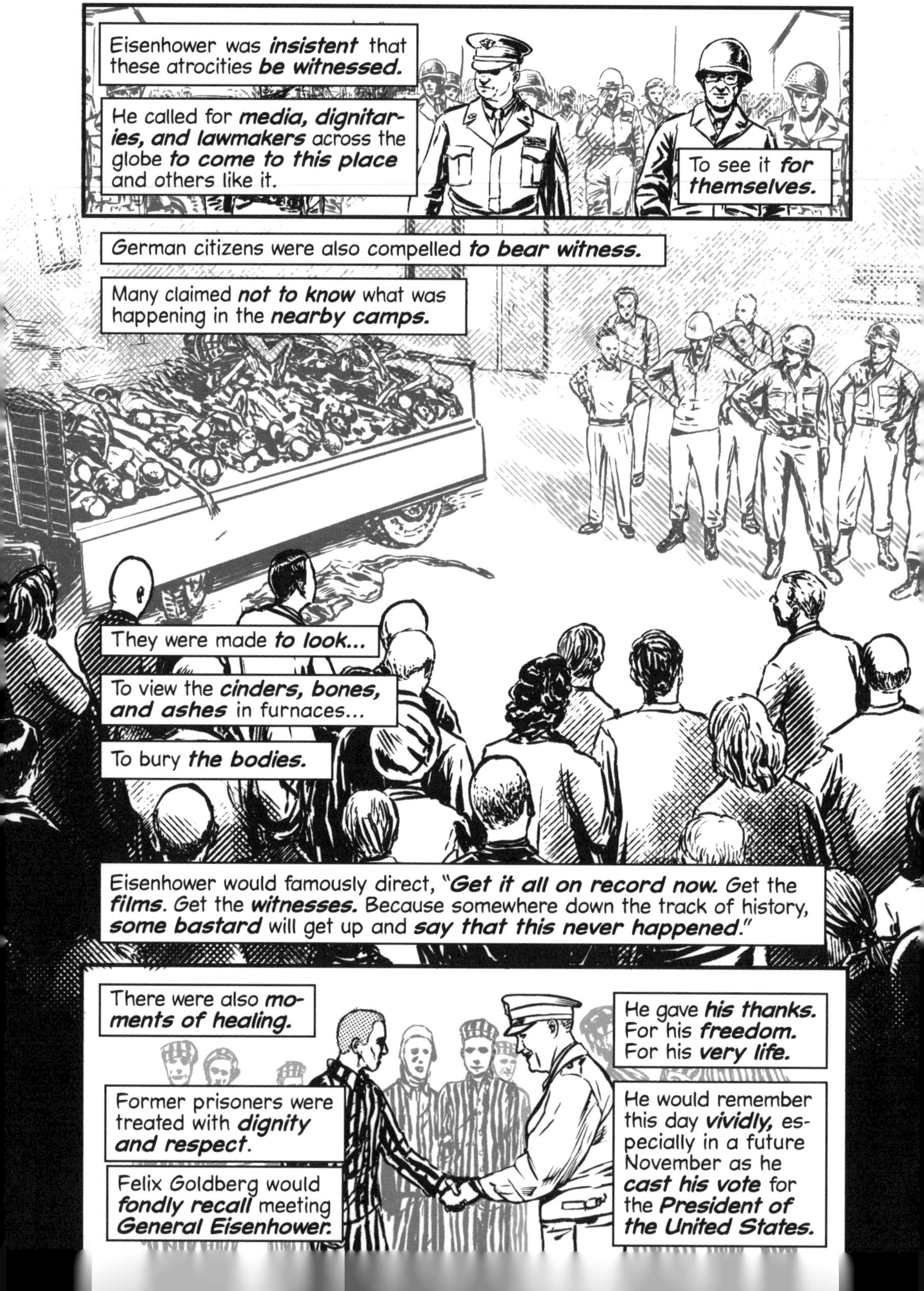

Eisenhower was insistent that these atrocities be witnessed.
He called for media, dignitaries, and lawmakers across the globe to come to this place and others like it.
To see it for themselves.
German citizens were also compelled to bear witness.
Many claimed not to know what was happening in the nearby camps.
They were made to look...
To view the cinders, bones, and ashes in furnaces...
To bury the bodies.
Eisenhower would famously direct, "Get it all on record now. Get the films. Get the witnesses. Because somewhere down the track of history, some bastard will get up and say that this never happened."
There were also moments of healing.
Former prisoners were treated with dignity and respect.
Felix Goldberg would fondly recall meeting General Eisenhower.
He gave his thanks. For his freedom. For his very life.
He would remember this day vividly, especially in a future November as he cast his vote for the President of the United States.

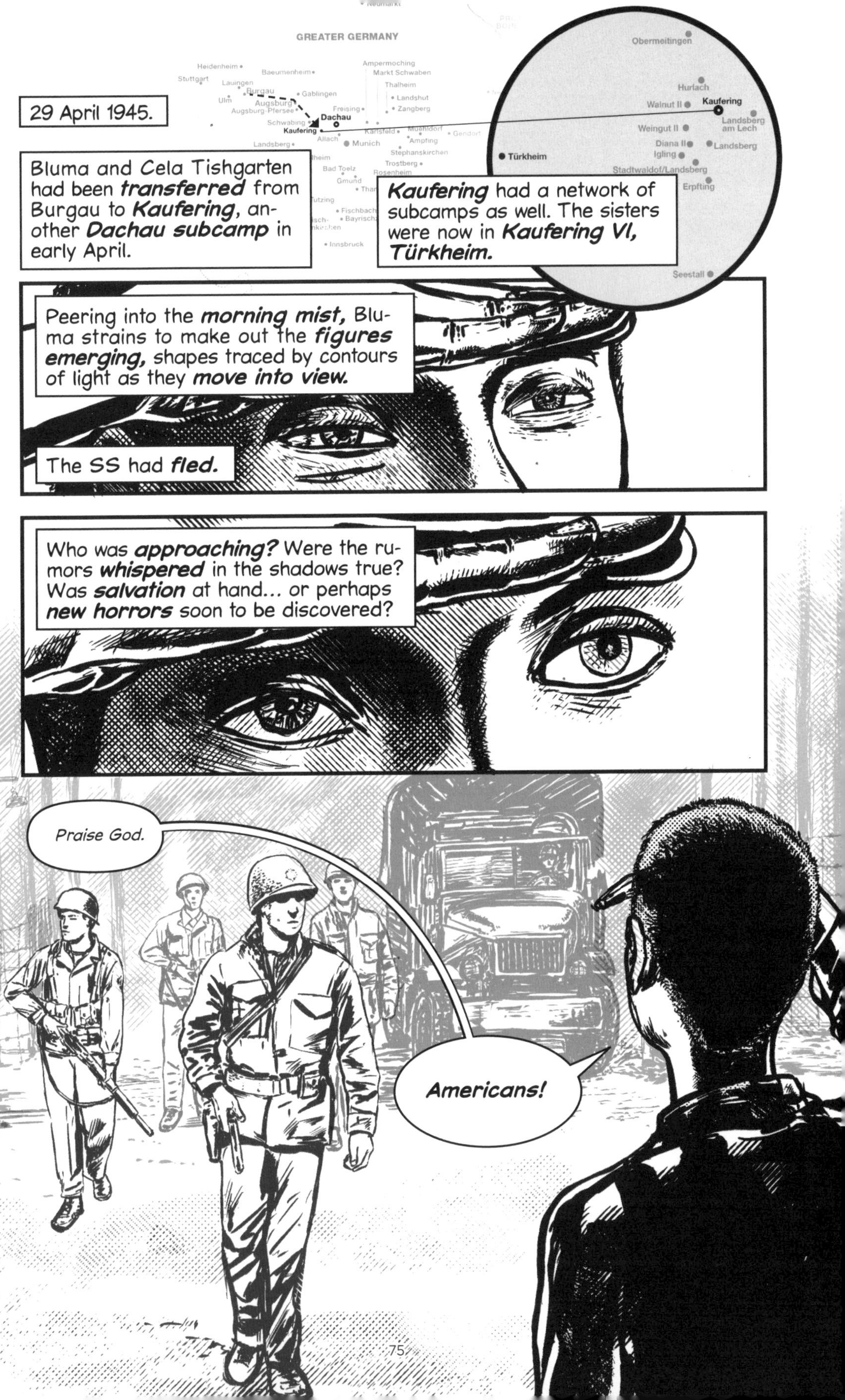

GREATER GERMANY
Heidenheim
Stuttgart
Lauingen
Baeumenheim
Ampermoching
Markt Schwaben
Thalheim
Burgau
Gablingen
Ulm
Augsburg
Augsburg-Pfersee
Landshut
Zangberg
Freising
Dachau
Schwabing
Kaufering
Karlsfeld
Muehldorf
Allach
Munich
Ampfing
Gendorf
Landsberg
Stephanskirchen
Trostberg
Bad Toelz
Rosenheim
Gmund
Fischbach
Innsbruck
Obermeitingen
Hurlach
Walnut II
Kaufering
Landsberg am Lech
Weingut II
Diana II
Landsberg
Igling
Türkheim
Stadtwaldof/Landsberg
Erpfting
Seestall
29 April 1945.
Bluma and Cela Tishgarten had been ***transferred*** from Burgau to ***Kaufering***, another ***Dachau subcamp*** in early April.
Kaufering had a network of subcamps as well. The sisters were now in ***Kaufering VI, Türkheim.***
Peering into the ***morning mist,*** Bluma strains to make out the ***figures emerging,*** shapes traced by contours of light as they ***move into view.***
The SS had ***fled.***
Who was ***approaching?*** Were the rumors ***whispered*** in the shadows true? Was ***salvation*** at hand... or perhaps ***new horrors*** soon to be discovered?
Praise God.
Americans!

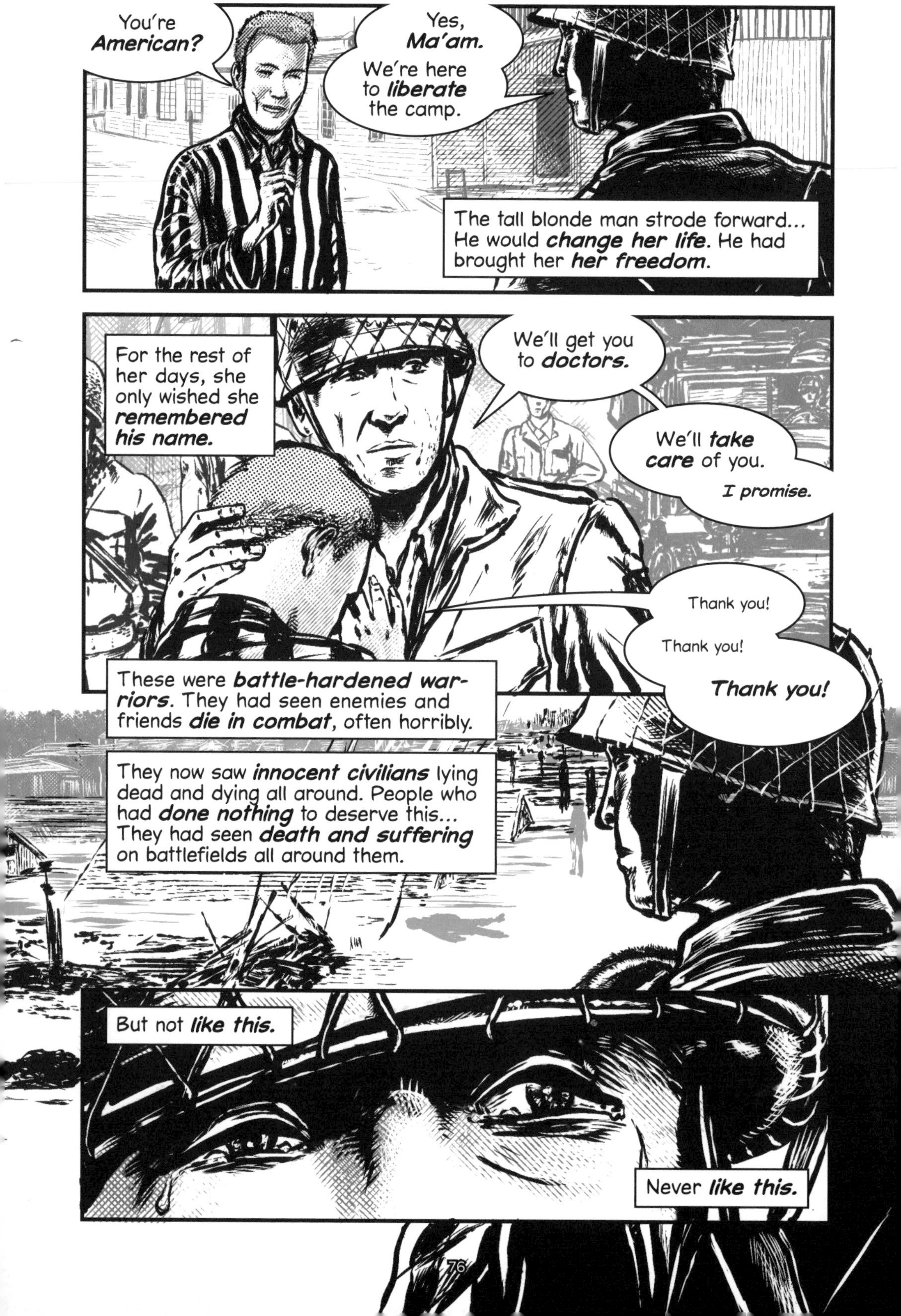

You're *American?*
Yes, *Ma'am.*
We're here to *liberate* the camp.
The tall blonde man strode forward... He would *change her life*. He had brought her *her freedom*.
For the rest of her days, she only wished she *remembered his name.*
We'll get you to *doctors.*
We'll *take care* of you.
I promise.
Thank you!
Thank you!
Thank you!
These were *battle-hardened warriors*. They had seen enemies and friends *die in combat*, often horribly.
They now saw *innocent civilians* lying dead and dying all around. People who had *done nothing* to deserve this... They had seen *death and suffering* on battlefields all around them.
But not *like this.*
Never *like this.*

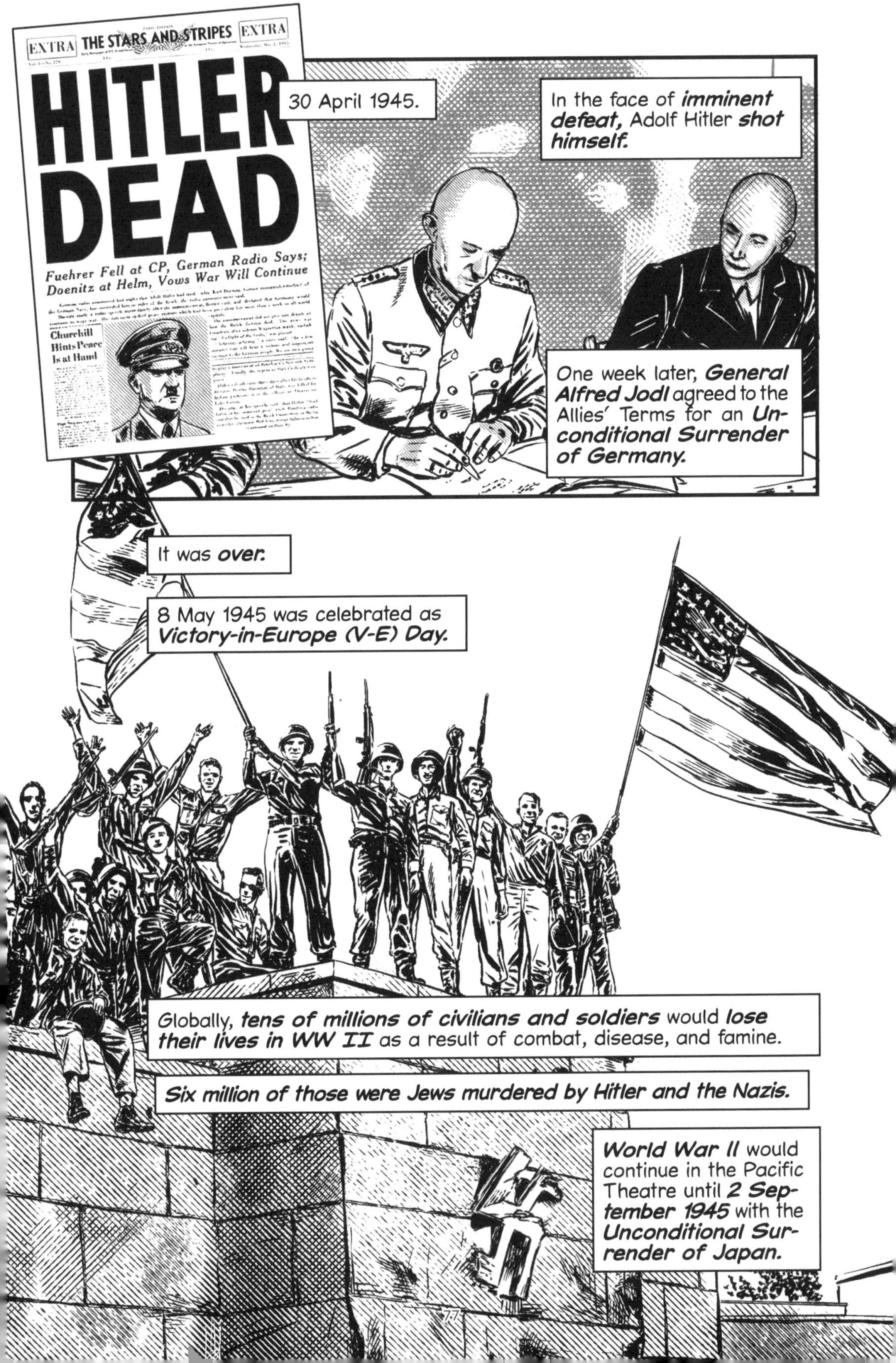
EXTRA
THE STARS AND STRIPES
EXTRA
HITLER DEAD
Fuehrer Fell at CP, German Radio Says; Doenitz at Helm, Vows War Will Continue
Churchill Hints Peace Is at Hand
30 April 1945.
In the face of ***imminent defeat,*** Adolf Hitler ***shot himself.***
One week later, ***General Alfred Jodl*** agreed to the Allies' Terms for an ***Unconditional Surrender of Germany.***
It was ***over.***
8 May 1945 was celebrated as ***Victory-in-Europe (V-E) Day.***
Globally, ***tens of millions of civilians and soldiers*** would ***lose their lives in WW II*** as a result of combat, disease, and famine.
Six million of those were Jews murdered by Hitler and the Nazis.
World War II would continue in the Pacific Theatre until ***2 September 1945*** with the ***Unconditional Surrender of Japan.***

LANDSBERG, GERMANY

MAY 1945 – SEPTEMBER 1949

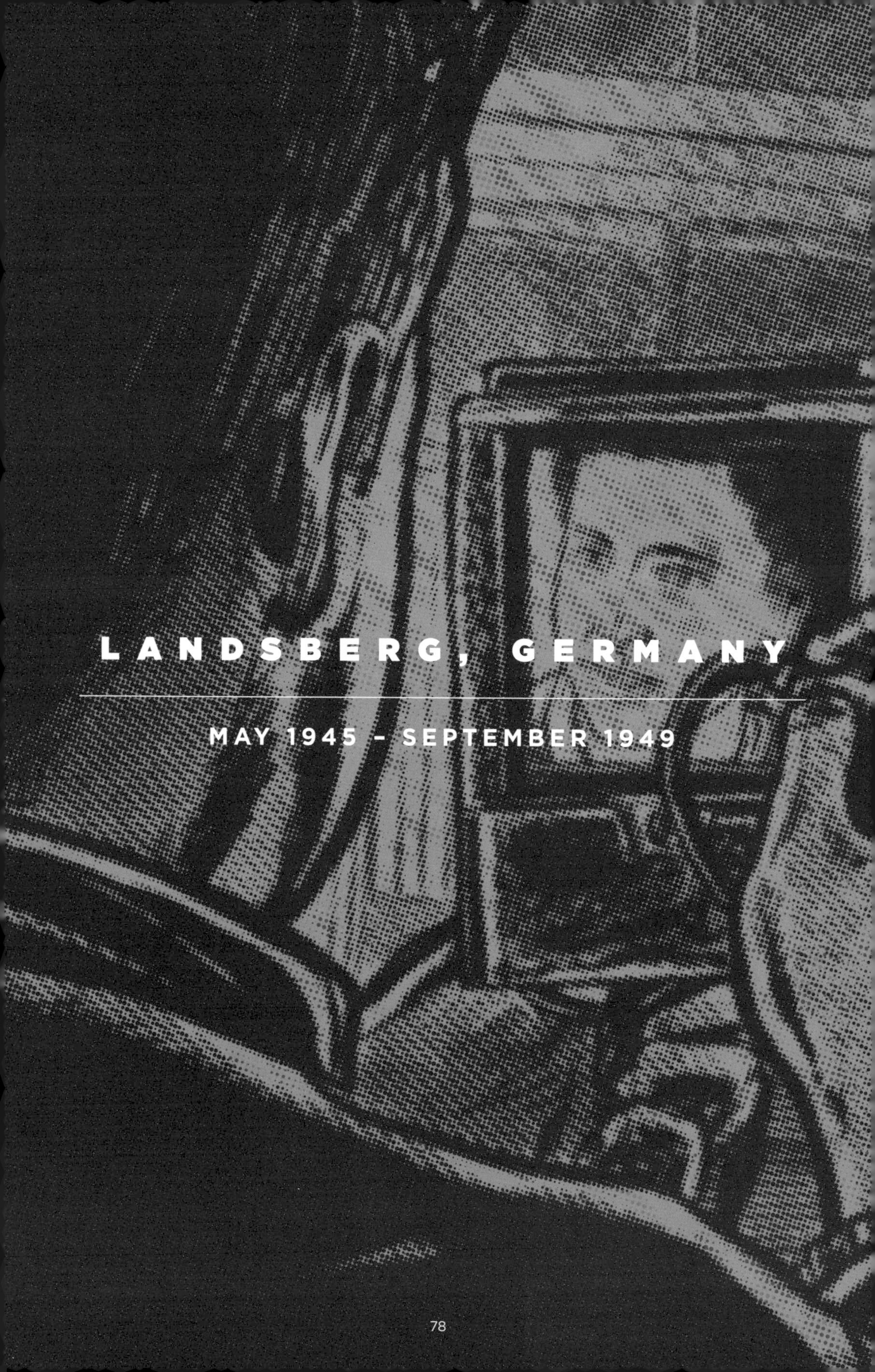

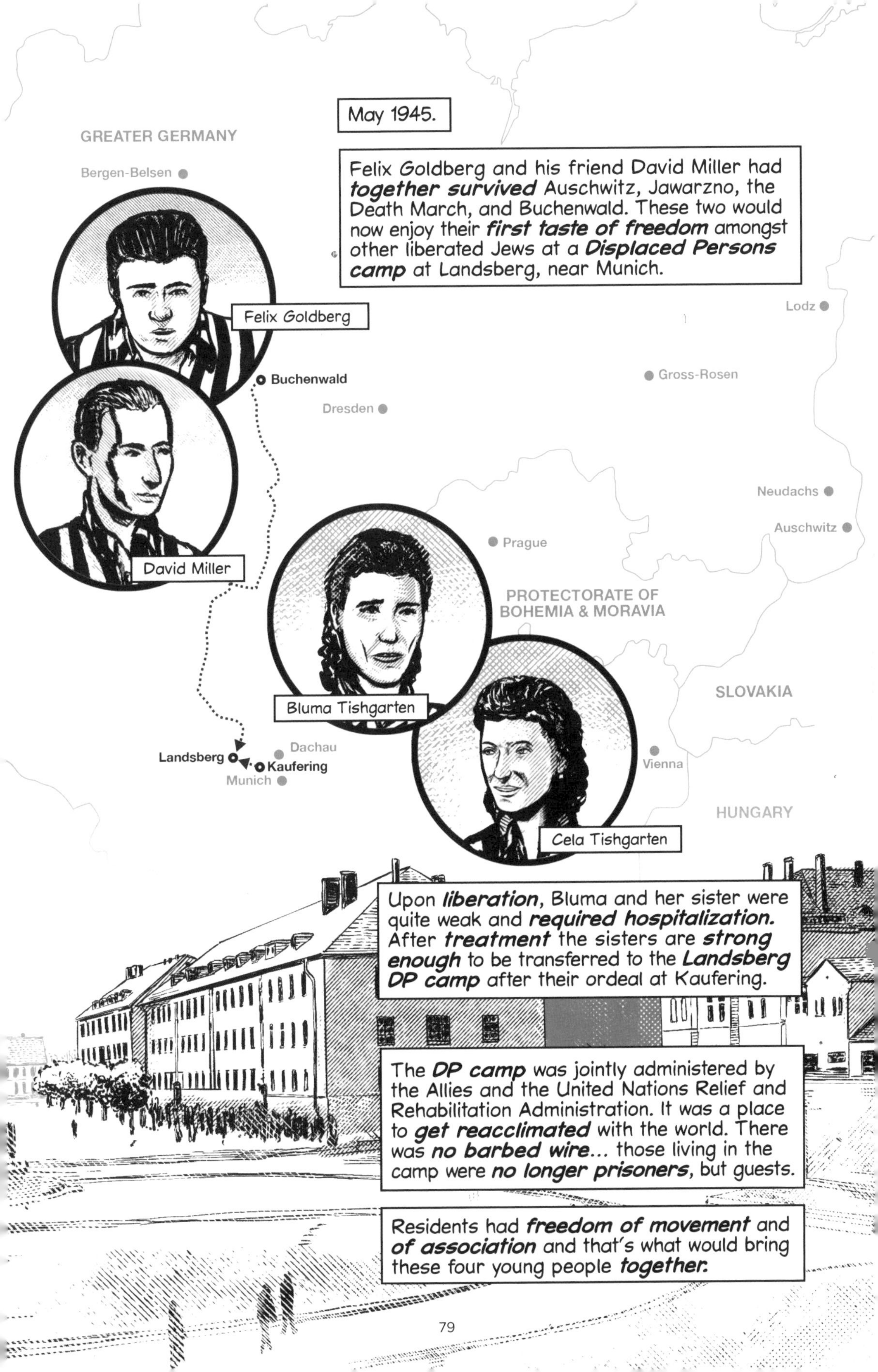

May 1945.
Felix Goldberg and his friend David Miller had together survived Auschwitz, Jawarzno, the Death March, and Buchenwald. These two would now enjoy their first taste of freedom amongst other liberated Jews at a Displaced Persons camp at Landsberg, near Munich.
GREATER GERMANY
Bergen-Belsen
Felix Goldberg
Lodz
Buchenwald
Gross-Rosen
Dresden
David Miller
Neudachs
Auschwitz
Prague
PROTECTORATE OF BOHEMIA & MORAVIA
Bluma Tishgarten
SLOVAKIA
Dachau
Landsberg
Kaufering
Munich
Vienna
HUNGARY
Cela Tishgarten
Upon liberation, Bluma and her sister were quite weak and required hospitalization. After treatment the sisters are strong enough to be transferred to the Landsberg DP camp after their ordeal at Kaufering.
The DP camp was jointly administered by the Allies and the United Nations Relief and Rehabilitation Administration. It was a place to get reacclimated with the world. There was no barbed wire... those living in the camp were no longer prisoners, but guests.
Residents had freedom of movement and of association and that's what would bring these four young people together.

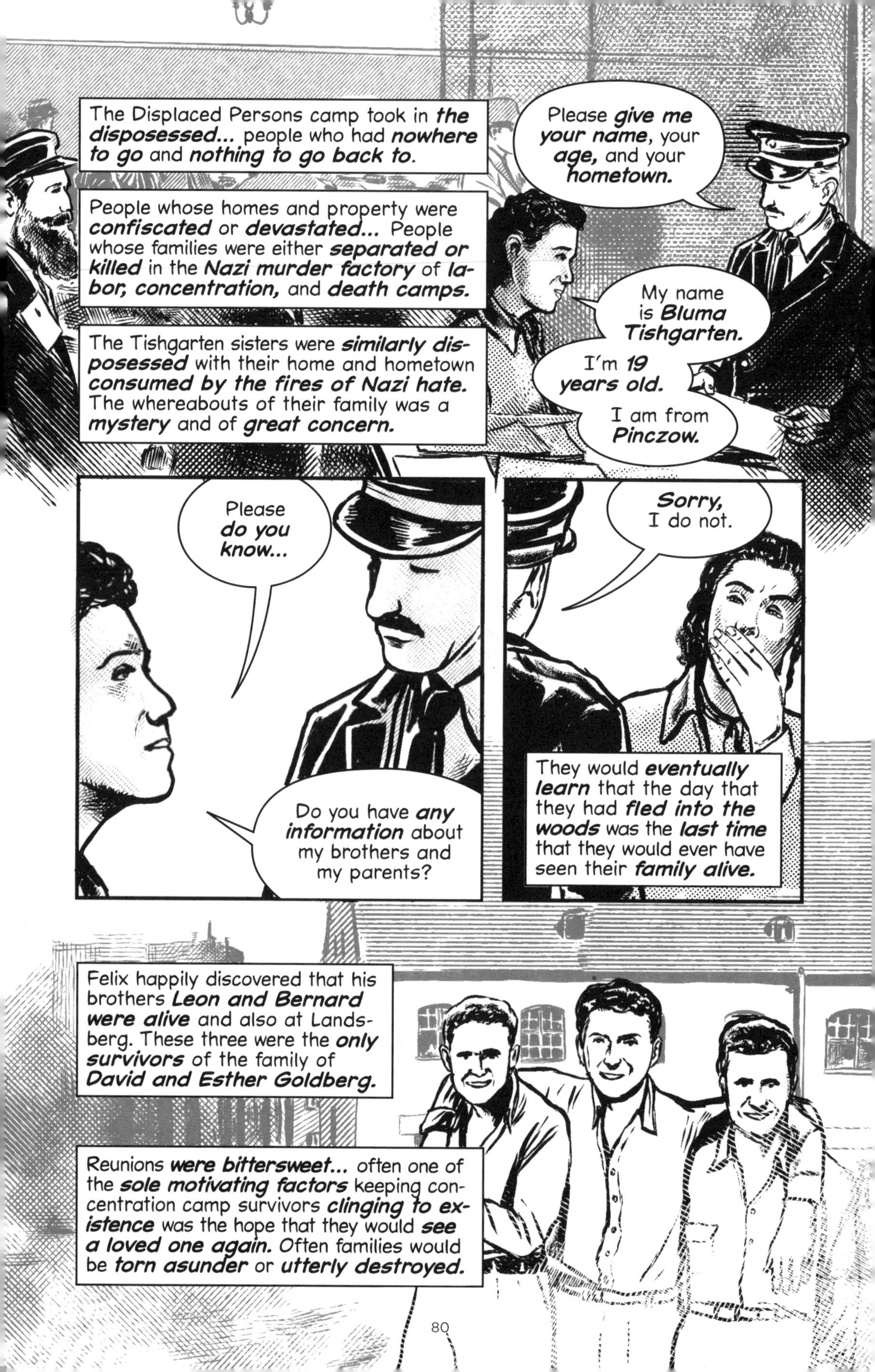
The Displaced Persons camp took in the disposessed... people who had nowhere to go and nothing to go back to.
Please give me your name, your age, and your hometown.
People whose homes and property were confiscated or devastated... People whose families were either separated or killed in the Nazi murder factory of labor, concentration, and death camps.
My name is Bluma Tishgarten.
The Tishgarten sisters were similarly disposessed with their home and hometown consumed by the fires of Nazi hate. The whereabouts of their family was a mystery and of great concern.
I'm 19 years old.
I am from Pinczow.
Please do you know...
Do you have any information about my brothers and my parents?
Sorry, I do not.
They would eventually learn that the day that they had fled into the woods was the last time that they would ever have seen their family alive.
Felix happily discovered that his brothers Leon and Bernard were alive and also at Landsberg. These three were the only survivors of the family of David and Esther Goldberg.
Reunions were bittersweet... often one of the sole motivating factors keeping concentration camp survivors clinging to existence was the hope that they would see a loved one again. Often families would be torn asunder or utterly destroyed.

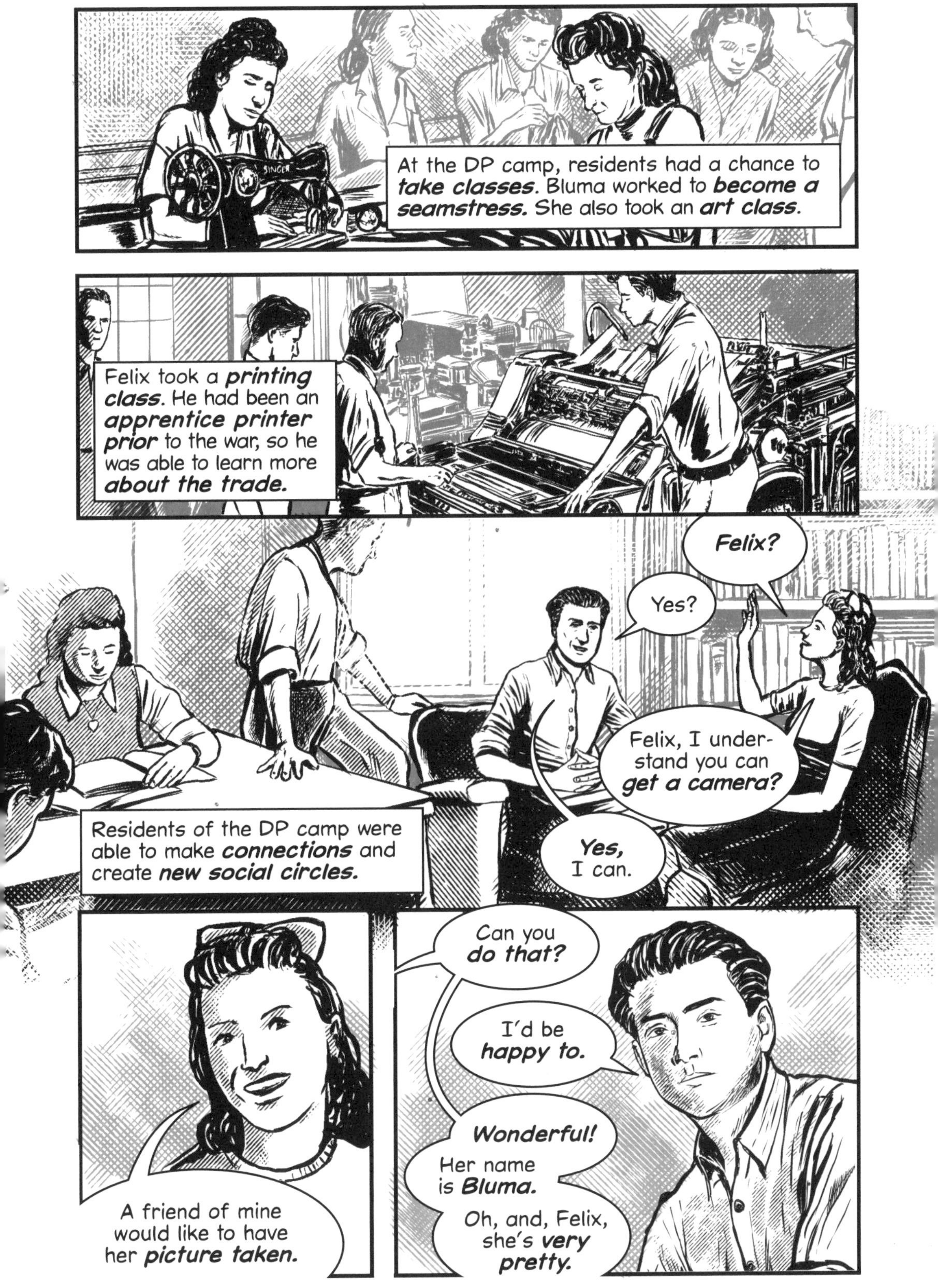
At the DP camp, residents had a chance to ***take classes***. Bluma worked to ***become a seamstress.*** She also took an ***art class***.
Felix took a ***printing class***. He had been an ***apprentice printer prior*** to the war, so he was able to learn more ***about the trade.***
Felix?
Yes?
Felix, I understand you can ***get a camera?***
Residents of the DP camp were able to make ***connections*** and create ***new social circles.***
Yes, I can.
A friend of mine would like to have her ***picture taken.***
Can you ***do that?***
I'd be ***happy to.***
Wonderful!
Her name is ***Bluma.***
Oh, and, Felix, she's ***very pretty.***

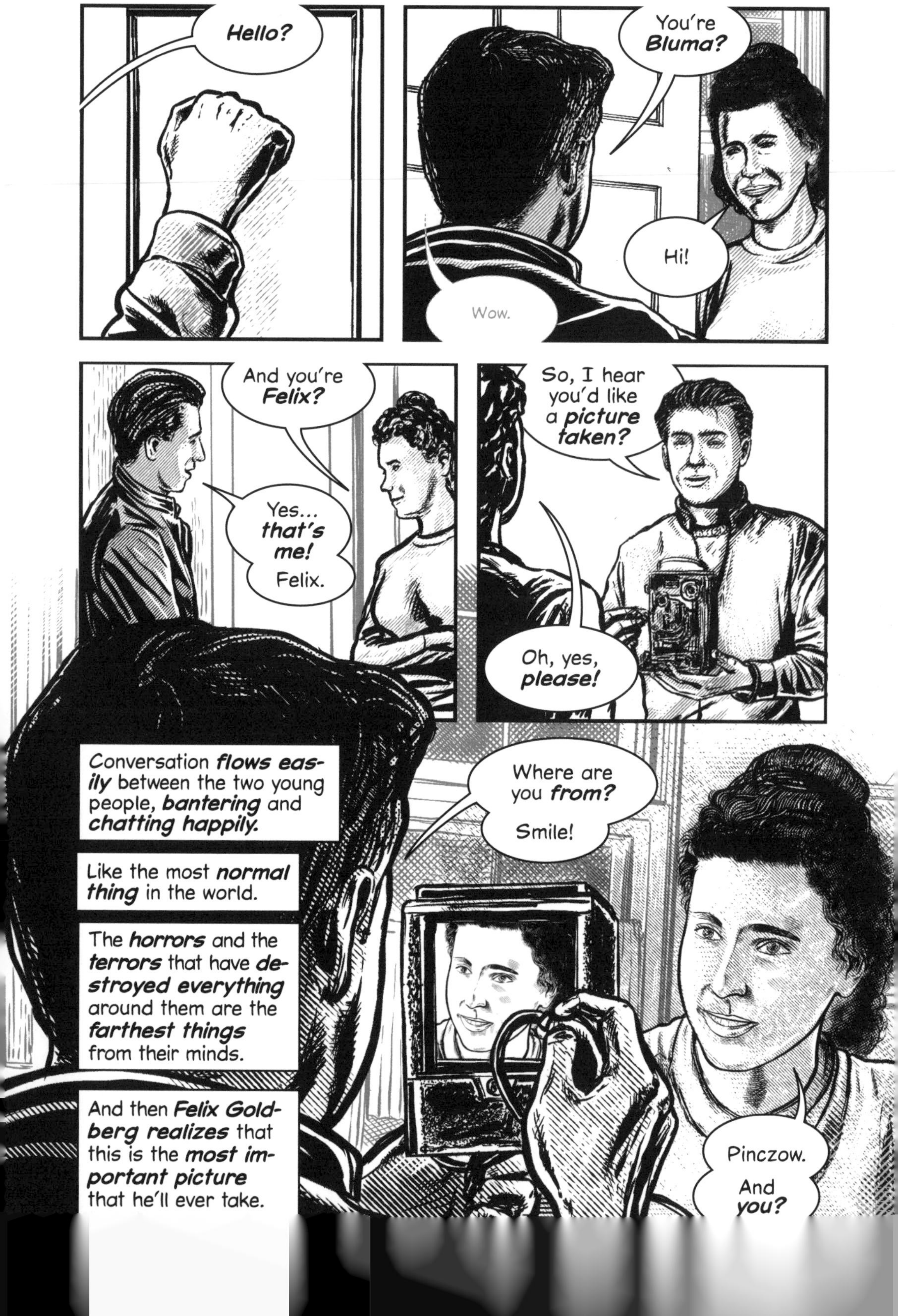
Hello?
You're Bluma?
Hi!
Wow.
And you're Felix?
Yes... that's me!
Felix.
So, I hear you'd like a picture taken?
Oh, yes, please!
Conversation flows easily between the two young people, bantering and chatting happily.
Like the most normal thing in the world.
The horrors and the terrors that have destroyed everything around them are the farthest things from their minds.
And then Felix Goldberg realizes that this is the most important picture that he'll ever take.
Where are you from?
Smile!
Pinczow.
And you?

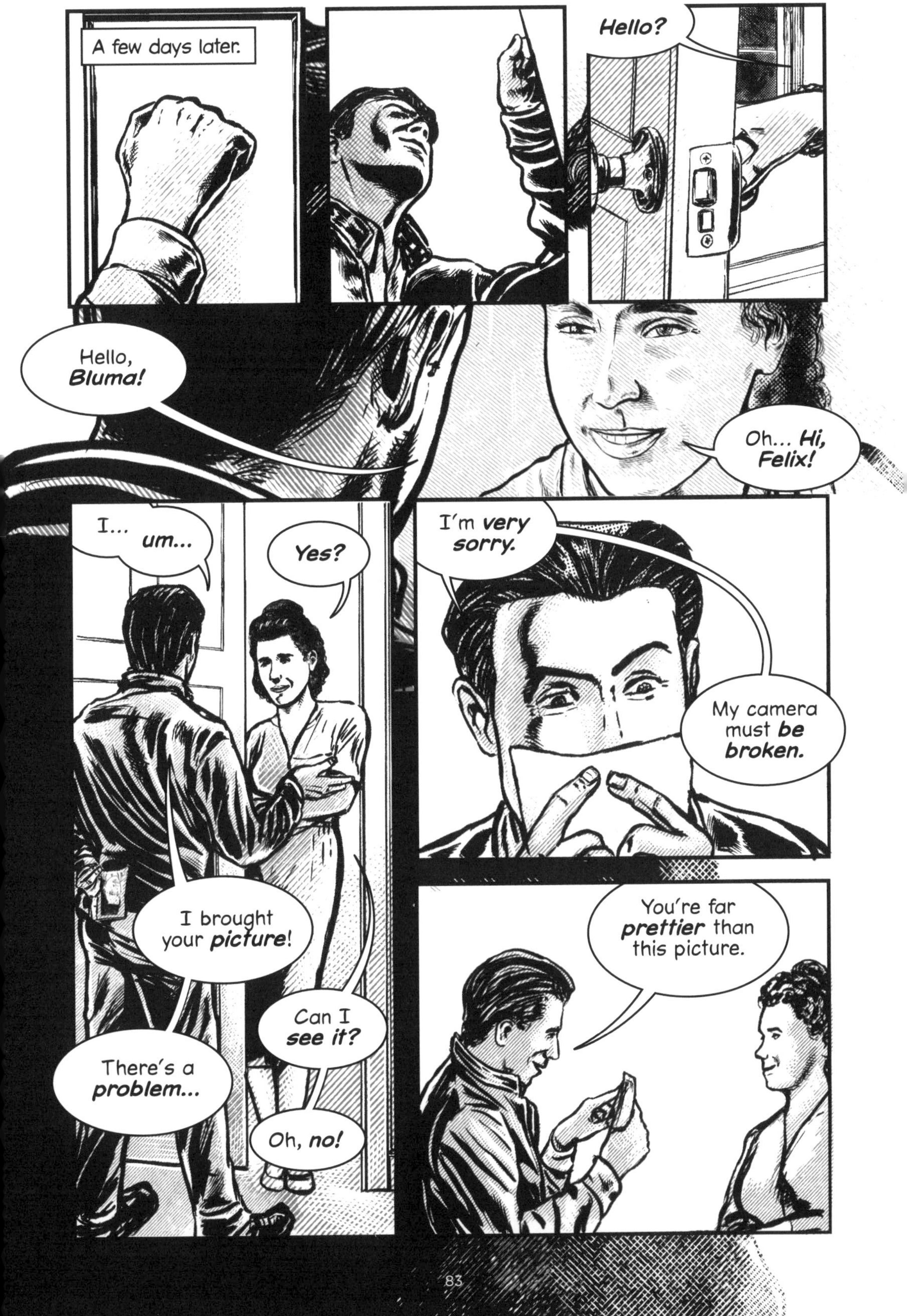
A few days later.
Hello?
Hello, Bluma!
Oh... Hi, Felix!
I... um...
Yes?
I brought your picture!
There's a problem...
Can I see it?
Oh, no!
I'm very sorry.
My camera must be broken.
You're far prettier than this picture.

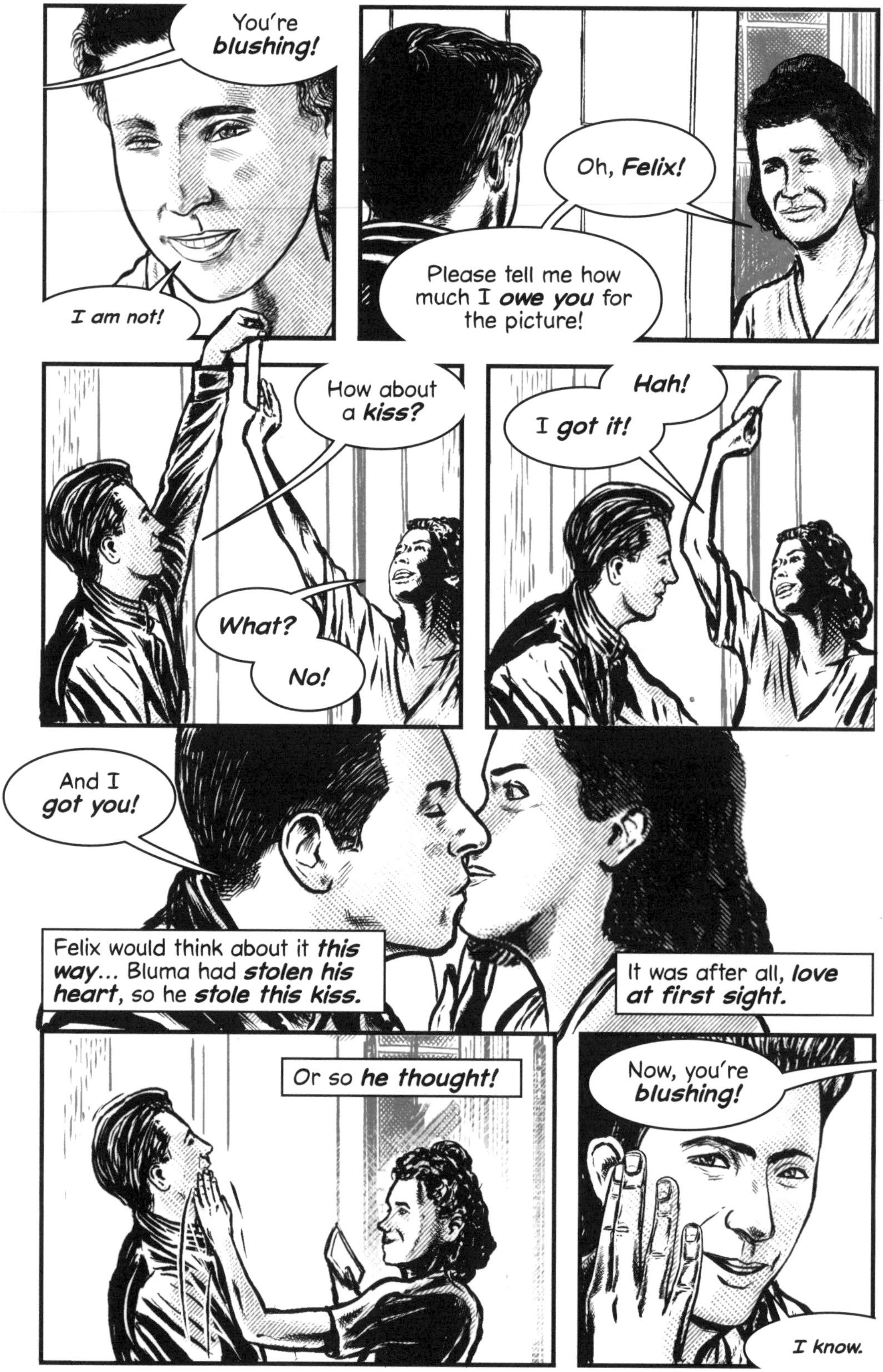
You're blushing!
I am not!
Oh, Felix!
Please tell me how much I owe you for the picture!
How about a kiss?
What?
No!
Hah!
I got it!
And I got you!
Felix would think about it this way... Bluma had stolen his heart, so he stole this kiss.
It was after all, love at first sight.
Or so he thought!
Now, you're blushing!
I know.

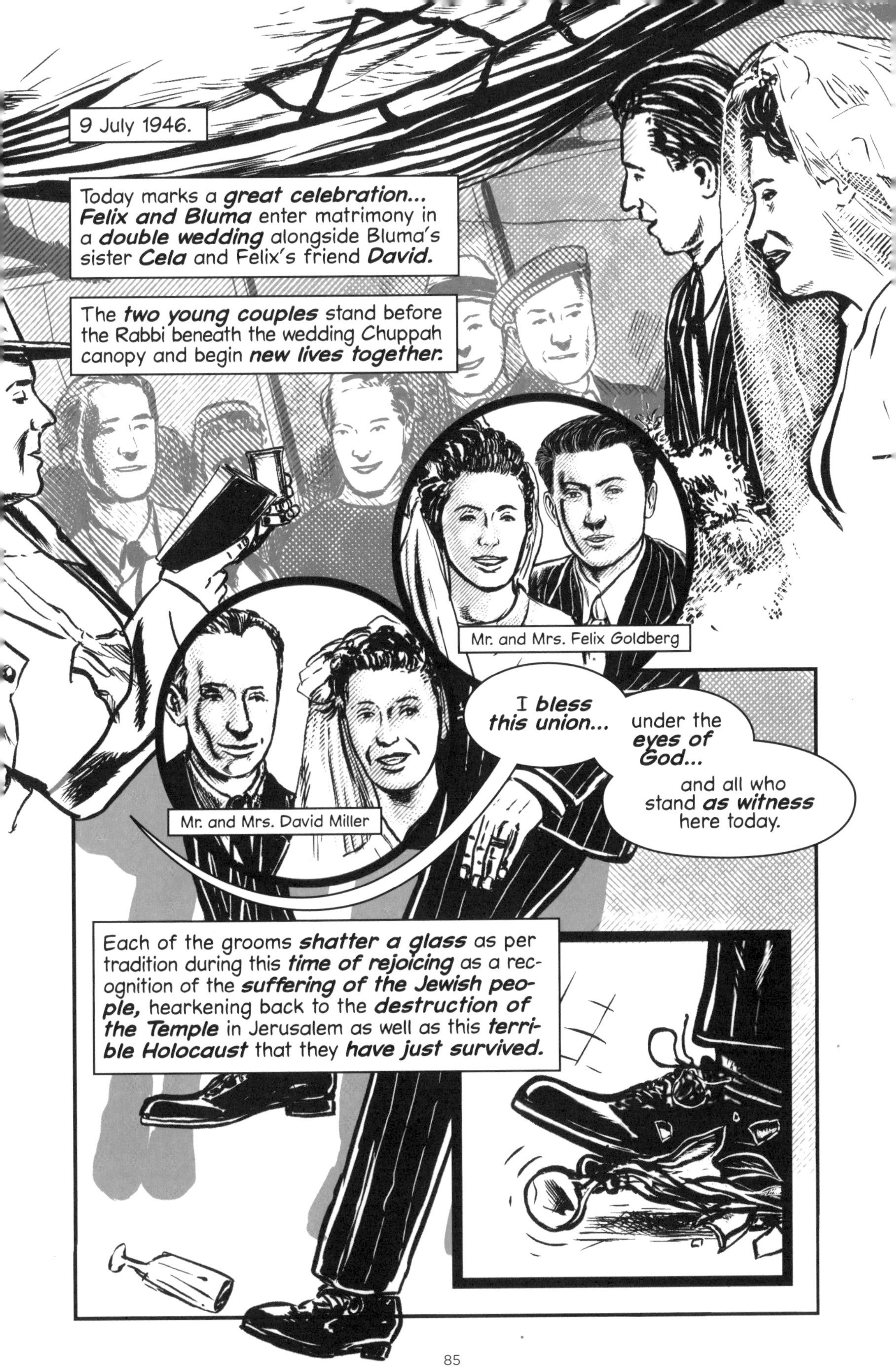

9 July 1946.
Today marks a ***great celebration...*** ***Felix and Bluma*** enter matrimony in a ***double wedding*** alongside Bluma's sister ***Cela*** and Felix's friend ***David.***
The ***two young couples*** stand before the Rabbi beneath the wedding Chuppah canopy and begin ***new lives together.***
Mr. and Mrs. Felix Goldberg
Mr. and Mrs. David Miller
I ***bless this union...***
under the ***eyes of God...***
and all who stand ***as witness*** here today.
Each of the grooms ***shatter a glass*** as per tradition during this ***time of rejoicing*** as a recognition of the ***suffering of the Jewish people,*** hearkening back to the ***destruction of the Temple*** in Jerusalem as well as this ***terrible Holocaust*** that they ***have just survived.***

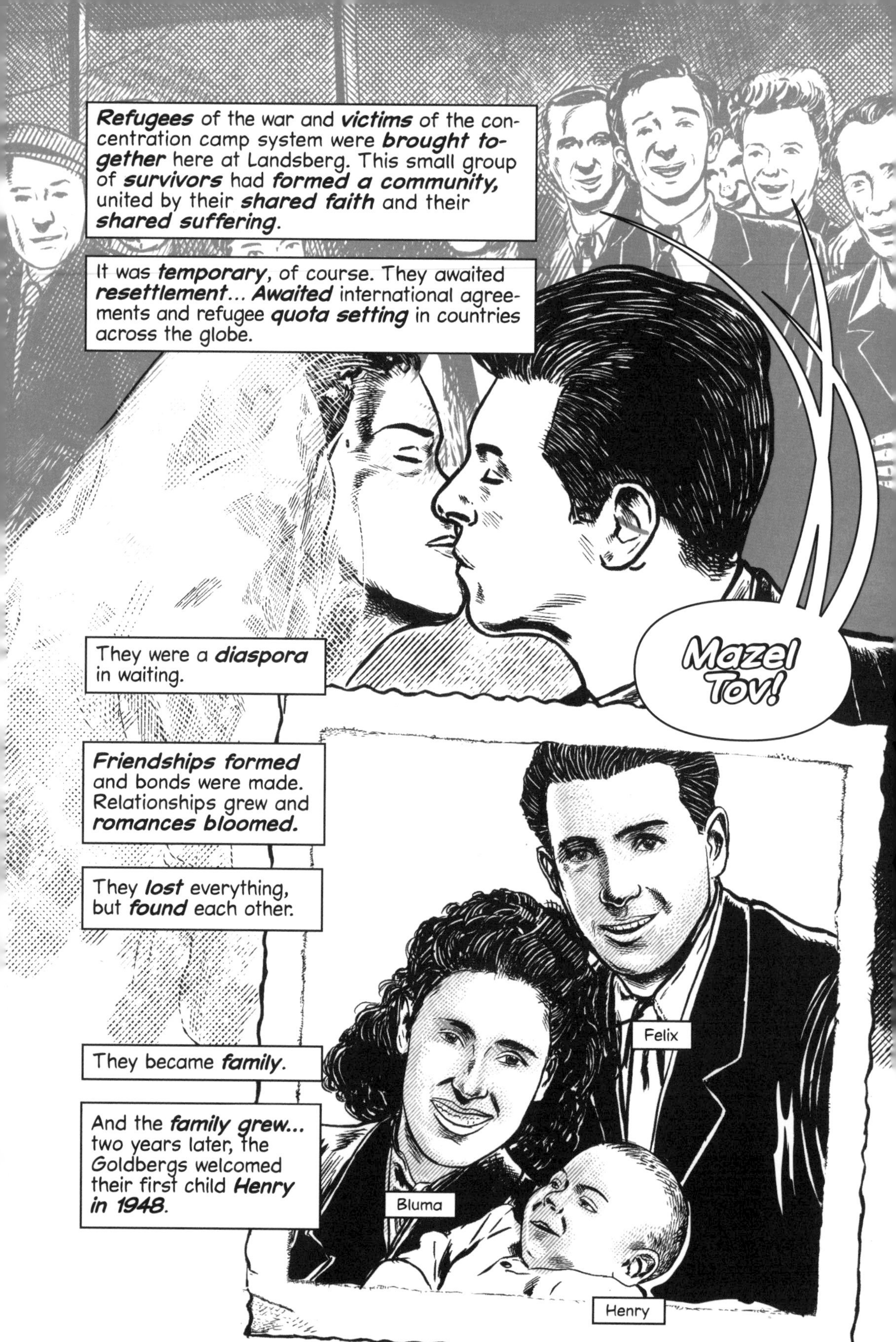

Refugees of the war and victims of the concentration camp system were brought together here at Landsberg. This small group of survivors had formed a community, united by their shared faith and their shared suffering.
It was temporary, of course. They awaited resettlement... Awaited international agreements and refugee quota setting in countries across the globe.
They were a diaspora in waiting.
Mazel Tov!
Friendships formed and bonds were made. Relationships grew and romances bloomed.
They lost everything, but found each other.
They became family.
And the family grew... two years later, the Goldbergs welcomed their first child Henry in 1948.
Felix
Bluma
Henry

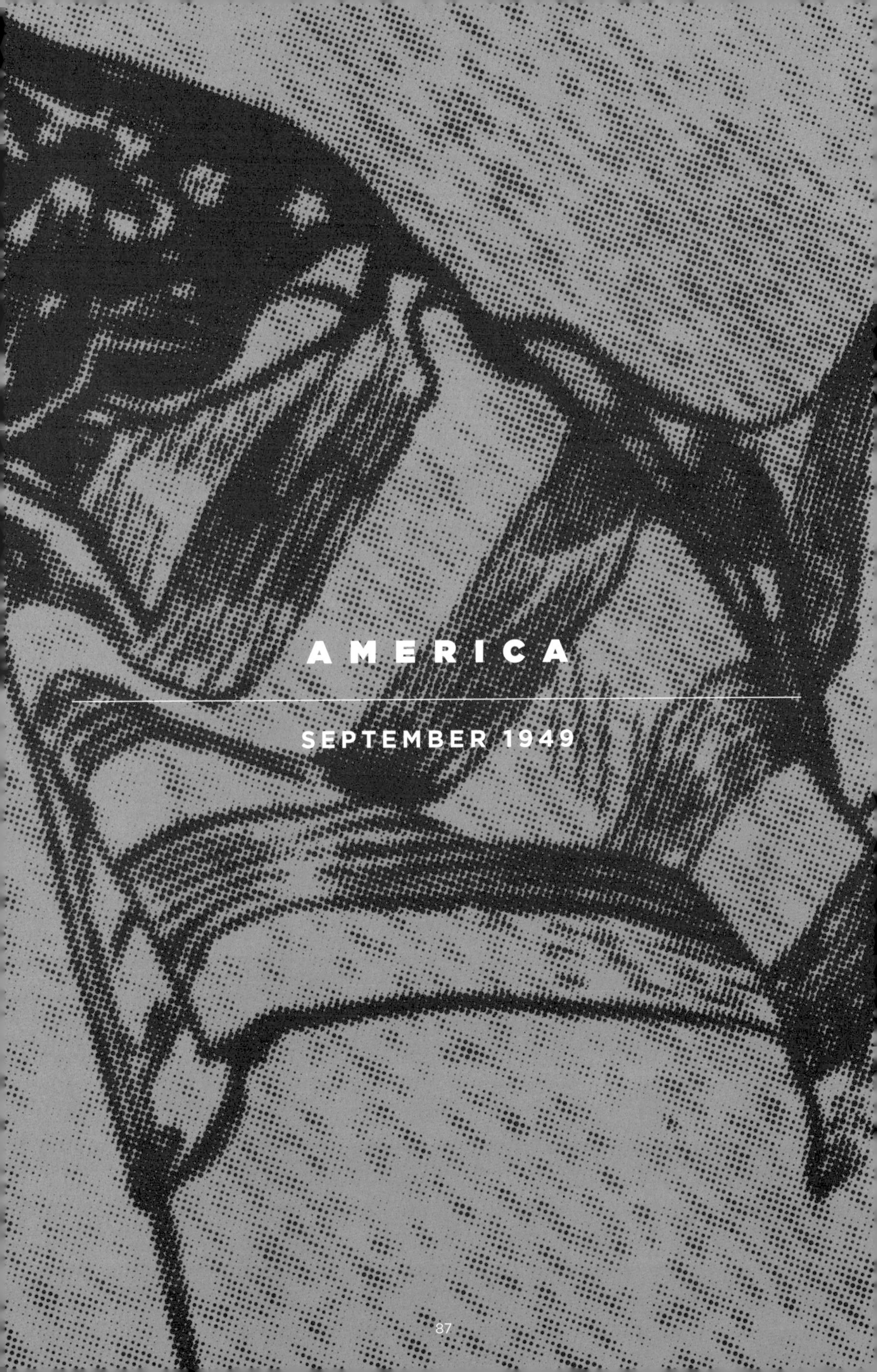

AMERICA

SEPTEMBER 1949

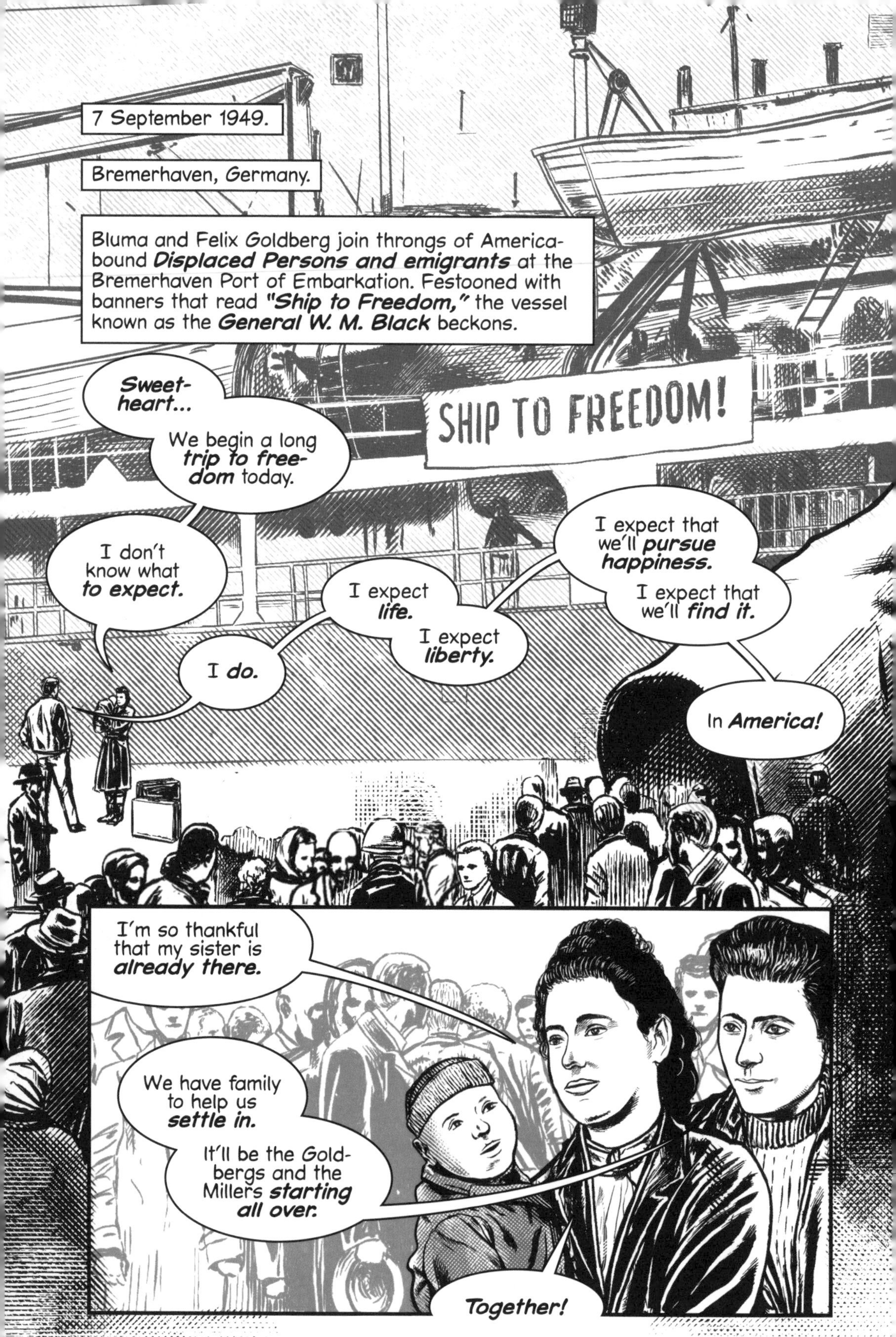
7 September 1949.
Bremerhaven, Germany.
Bluma and Felix Goldberg join throngs of America-bound ***Displaced Persons and emigrants*** at the Bremerhaven Port of Embarkation. Festooned with banners that read ***"Ship to Freedom,"*** the vessel known as the ***General W. M. Black*** beckons.
Sweet-heart...
We begin a long trip to free-dom today.
SHIP TO FREEDOM!
I don't know what to expect.
I do.
I expect life.
I expect liberty.
I expect that we'll pursue happiness.
I expect that we'll find it.
In America!
I'm so thankful that my sister is already there.
We have family to help us settle in.
It'll be the Gold-bergs and the Millers starting all over.
Together!

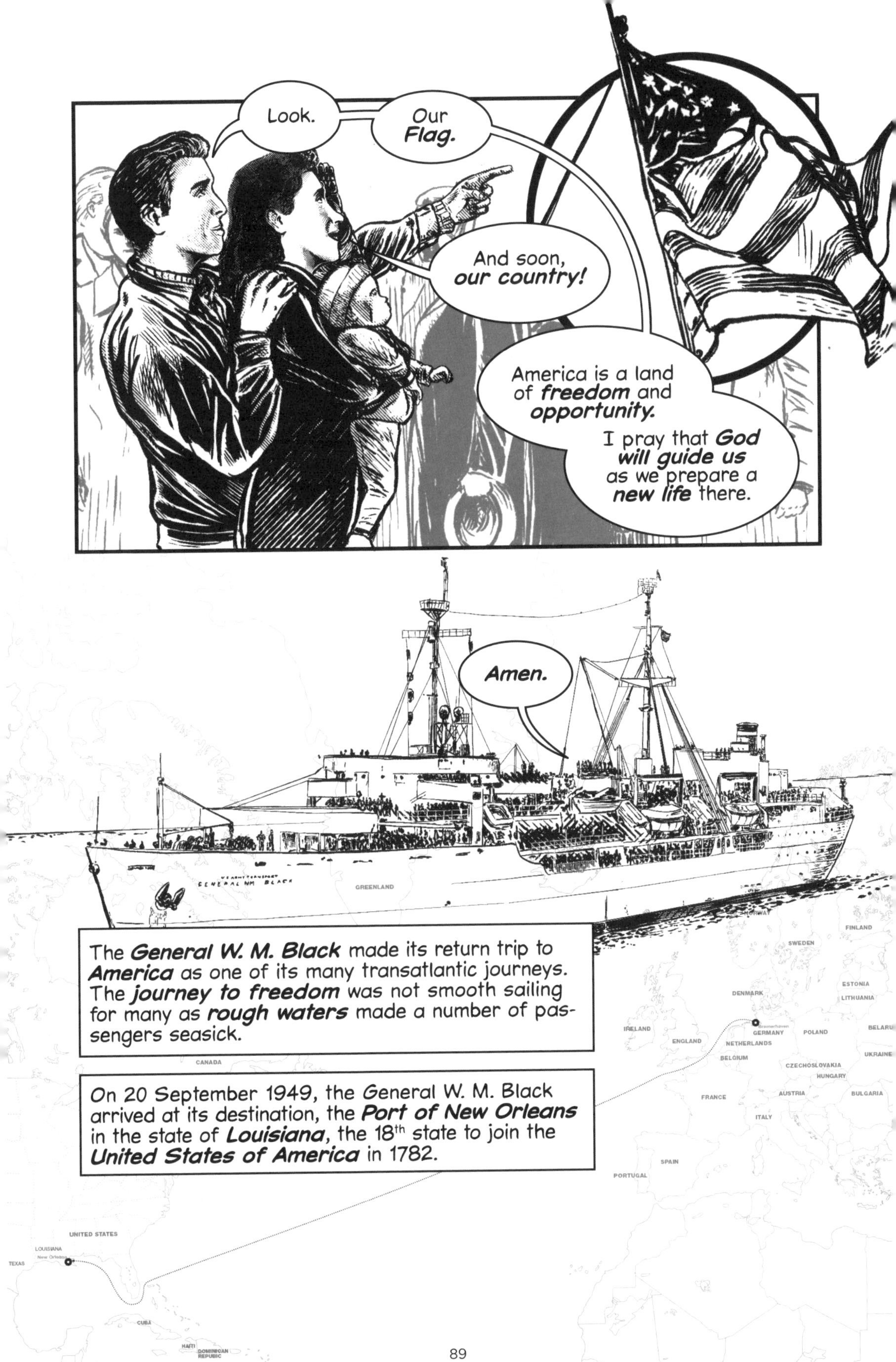
Look.
Our Flag.
And soon, our country!
America is a land of freedom and opportunity.
I pray that God will guide us as we prepare a new life there.
Amen.
GREENLAND
The General W. M. Black made its return trip to America as one of its many transatlantic journeys. The journey to freedom was not smooth sailing for many as rough waters made a number of passengers seasick.
On 20 September 1949, the General W. M. Black arrived at its destination, the Port of New Orleans in the state of Louisiana, the 18th state to join the United States of America in 1782.
FINLAND
SWEDEN
ESTONIA
LITHUANIA
DENMARK
IRELAND
ENGLAND
Bremerhaven
GERMANY
NETHERLANDS
POLAND
BELGIUM
UKRAINE
CZECHOSLOVAKIA
HUNGARY
CANADA
FRANCE
AUSTRIA
BULGARIA
ITALY
SPAIN
PORTUGAL
UNITED STATES
LOUISIANA
New Orleans
TEXAS
CUBA
HAITI
DOMINICAN REPUBLIC

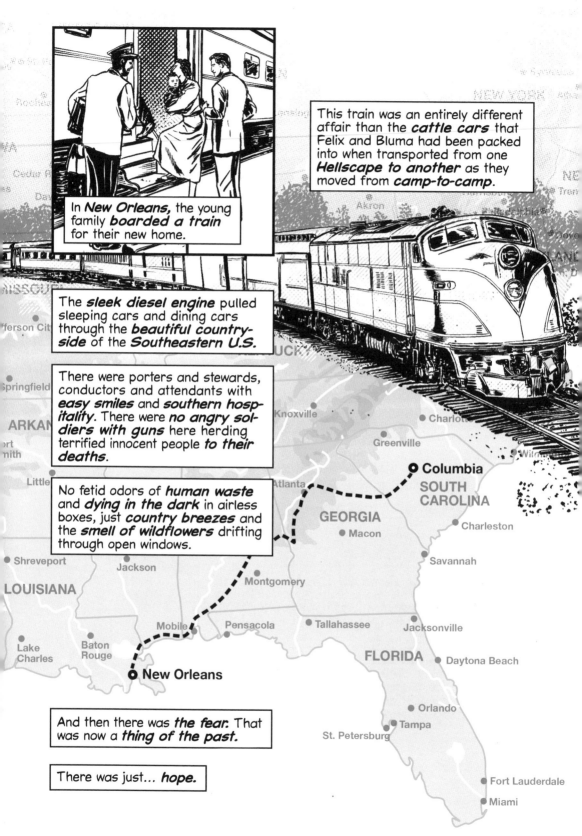

In **New Orleans,** the young family **boarded a train** for their new home.

This train was an entirely different affair than the **cattle cars** that Felix and Bluma had been packed into when transported from one **Hellscape to another** as they moved from **camp-to-camp.**

The **sleek diesel engine** pulled sleeping cars and dining cars through the **beautiful country-side** of the **Southeastern U.S.**

There were porters and stewards, conductors and attendants with **easy smiles** and **southern hospitality.** There were **no angry soldiers with guns** here herding terrified innocent people **to their deaths.**

No fetid odors of **human waste** and **dying in the dark** in airless boxes, just **country breezes** and the **smell of wildflowers** drifting through open windows.

And then there was **the fear.** That was now a **thing of the past.**

There was just... **hope.**

Columbia
SOUTH CAROLINA
Charleston
GEORGIA
Macon
Savannah
Knoxville
Charlotte
Greenville
Wilmington
Atlanta
Shreveport
Jackson
Montgomery
LOUISIANA
Mobile
Pensacola
Tallahassee
Jacksonville
Lake Charles
Baton Rouge
FLORIDA
Daytona Beach
New Orleans
Orlando
Tampa
St. Petersburg
Fort Lauderdale
Miami
Springfield
Little
Jefferson City
ARKANSAS
Fort Smith
MISSOURI

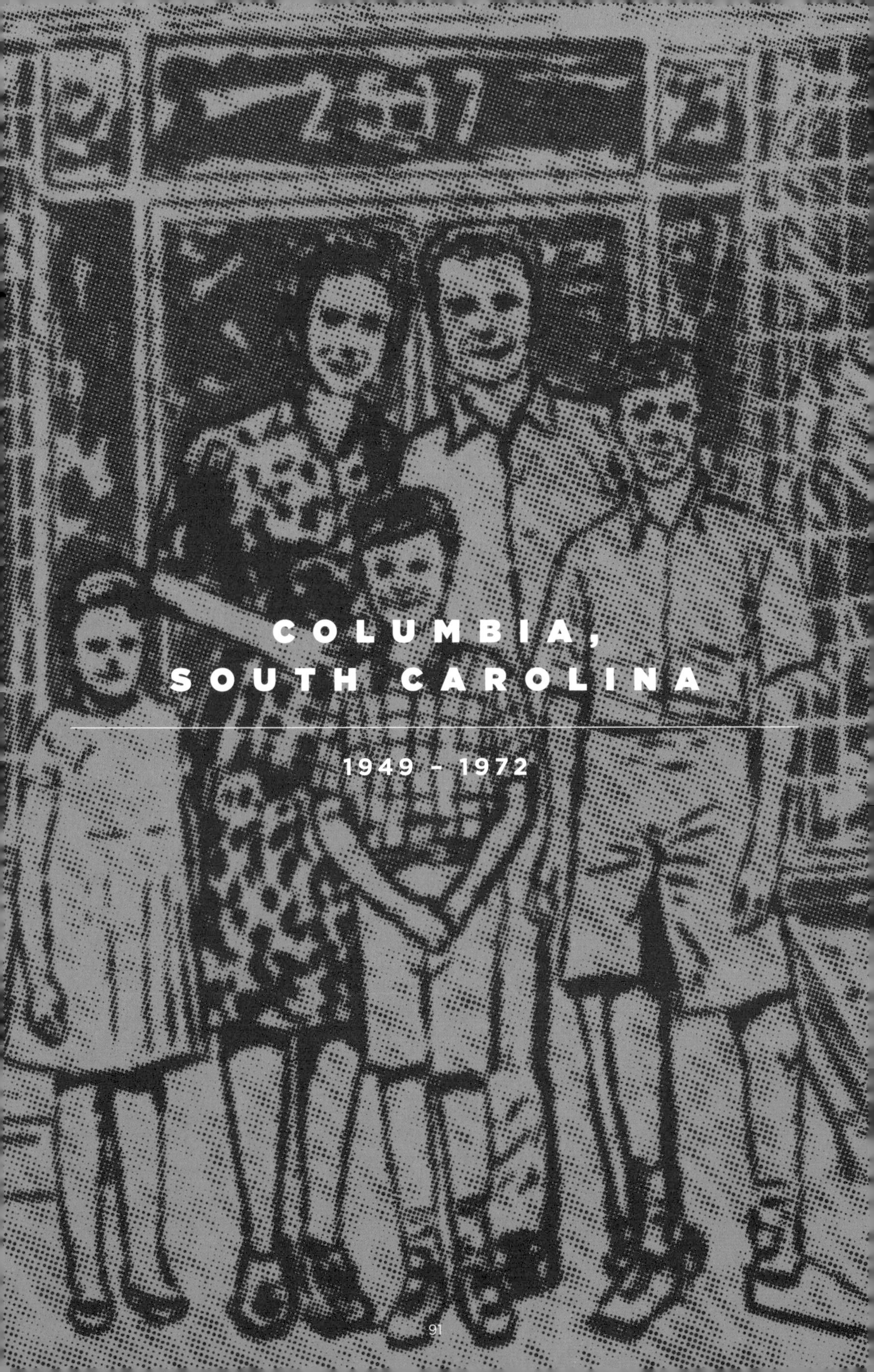

COLUMBIA, SOUTH CAROLINA

1949 – 1972

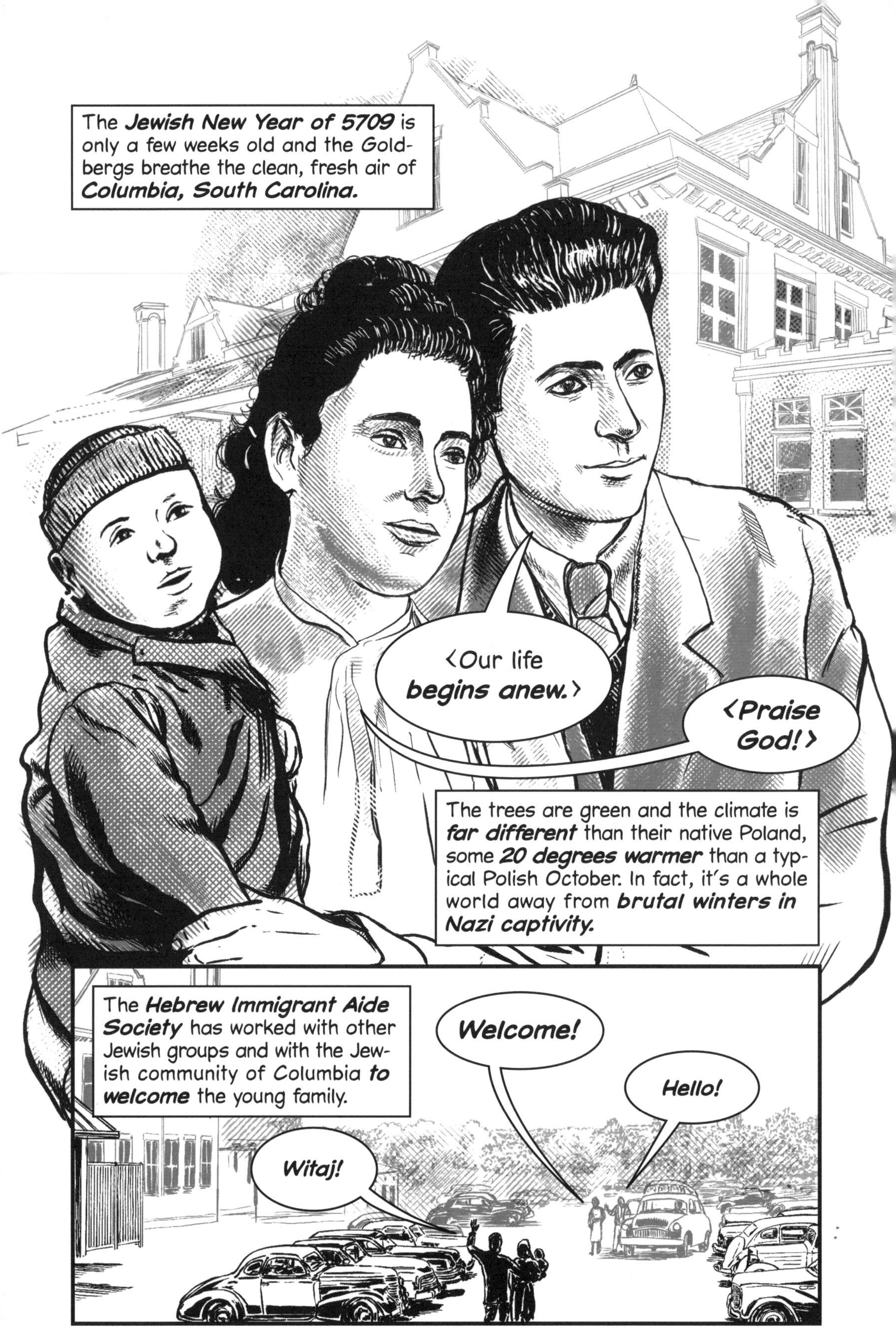
The Jewish New Year of 5709 is only a few weeks old and the Goldbergs breathe the clean, fresh air of Columbia, South Carolina.
<Our life begins anew.>
<Praise God!>
The trees are green and the climate is far different than their native Poland, some 20 degrees warmer than a typical Polish October. In fact, it's a whole world away from brutal winters in Nazi captivity.
The Hebrew Immigrant Aide Society has worked with other Jewish groups and with the Jewish community of Columbia to welcome the young family.
Welcome!
Hello!
Witaj!

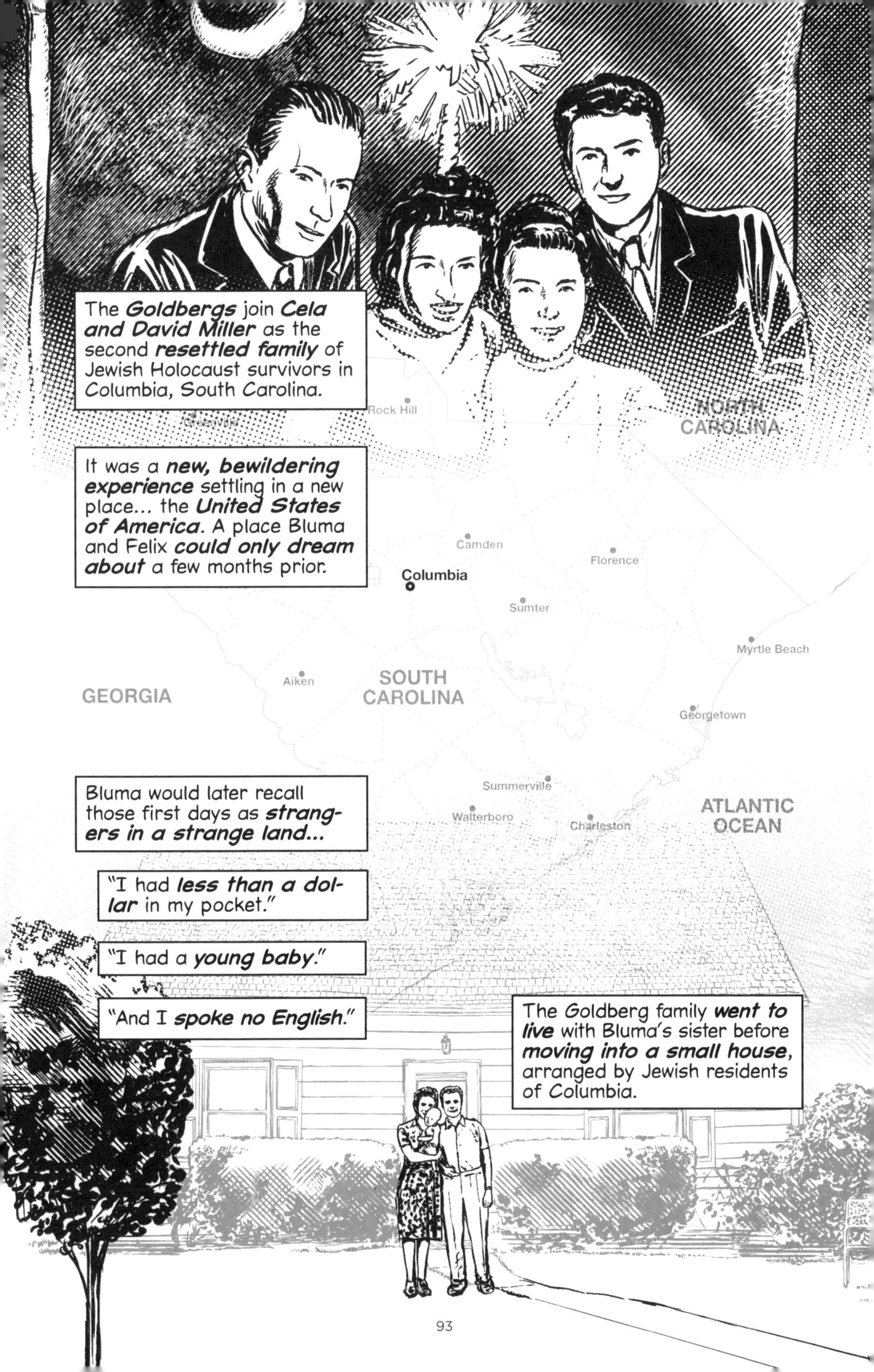
The ***Goldbergs*** join ***Cela and David Miller*** as the second ***resettled family*** of Jewish Holocaust survivors in Columbia, South Carolina.
It was a ***new, bewildering experience*** settling in a new place... the ***United States of America***. A place Bluma and Felix ***could only dream about*** a few months prior.
Rock Hill
Greenville
NORTH CAROLINA
Camden
Florence
Columbia
Sumter
Myrtle Beach
Aiken
SOUTH CAROLINA
GEORGIA
Georgetown
Summerville
Walterboro
Charleston
ATLANTIC OCEAN
Bluma would later recall those first days as ***strangers in a strange land...***
"I had ***less than a dollar*** in my pocket."
"I had a ***young baby***."
"And I ***spoke no English***."
The Goldberg family ***went to live*** with Bluma's sister before ***moving into a small house***, arranged by Jewish residents of Columbia.

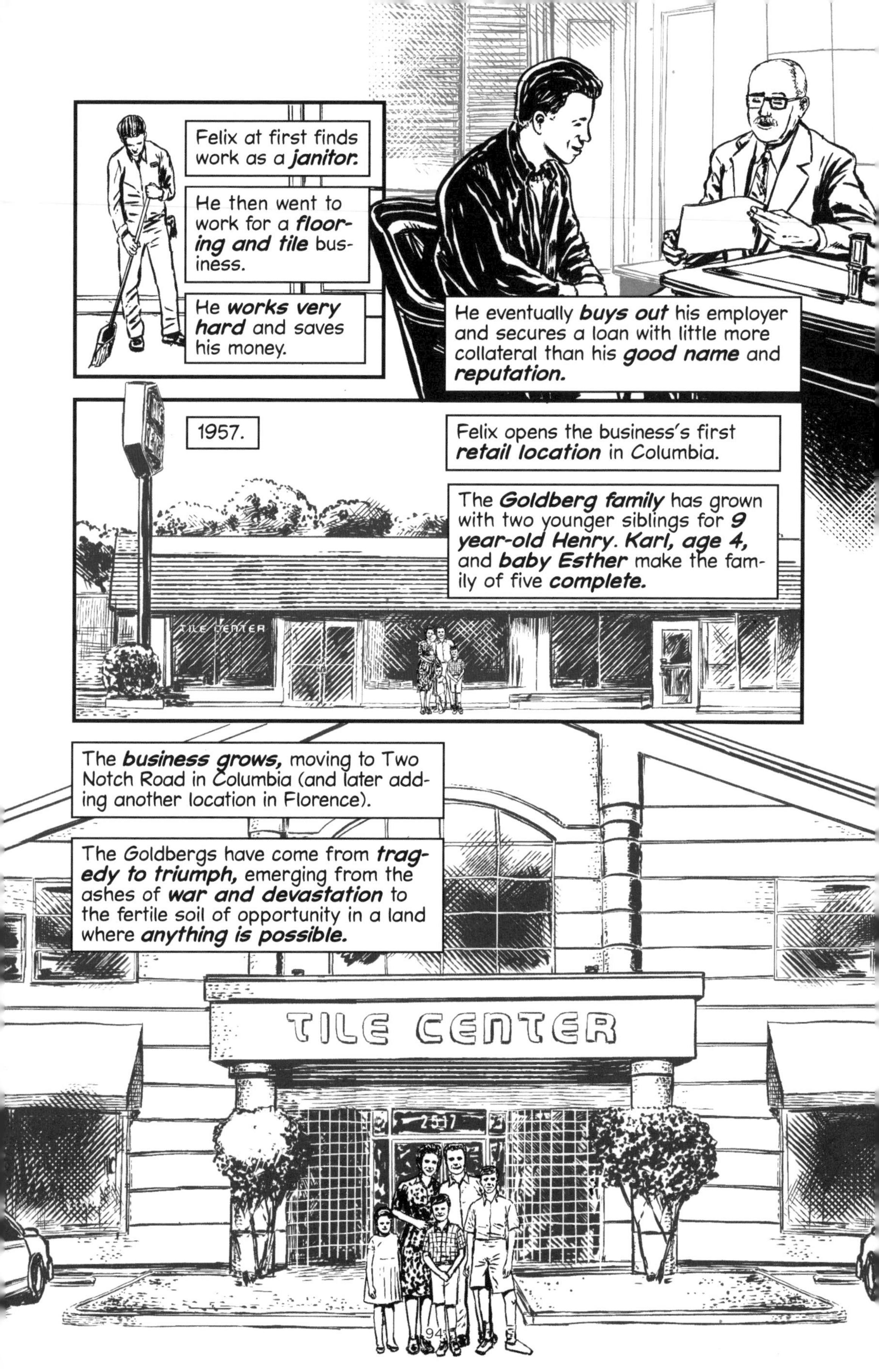
Felix at first finds work as a ***janitor.***
He then went to work for a ***flooring and tile*** business.
He ***works very hard*** and saves his money.
He eventually ***buys out*** his employer and secures a loan with little more collateral than his ***good name*** and ***reputation.***
1957.
Felix opens the business's first ***retail location*** in Columbia.
The ***Goldberg family*** has grown with two younger siblings for ***9 year-old Henry. Karl, age 4,*** and ***baby Esther*** make the family of five ***complete.***
TILE CENTER
The ***business grows,*** moving to Two Notch Road in Columbia (and later adding another location in Florence).
The Goldbergs have come from ***tragedy to triumph,*** emerging from the ashes of ***war and devastation*** to the fertile soil of opportunity in a land where ***anything is possible.***
TILE CENTER
2517

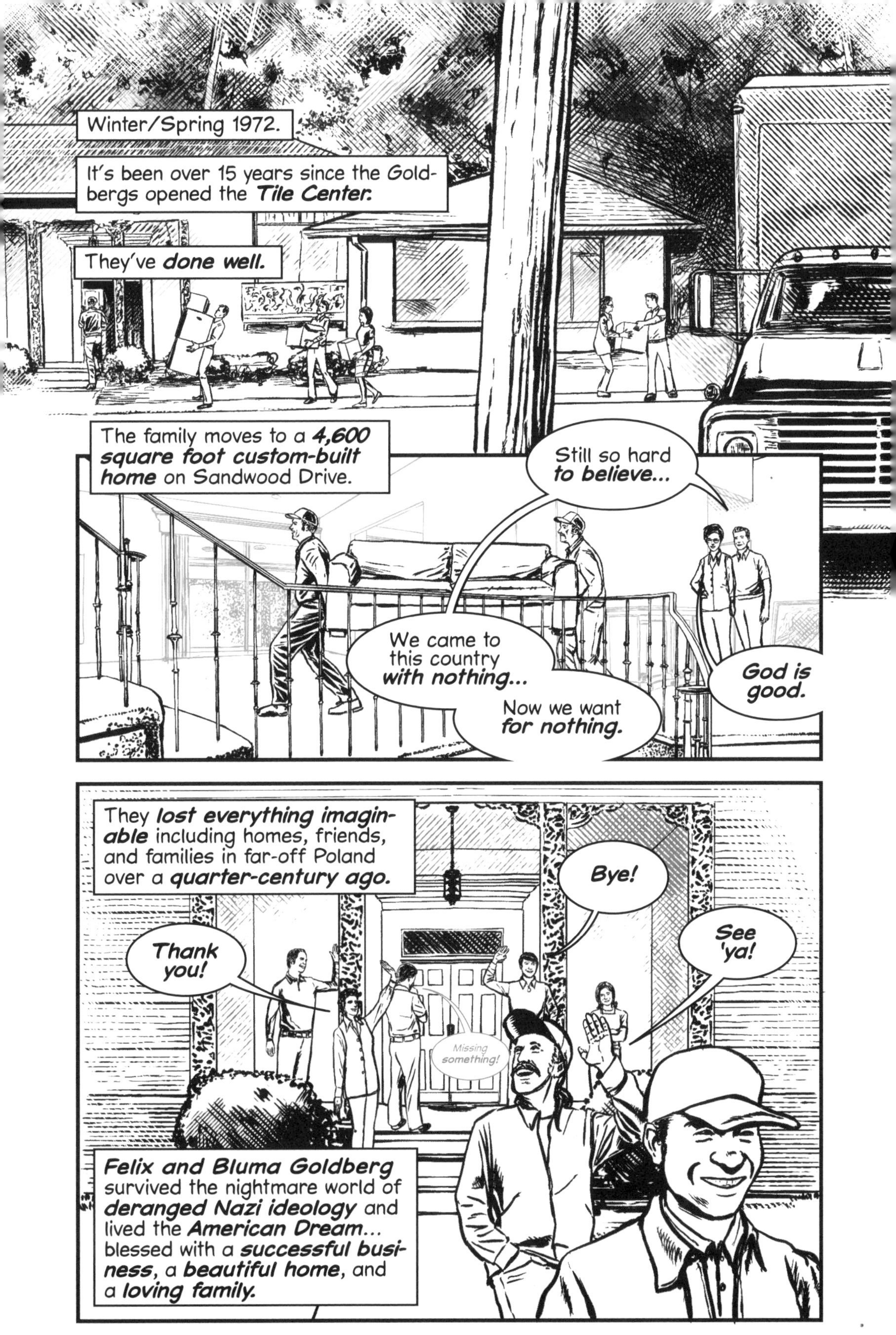
Winter/Spring 1972.
It's been over 15 years since the Goldbergs opened the Tile Center.
They've done well.
The family moves to a 4,600 square foot custom-built home on Sandwood Drive.
Still so hard to believe...
We came to this country with nothing...
Now we want for nothing.
God is good.
They lost everything imaginable including homes, friends, and families in far-off Poland over a quarter-century ago.
Bye!
Thank you!
See 'ya!
Missing something!
Felix and Bluma Goldberg survived the nightmare world of deranged Nazi ideology and lived the American Dream... blessed with a successful business, a beautiful home, and a loving family.

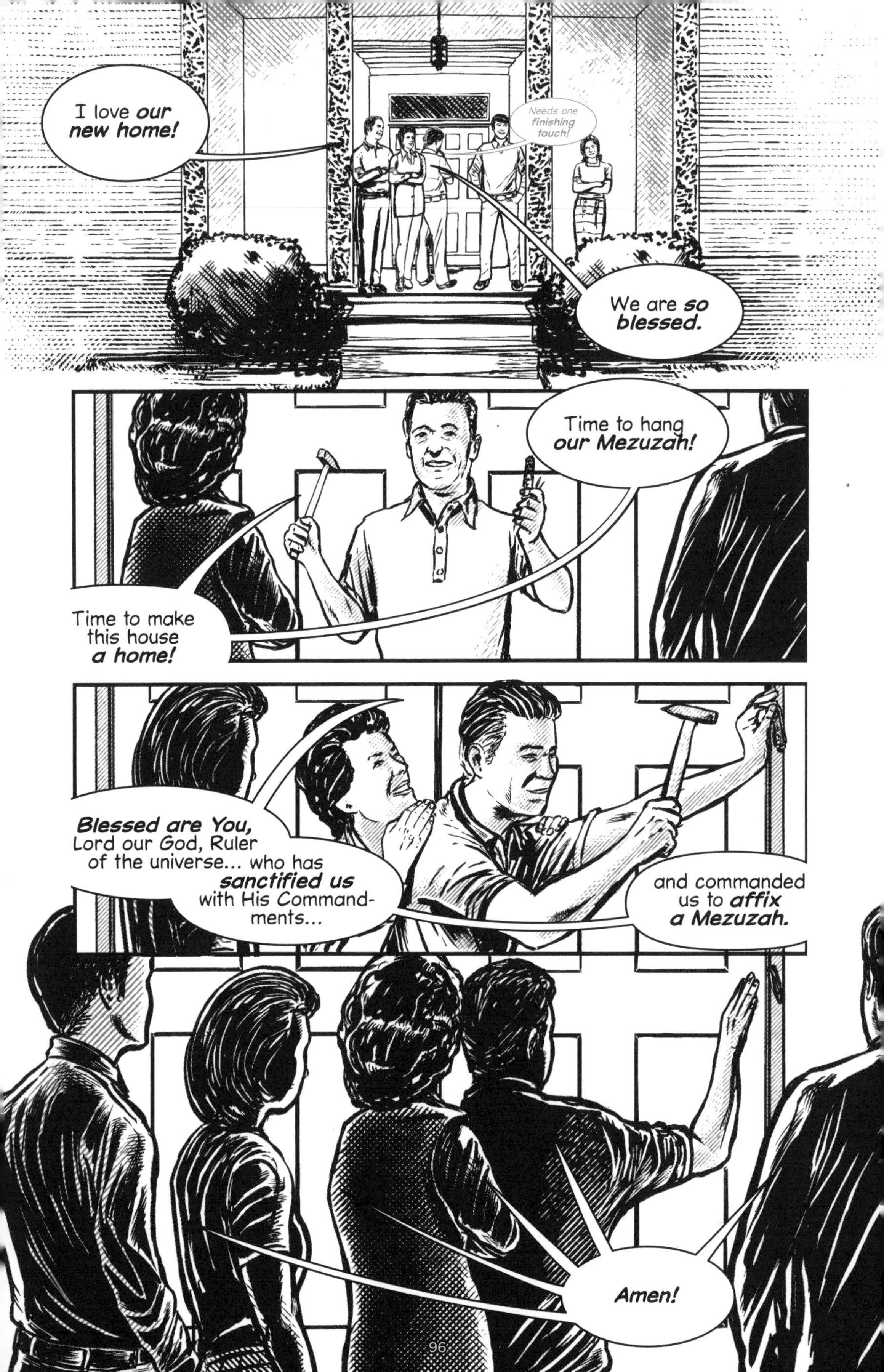
I love our new home!
Needs one finishing touch!
We are so blessed.
Time to hang our Mezuzah!
Time to make this house a home!
Blessed are You, Lord our God, Ruler of the universe... who has sanctified us with His Commandments...
and commanded us to affix a Mezuzah.
Amen!

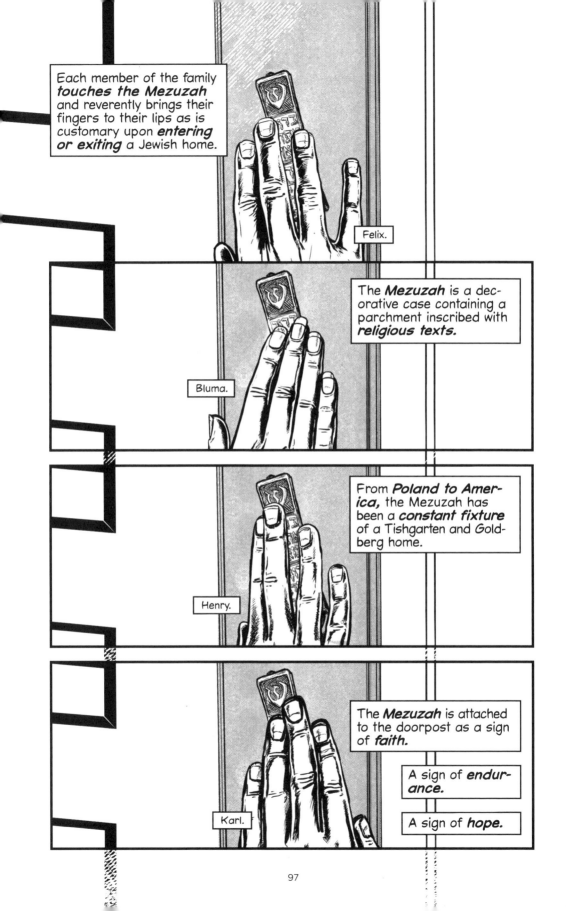

Each member of the family **touches the Mezuzah** and reverently brings their fingers to their lips as is customary upon *entering or exiting* a Jewish home.

Felix.

The **Mezuzah** is a decorative case containing a parchment inscribed with **religious texts.**

Bluma.

From **Poland to America,** the Mezuzah has been a **constant fixture** of a Tishgarten and Goldberg home.

Henry.

The **Mezuzah** is attached to the doorpost as a sign of *faith.*

A sign of *endurance.*

A sign of *hope.*

Karl.

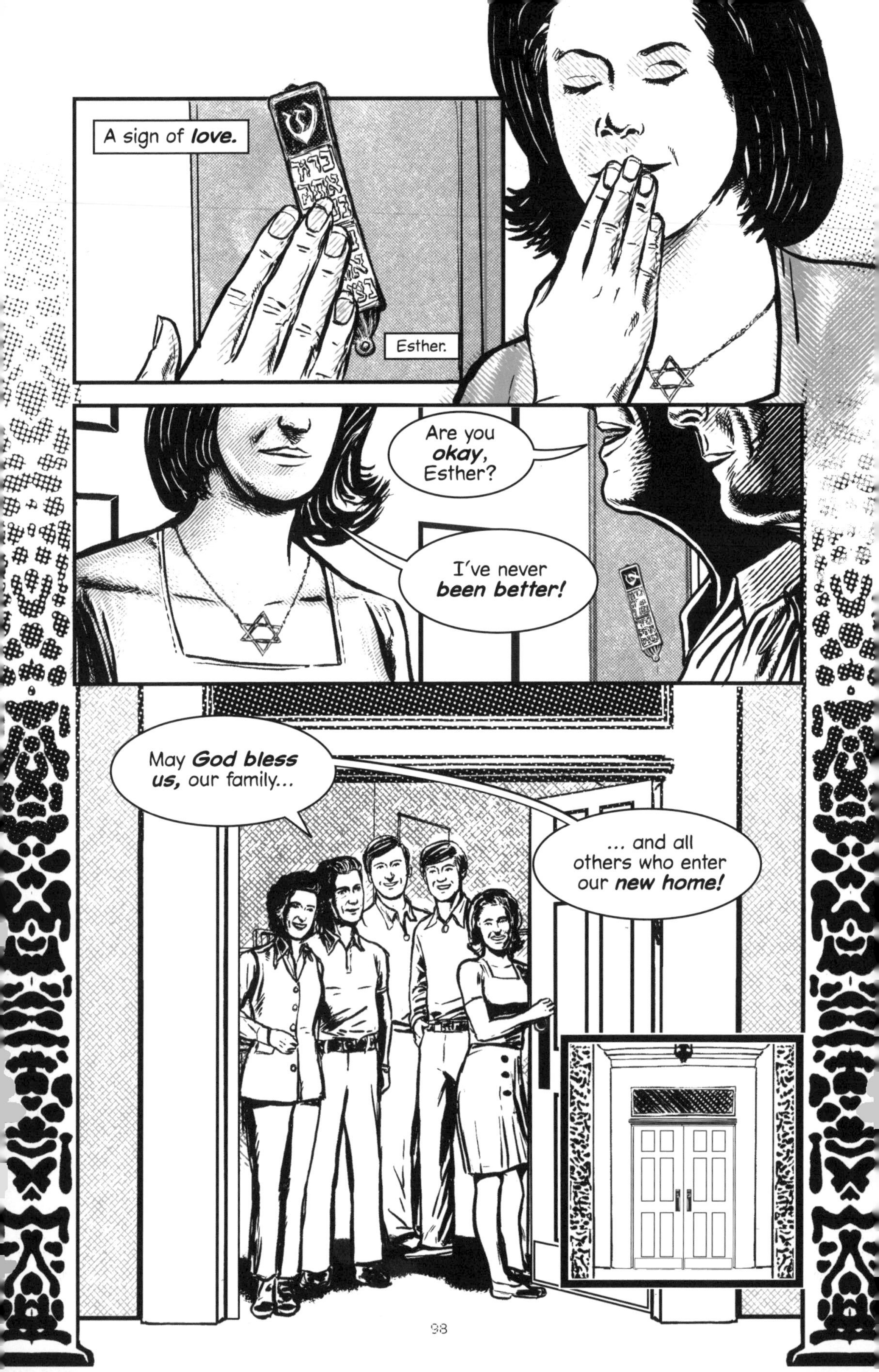
A sign of love.
Esther.
Are you okay, Esther?
I've never been better!
May God bless us, our family...
... and all others who enter our new home!

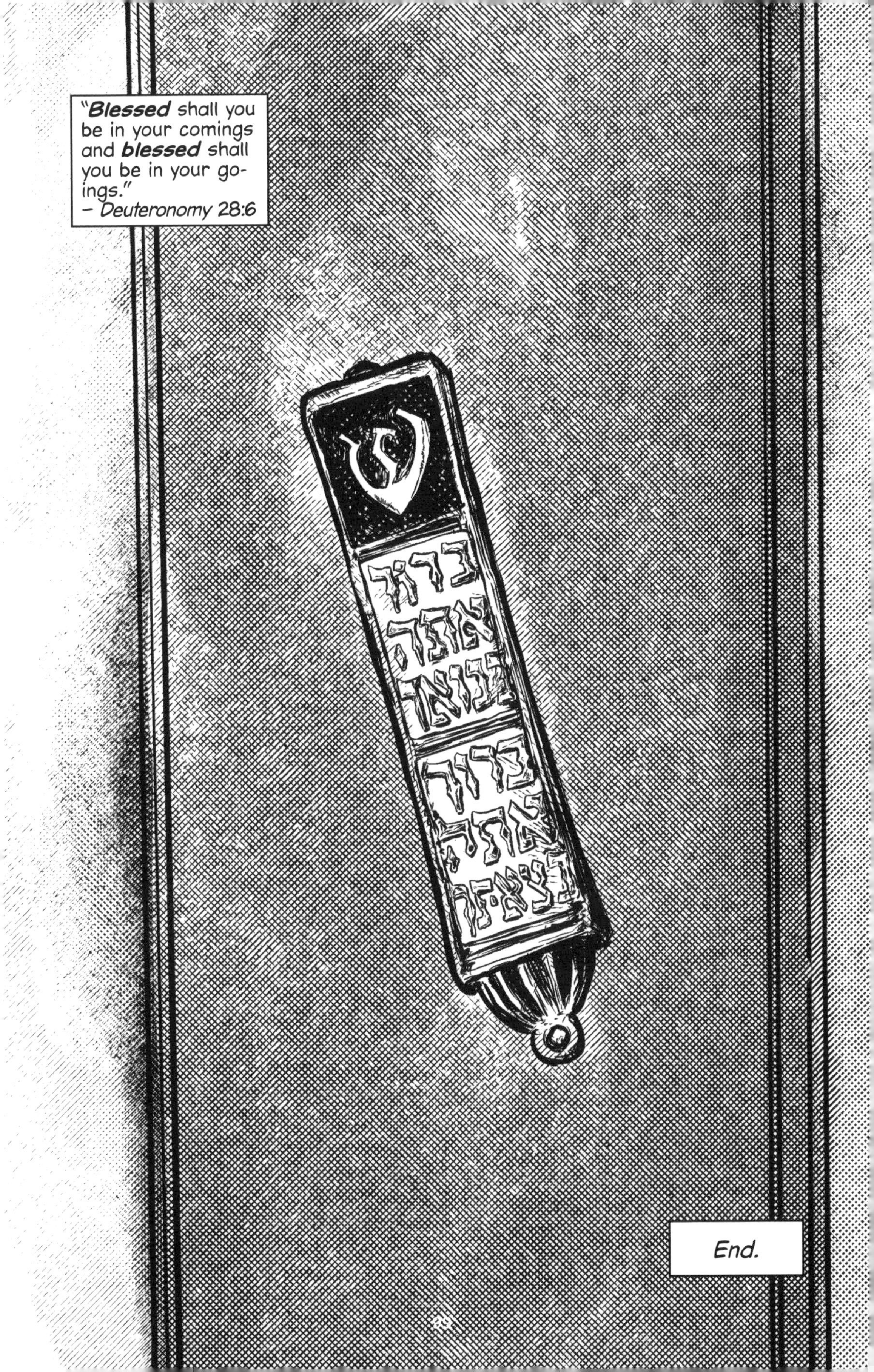
"**Blessed** shall you be in your comings and **blessed** shall you be in your goings."
– Deuteronomy 28:6
End.

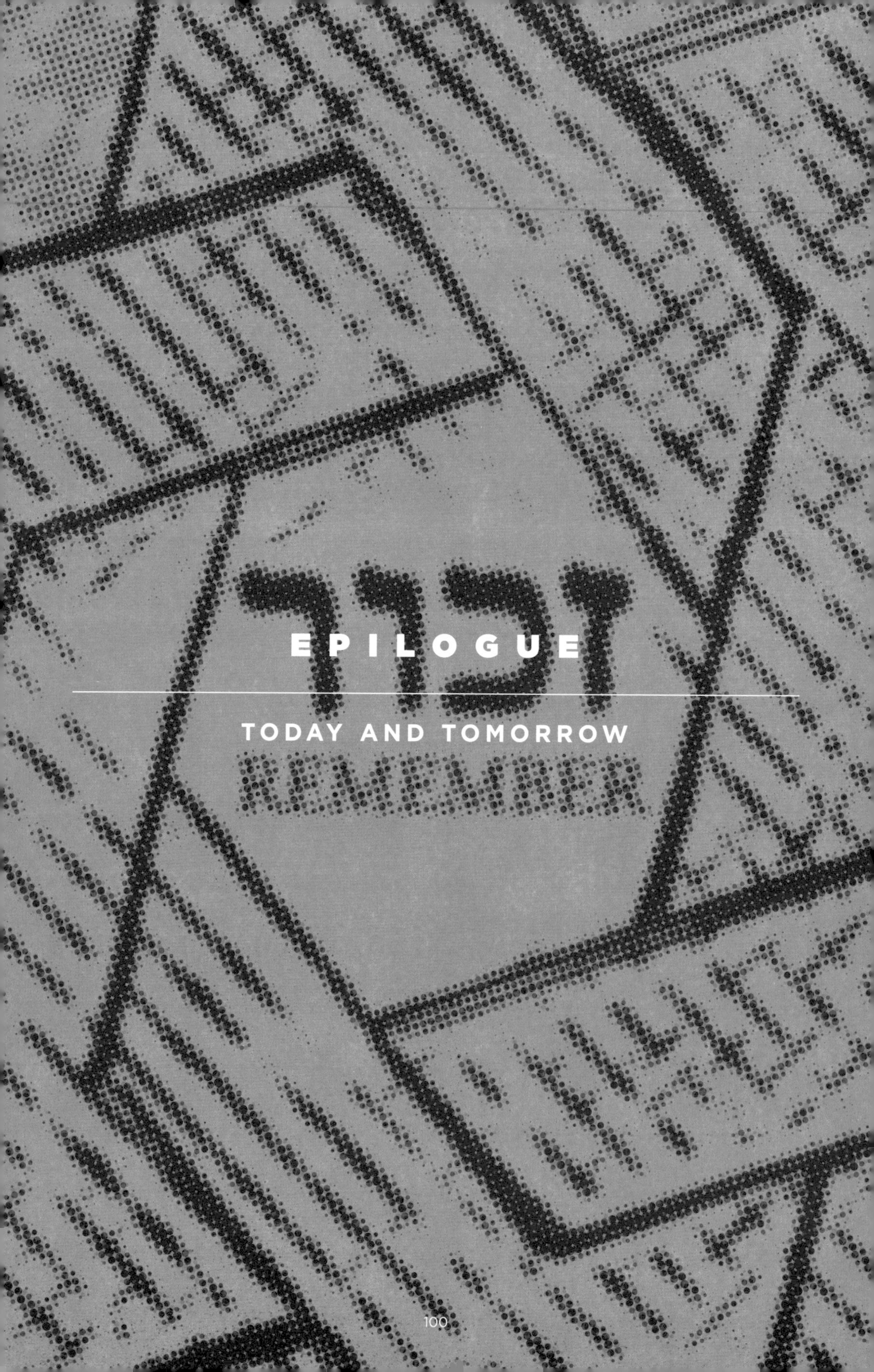
זכור
REMEMBER

EPILOGUE

TODAY AND TOMORROW

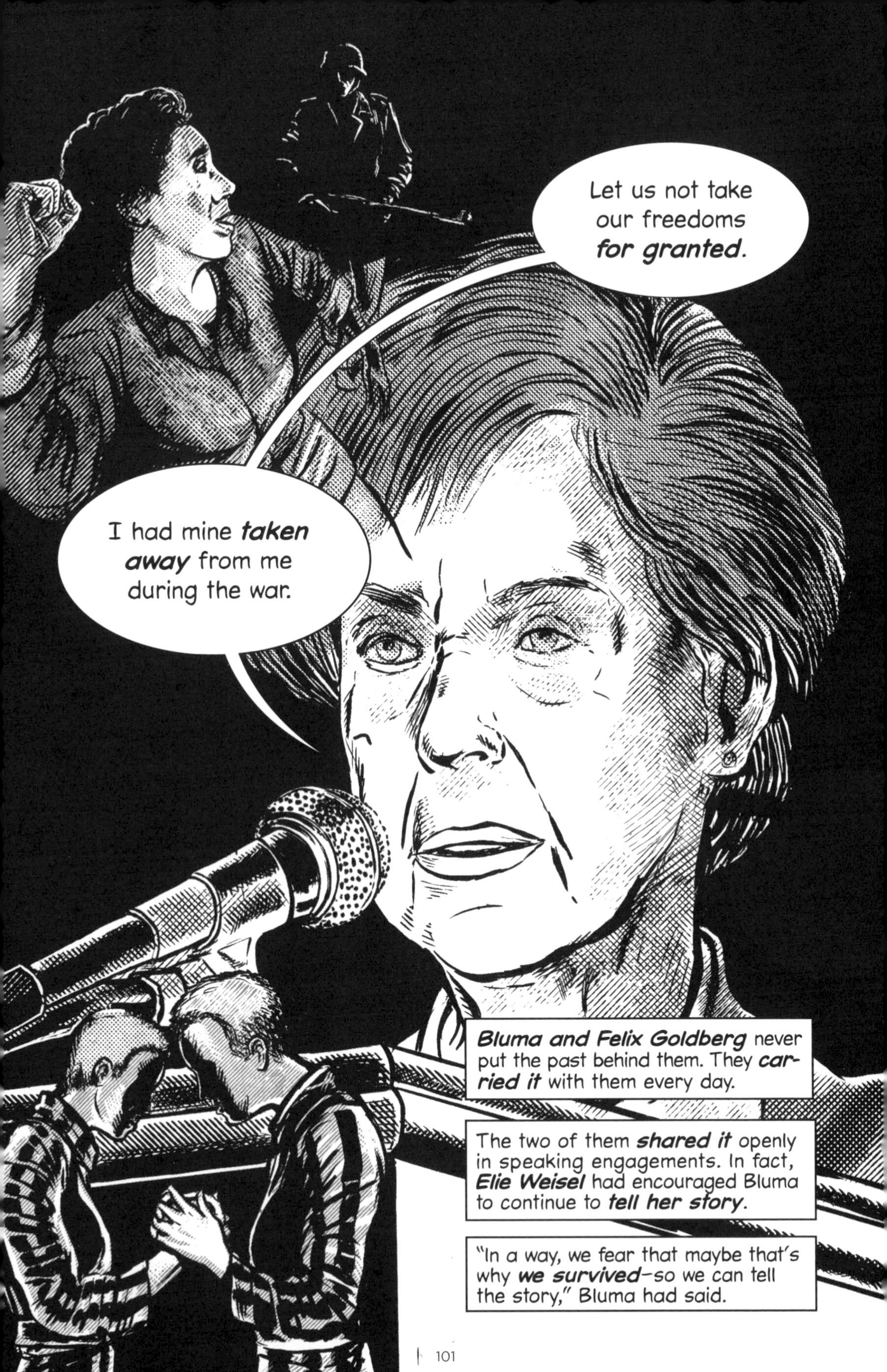

Let us not take our freedoms **for granted**.
I had mine **taken away** from me during the war.
Bluma and Felix Goldberg never put the past behind them. They **carried it** with them every day.
The two of them **shared it** openly in speaking engagements. In fact, **Elie Weisel** had encouraged Bluma to continue to **tell her story**.
"In a way, we fear that maybe that's why **we survived**—so we can tell the story," Bluma had said.

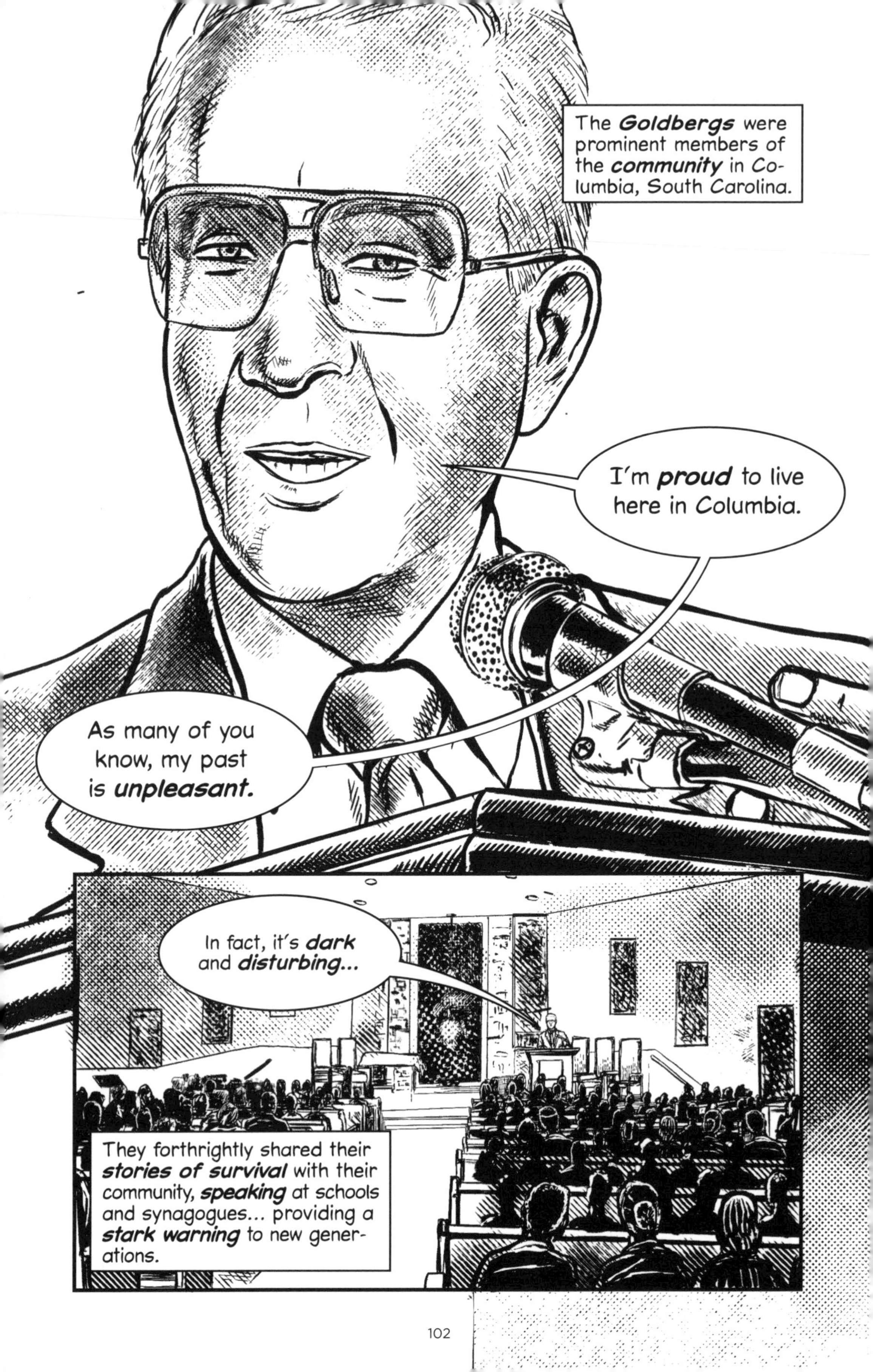
The Goldbergs were prominent members of the community in Columbia, South Carolina.
I'm proud to live here in Columbia.
As many of you know, my past is unpleasant.
In fact, it's dark and disturbing...
They forthrightly shared their stories of survival with their community, speaking at schools and synagogues... providing a stark warning to new generations.

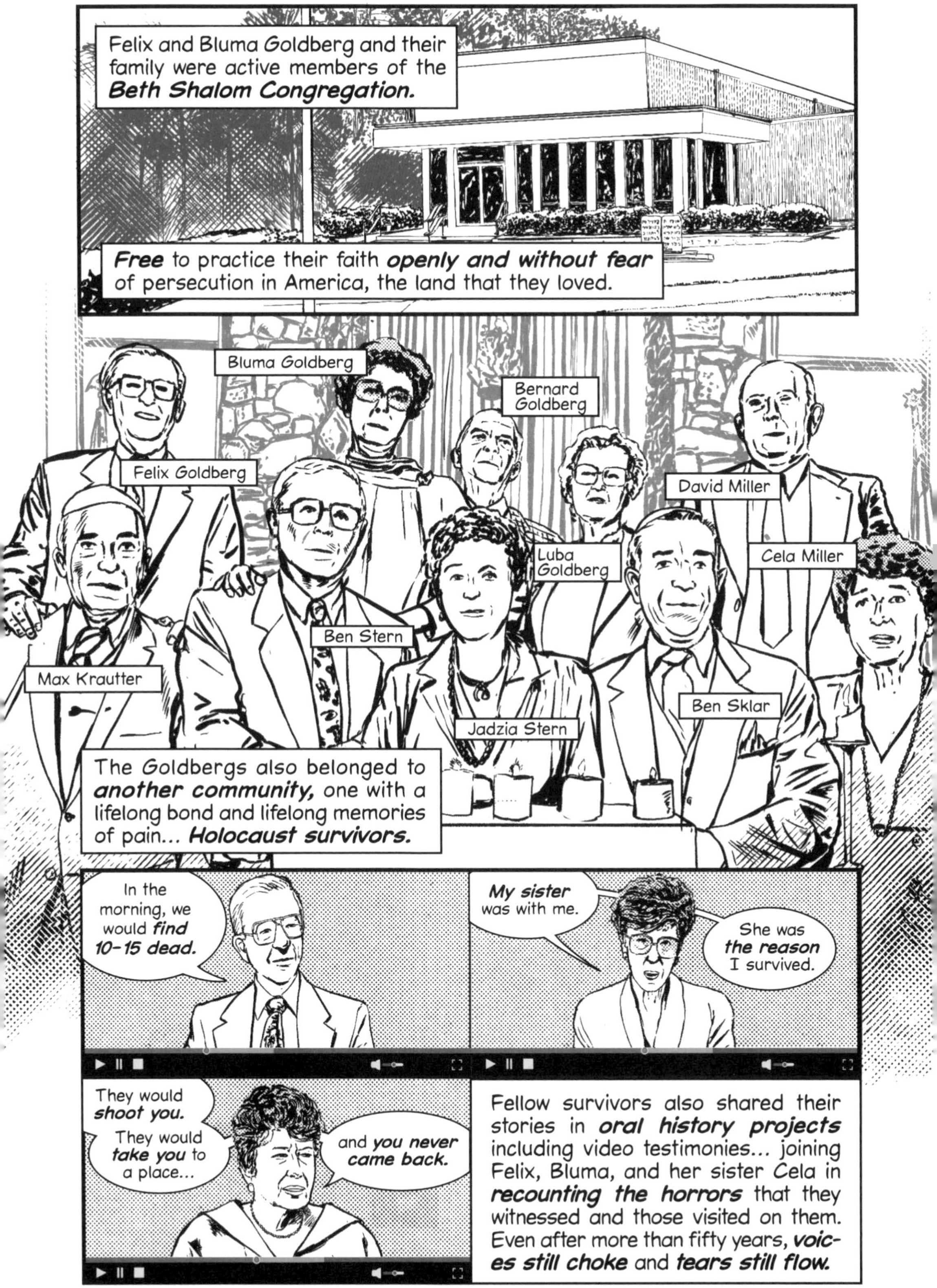

Felix and Bluma Goldberg and their family were active members of the *Beth Shalom Congregation.*
Free to practice their faith *openly and without fear* of persecution in America, the land that they loved.
Bluma Goldberg
Bernard Goldberg
Felix Goldberg
David Miller
Luba Goldberg
Cela Miller
Ben Stern
Max Krautter
Ben Sklar
Jadzia Stern
The Goldbergs also belonged to *another community,* one with a lifelong bond and lifelong memories of pain... *Holocaust survivors.*
In the morning, we would *find 10-15 dead.*
My sister was with me.
She was *the reason* I survived.
They would *shoot you.*
They would *take you* to a place...
and *you never came back.*
Fellow survivors also shared their stories in *oral history projects* including video testimonies... joining Felix, Bluma, and her sister Cela in *recounting the horrors* that they witnessed and those visited on them. Even after more than fifty years, *voices still choke* and *tears still flow.*

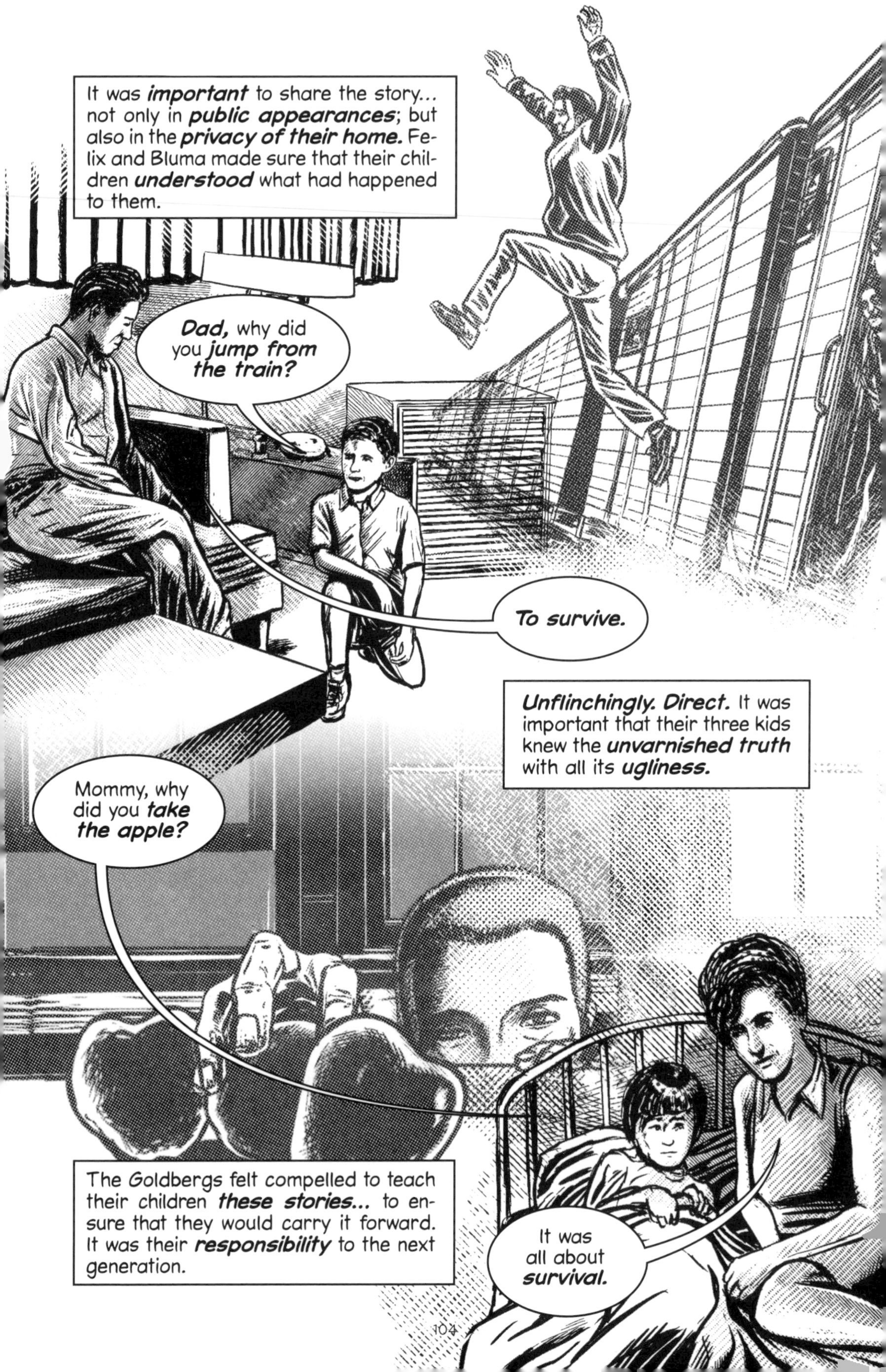

It was *important* to share the story... not only in *public appearances*; but also in the *privacy of their home.* Felix and Bluma made sure that their children *understood* what had happened to them.
Dad, why did you *jump from the train?*
To survive.
Unflinchingly. Direct. It was important that their three kids knew the *unvarnished truth* with all its *ugliness.*
Mommy, why did you *take the apple?*
The Goldbergs felt compelled to teach their children *these stories...* to ensure that they would carry it forward. It was their *responsibility* to the next generation.
It was all about *survival.*

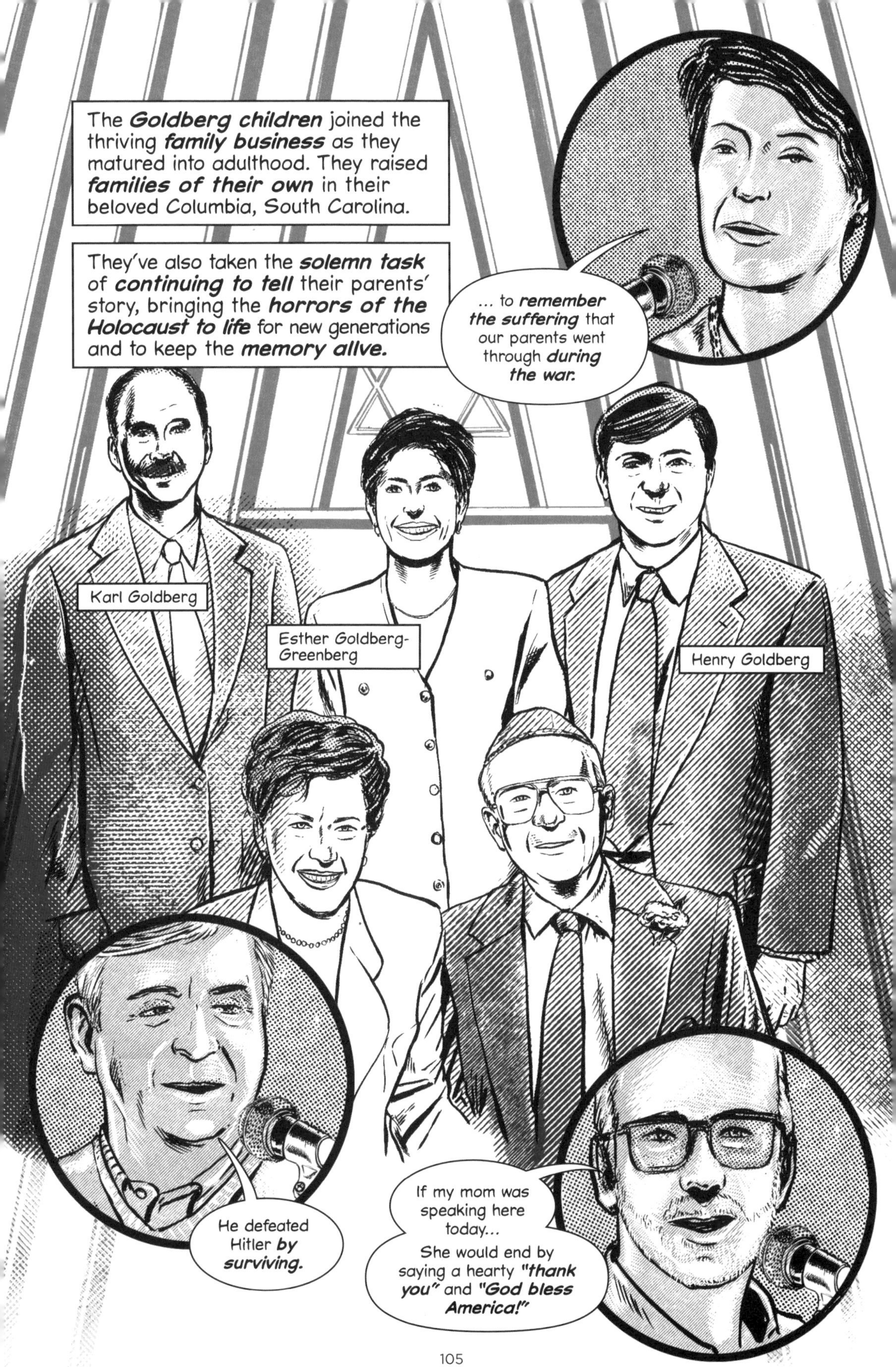

The *Goldberg children* joined the thriving *family business* as they matured into adulthood. They raised *families of their own* in their beloved Columbia, South Carolina.
They've also taken the *solemn task* of *continuing to tell* their parents' story, bringing the *horrors of the Holocaust to life* for new generations and to keep the *memory alive.*
... to *remember the suffering* that our parents went through *during the war.*
Karl Goldberg
Esther Goldberg-Greenberg
Henry Goldberg
He defeated Hitler *by surviving.*
If my mom was speaking here today...
She would end by saying a hearty *"thank you"* and *"God bless America!"*

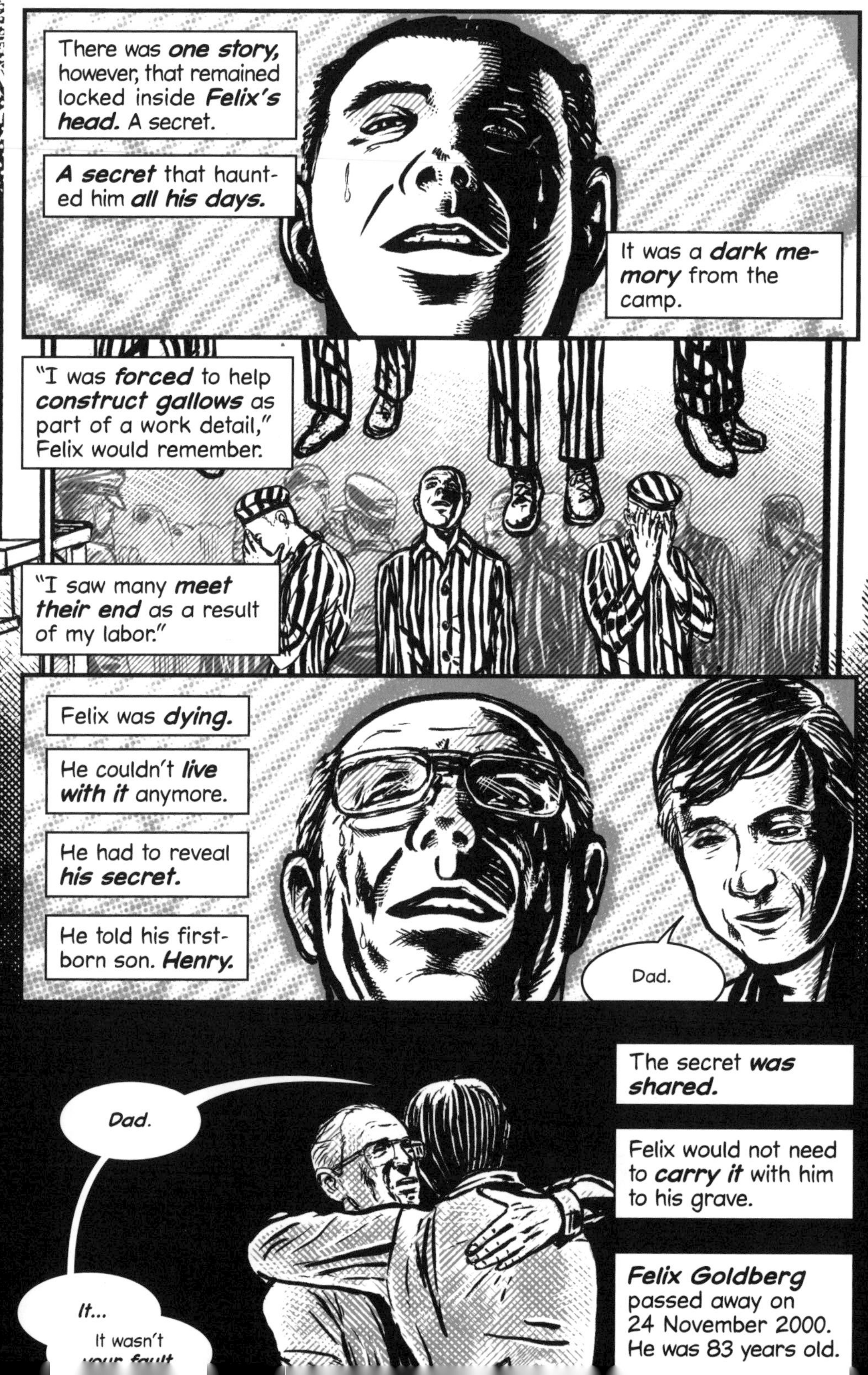
There was one story, however, that remained locked inside Felix's head. A secret.
A secret that haunted him all his days.
It was a dark memory from the camp.
"I was forced to help construct gallows as part of a work detail," Felix would remember.
"I saw many meet their end as a result of my labor."
Felix was dying.
He couldn't live with it anymore.
He had to reveal his secret.
He told his firstborn son. Henry.
Dad.
The secret was shared.
Dad.
Felix would not need to carry it with him to his grave.
It...
It wasn't
Felix Goldberg passed away on 24 November 2000. He was 83 years old.

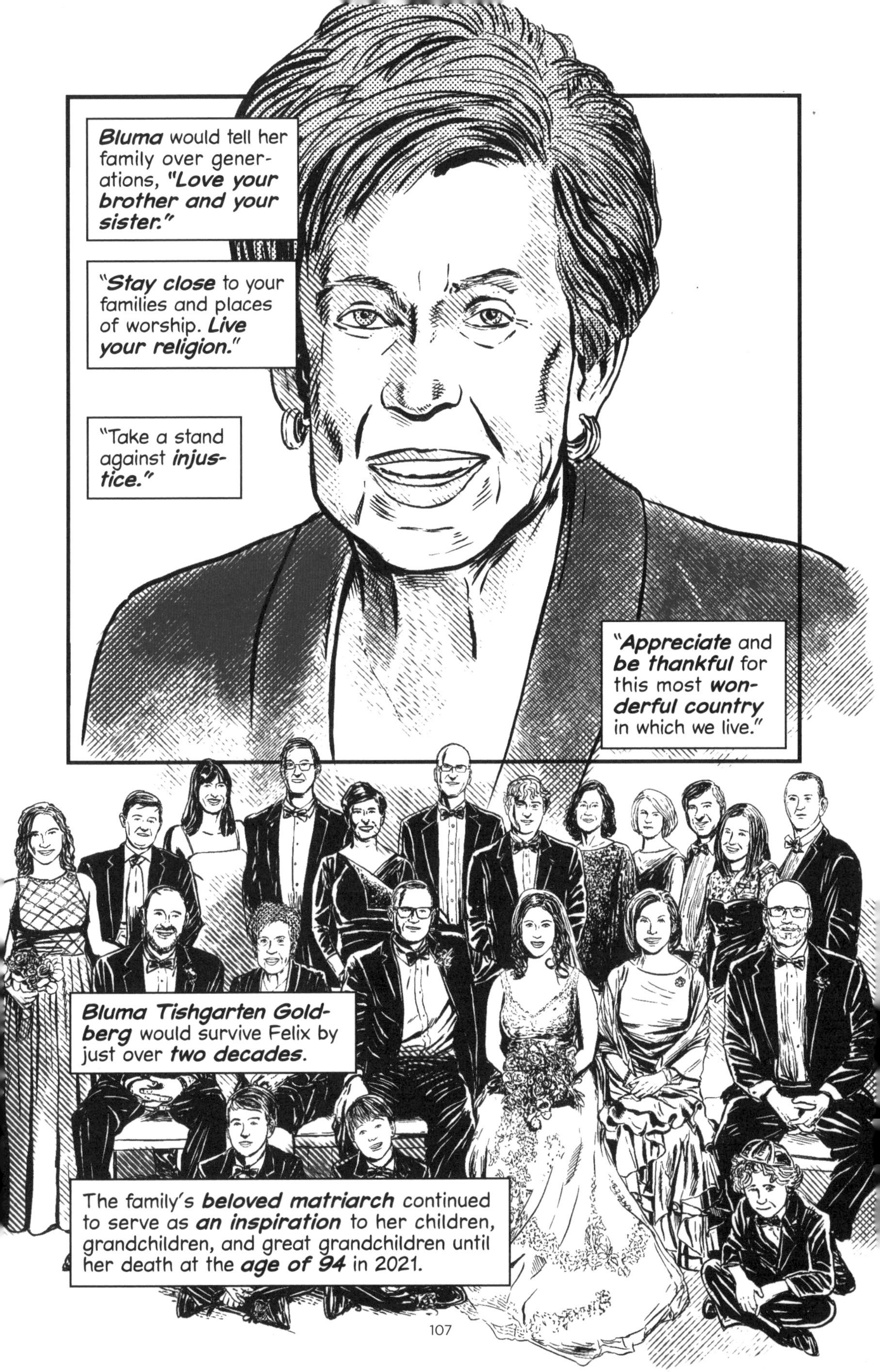

Bluma would tell her family over generations, "Love your brother and your sister."
"Stay close to your families and places of worship. Live your religion."
"Take a stand against injustice."
"Appreciate and be thankful for this most wonderful country in which we live."
Bluma Tishgarten Goldberg would survive Felix by just over two decades.
The family's beloved matriarch continued to serve as an inspiration to her children, grandchildren, and great grandchildren until her death at the age of 94 in 2021.

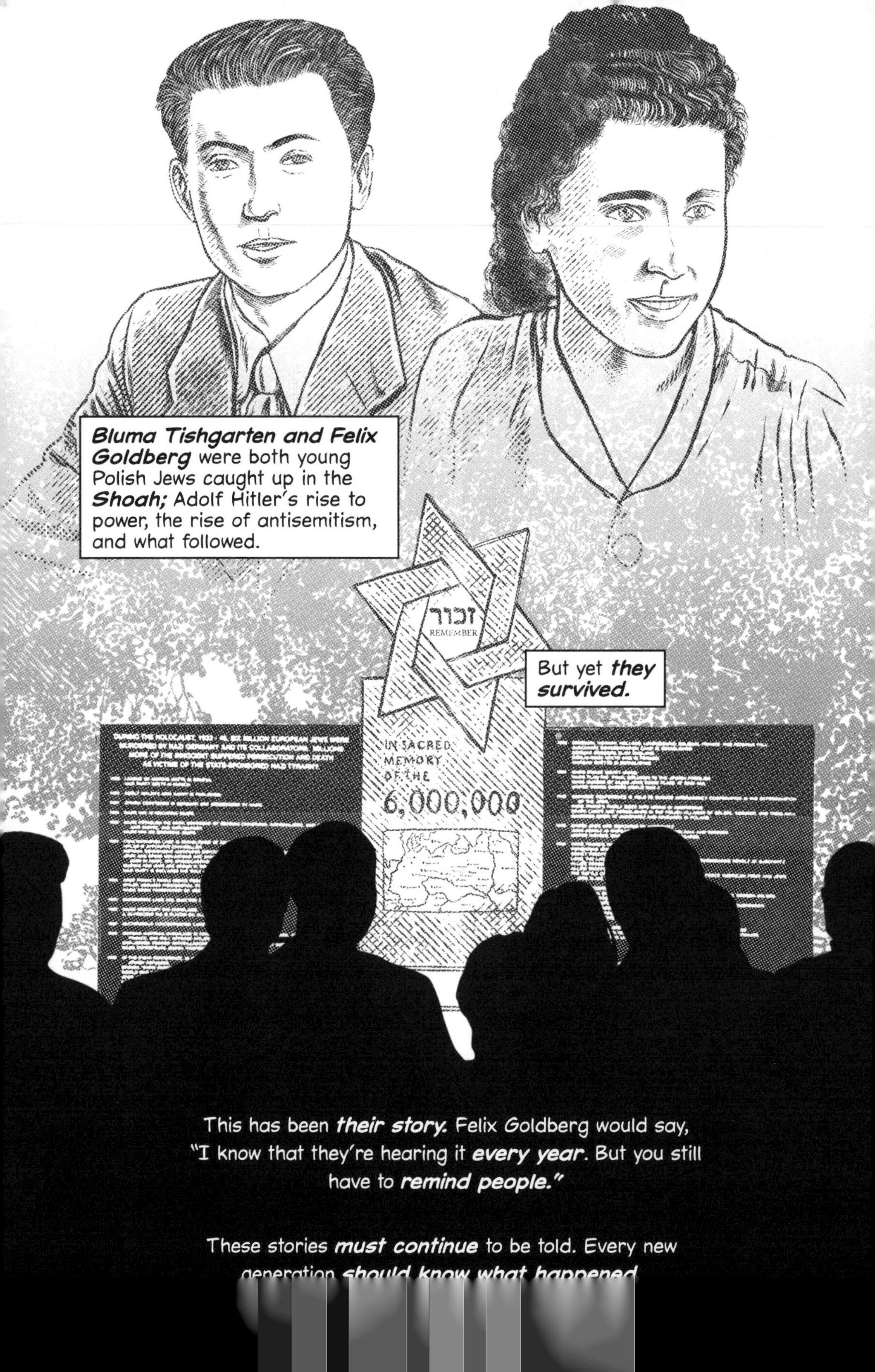

Bluma Tishgarten and Felix Goldberg were both young Polish Jews caught up in the **Shoah;** Adolf Hitler's rise to power, the rise of antisemitism, and what followed.
זכור
REMEMBER
But yet **they survived.**
IN SACRED MEMORY OF THE
6,000,000
This has been **their story.** Felix Goldberg would say, "I know that they're hearing it **every year**. But you still have to **remind people."**
These stories **must continue** to be told. Every new generation **should know what happened.**

Even though **World War II** and the **Holocaust** are long over... atrocities, genocide, intolerance, prejudice and antisemitism *still exist today.*

The phrase *"never forget"* was coined as a *reminder* for all of us to *remember* and to *study the past.* As William Faulkner said, *"The past is never dead. It's not even past."*

It's always with us — and if we're not careful — *it can repeat itself.*

Felix and Bluma Goldberg's story of survival warns us of what happened... and *reminds us of our duty* to never forget the six million who lost their lives and make sure *it never happens again.*

End.

AFTERWORD

BY JOHN SHABLESKI

Genocide, Ethnic Cleansing, Relocation, Lynching, Pogrom… these are but a few of the words or euphemisms that have been used throughout history to describe one of the most hideous aspects of the human race. There is not a place on any continent that is without stories of the slaughter of our fellow human beings. Throughout history "explorers and discoverers" led the first wave of the efforts to erase local native populations. Over the past 400 years of history in North America, we have killed or resettled the people who lived here for eons, we also enslaved an entire race of people who to this very day live with the threat of slaughter.

Even today we are still witness to the horrors of atrocities committed against people around the world. From the Sudanese and Rwandans to the Cambodians and Rohingya, Syrians, Kurds, Serbs and Croats. Ethnic cleansing is a new form of genocide that is very much in evidence.

With the focus of this particular story, and what makes it so incredibly horrifying, is that the Holocaust represents the moment human beings developed an industrial, scientific and mechanized approach to the slaughter of an entire race of people. Equally as frightening is the idea that the rest of the world sat back and simply watched as millions of people: children, women and men, mothers, sisters, brothers, sons, fathers, elders…. were all slaughtered.

From this event, out of literal ashes, we also discover the true strength of the human spirit. Anne Frank is often quoted as saying "In spite of everything, I still believe that people are really good at heart." When you read Bluma and Felix's story, you will see just how incredible the human spirit can be.

The images in this book are just a small sample of the daily struggles they faced along with thousands of other prisoners where every single moment was truly a life-or-death decision.

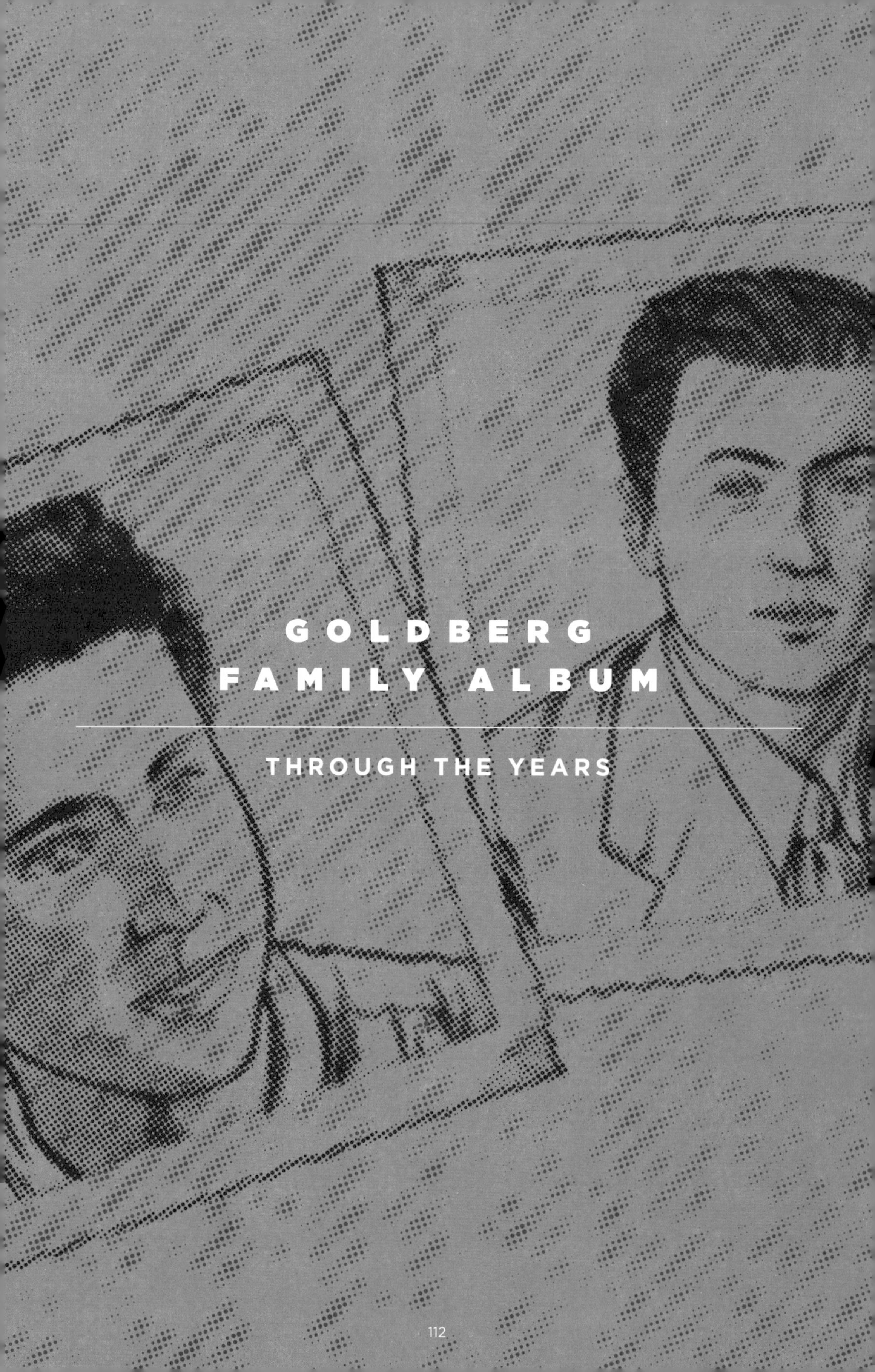

GOLDBERG FAMILY ALBUM

THROUGH THE YEARS

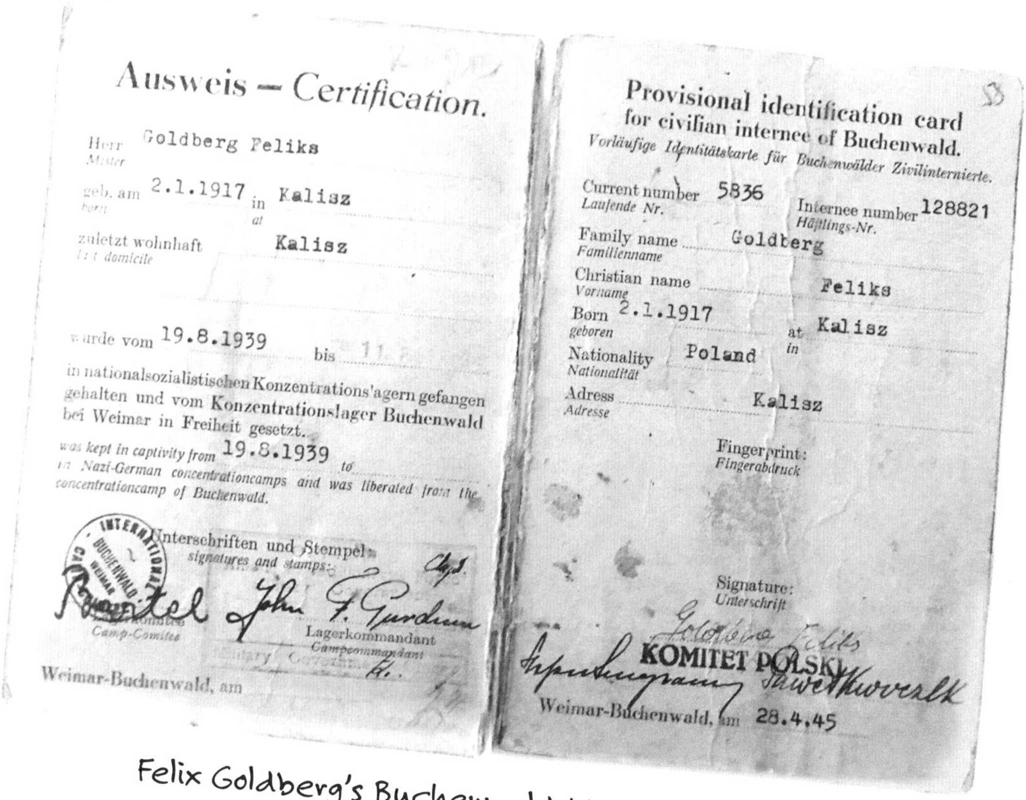

Ausweis – Certification.

Herr / Mister: Goldberg Feliks

geb. am / born: 2.1.1917 in / at: Kalisz

zuletzt wohnhaft / last domicile: Kalisz

wurde vom 19.8.1939 bis 11.

in nationalsozialistischen Konzentrationslagern gefangen gehalten und vom Konzentrationslager Buchenwald bei Weimar in Freiheit gesetzt.

was kept in captivity from 19.8.1939 to in Nazi-German concentrationcamps and was liberated from the concentrationcamp of Buchenwald.

Unterschriften und Stempel: / signatures and stamps:

Lagerkomitee / Camp-Comitee

Lagerkommandant / Campcommandant

Weimar-Buchenwald, am

Provisional identification card for civilian internee of Buchenwald.

Vorläufige Identitätskarte für Buchenwälder Zivilinternierte.

Current number / Laufende Nr.: 5836

Internee number / Häftlings-Nr.: 128821

Family name / Familienname: Goldberg

Christian name / Vorname: Feliks

Born / geboren: 2.1.1917 at / in: Kalisz

Nationality / Nationalität: Poland

Adress / Adresse: Kalisz

Fingerprint: / Fingerabdruck

Signature: / Unterschrift: Goldberg Feliks

KOMITET POLSKI

Weimar-Buchenwald, am 28.4.45

Felix Goldberg's Buchenwald Identification Card

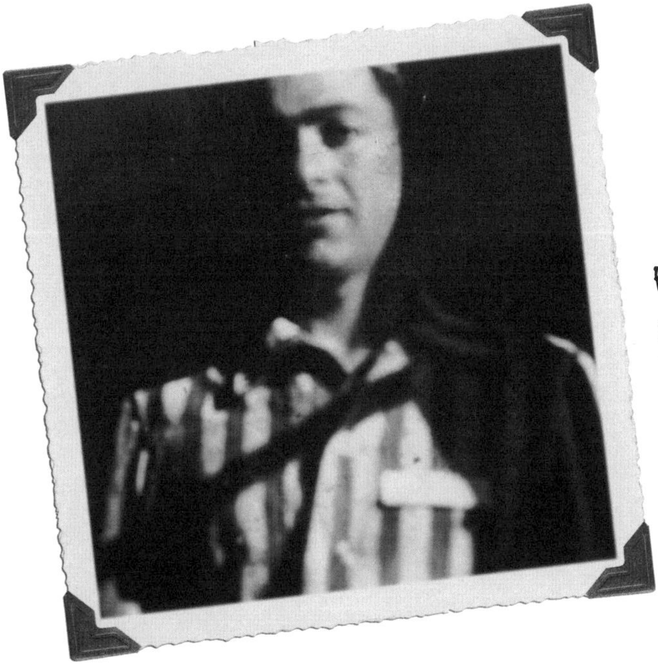

Felix Goldberg as seen shortly after his liberation from Buchenwald.

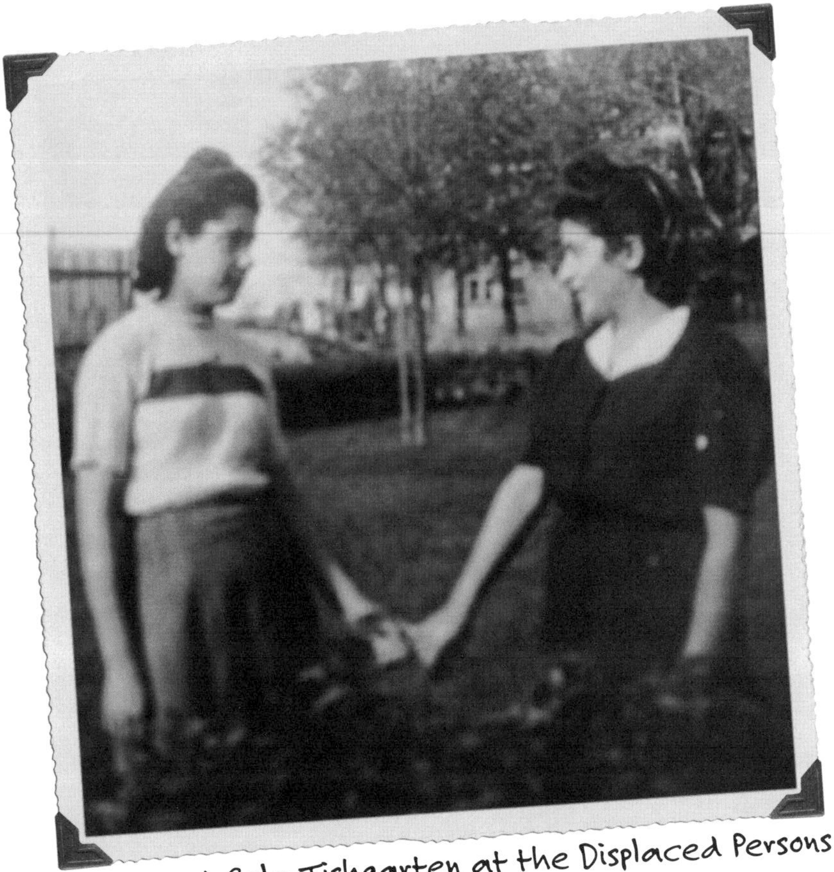

Bluma and Cela Tishgarten at the Displaced Persons Camp in Germany.

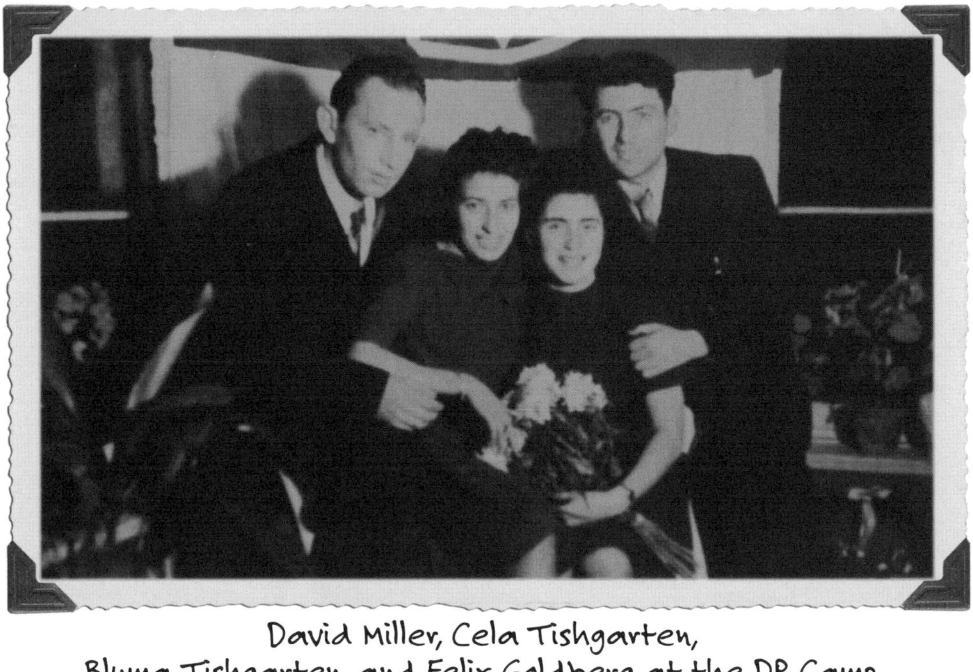

David Miller, Cela Tishgarten, Bluma Tishgarten, and Felix Goldberg at the DP Camp.

Wedding Day: A Double Wedding

On the Right:
Newlyweds
Mr & Mrs.
Felix Goldberg

Left: Mr & Mrs David Miller
(Cela had married Felix's best friend)

The happy couple
Bluma and Felix Goldberg
shortly after the birth
of their son Henry.

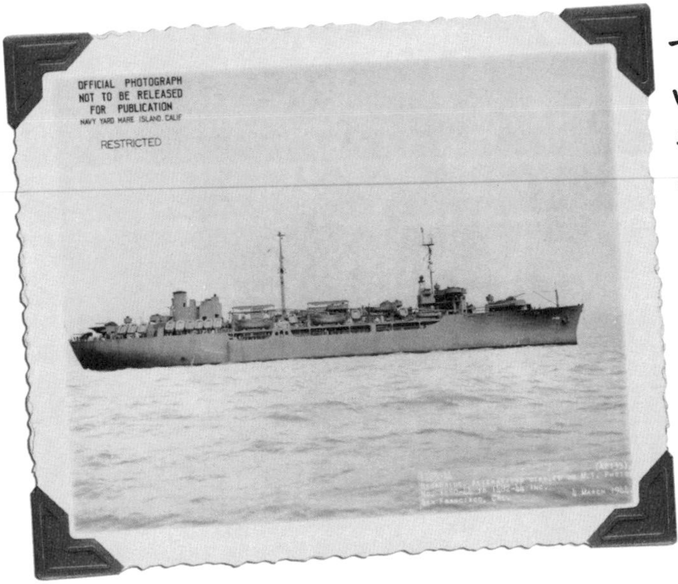
OFFICIAL PHOTOGRAPH
NOT TO BE RELEASED
FOR PUBLICATION
NAVY YARD MARE ISLAND, CALIF
RESTRICTED

The General W M Black, the transport ship that brought the Goldbergs and other displaced persons to America.

Raising a Family in America

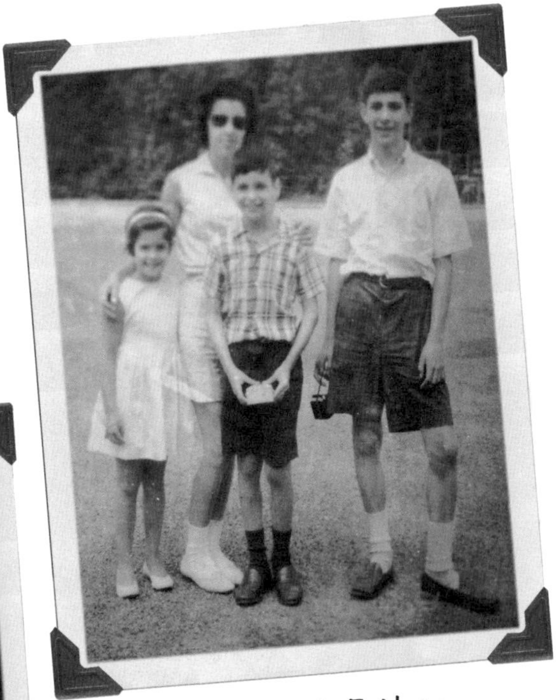

Bluma with Esther, Karl, and Henry (1963)

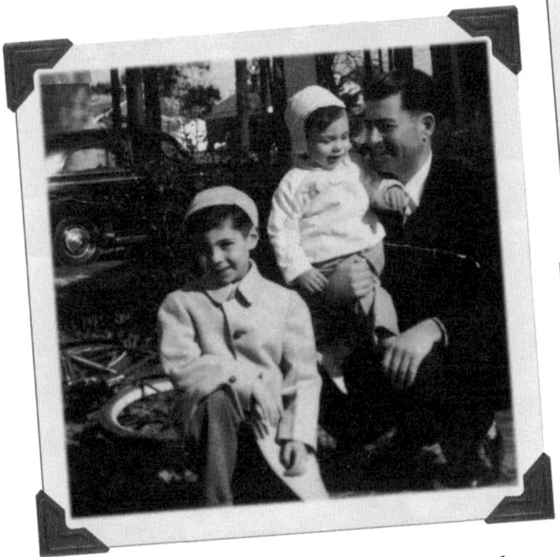

Felix with Henry and Karl (1954)

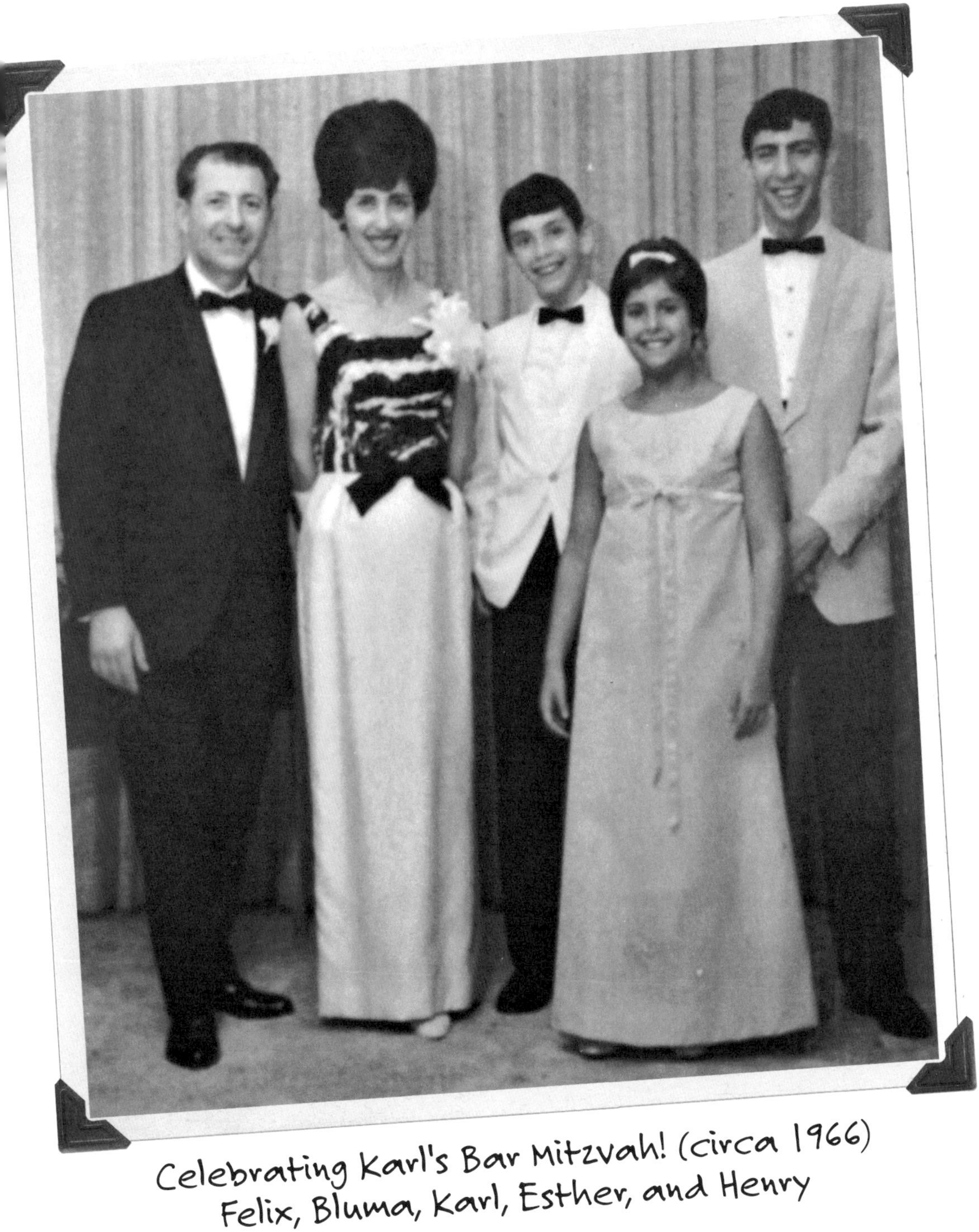

Celebrating Karl's Bar Mitzvah! (circa 1966)
Felix, Bluma, Karl, Esther, and Henry

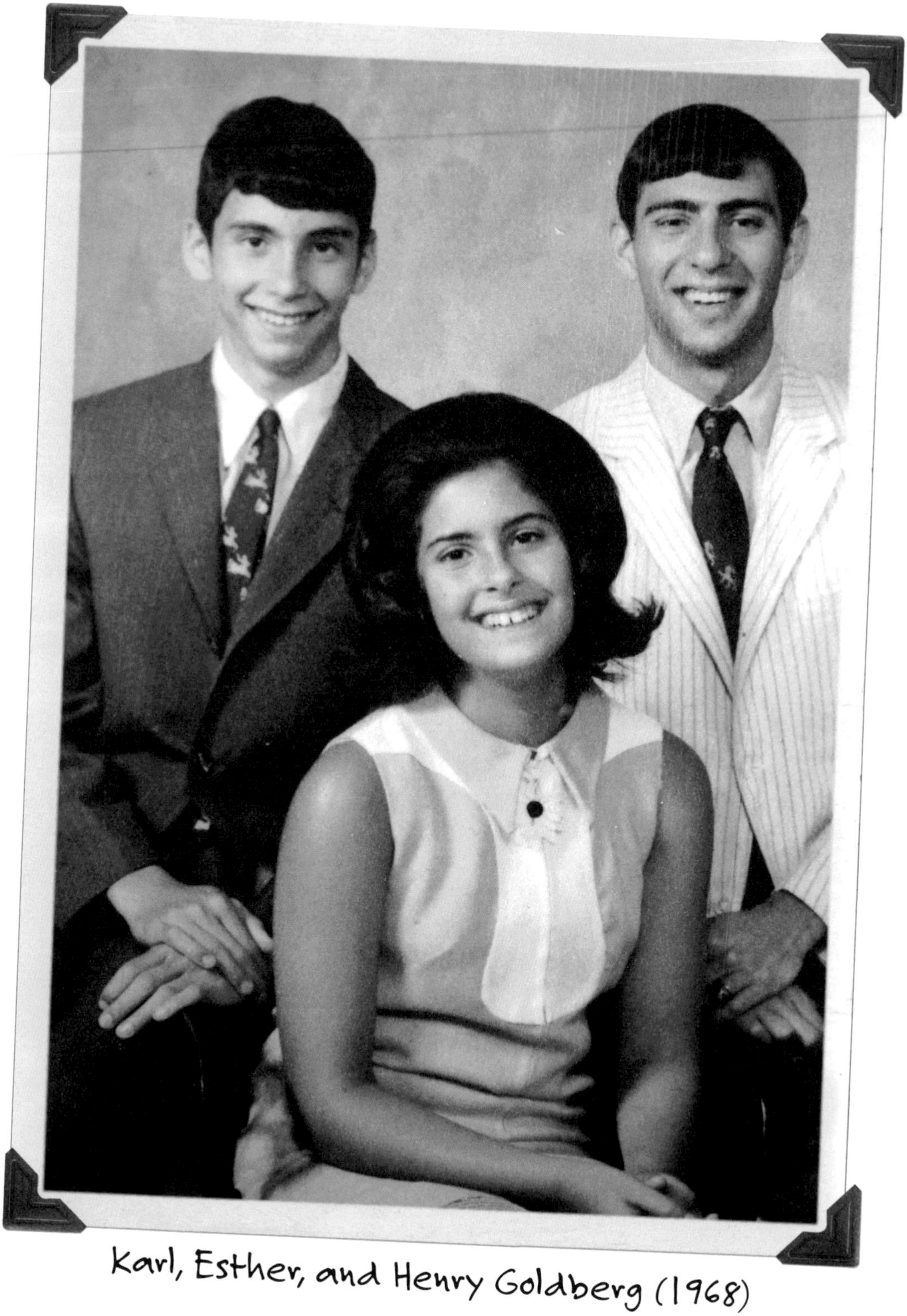

Karl, Esther, and Henry Goldberg (1968)

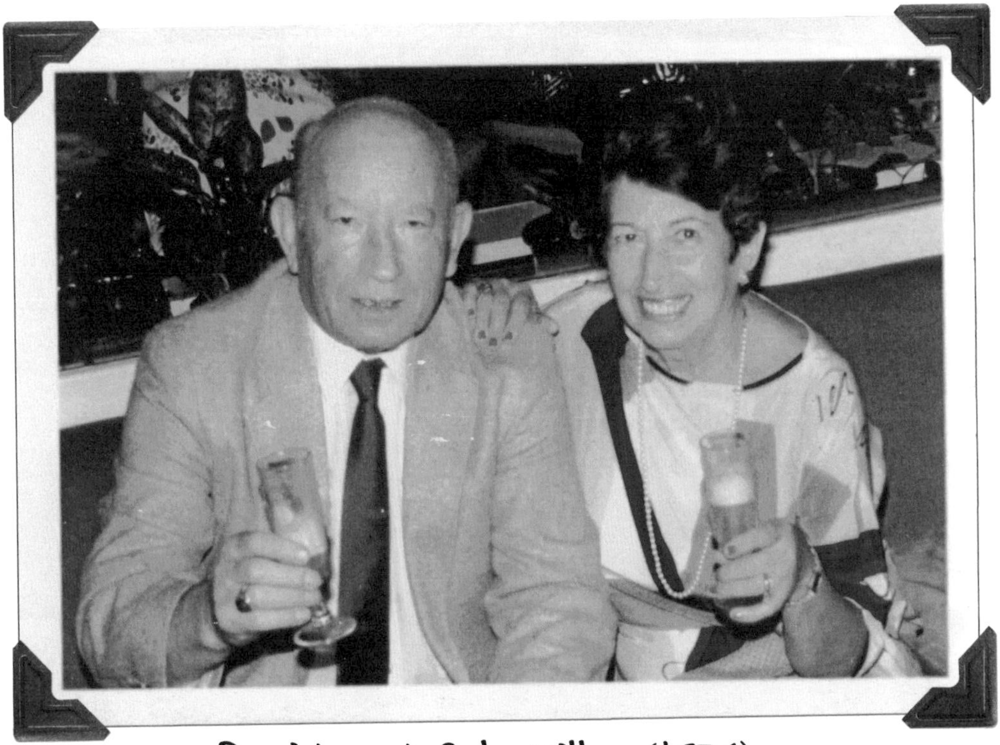

David and Cela Miller (1976)

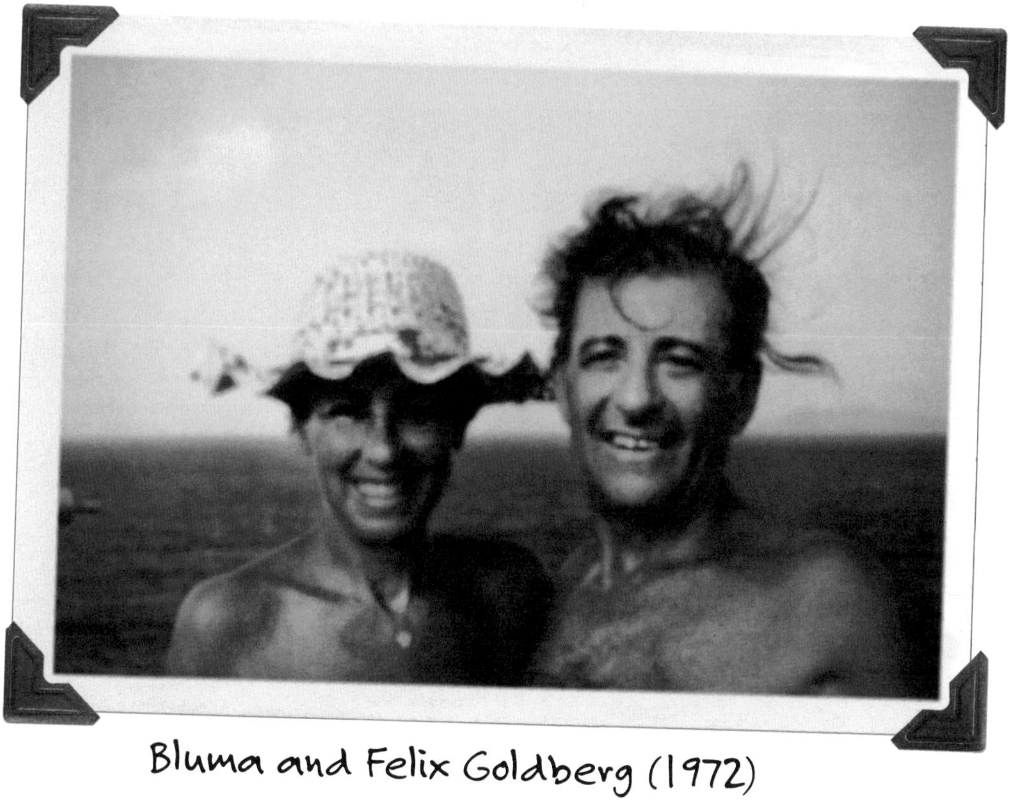

Bluma and Felix Goldberg (1972)

South Carolina Legislature Passes Resolution Recognizing Bluma Goldberg

2021-2022 Bill 3713

Left to right:
Henry Goldberg, Esther Greenberg,
SC State Rep Beth Bernstein,
Gloria Goldberg,
Karl Goldberg, Margo Goldberg,
Ira Greenberg
(20 June 2021)

Felix Goldberg, 1917-2000

Bluma Goldberg, 1926-2021

Learn more about the Goldbergs
and their entire journey
at the *Stories of Survival* website:
www.StoriesofSurvival.org

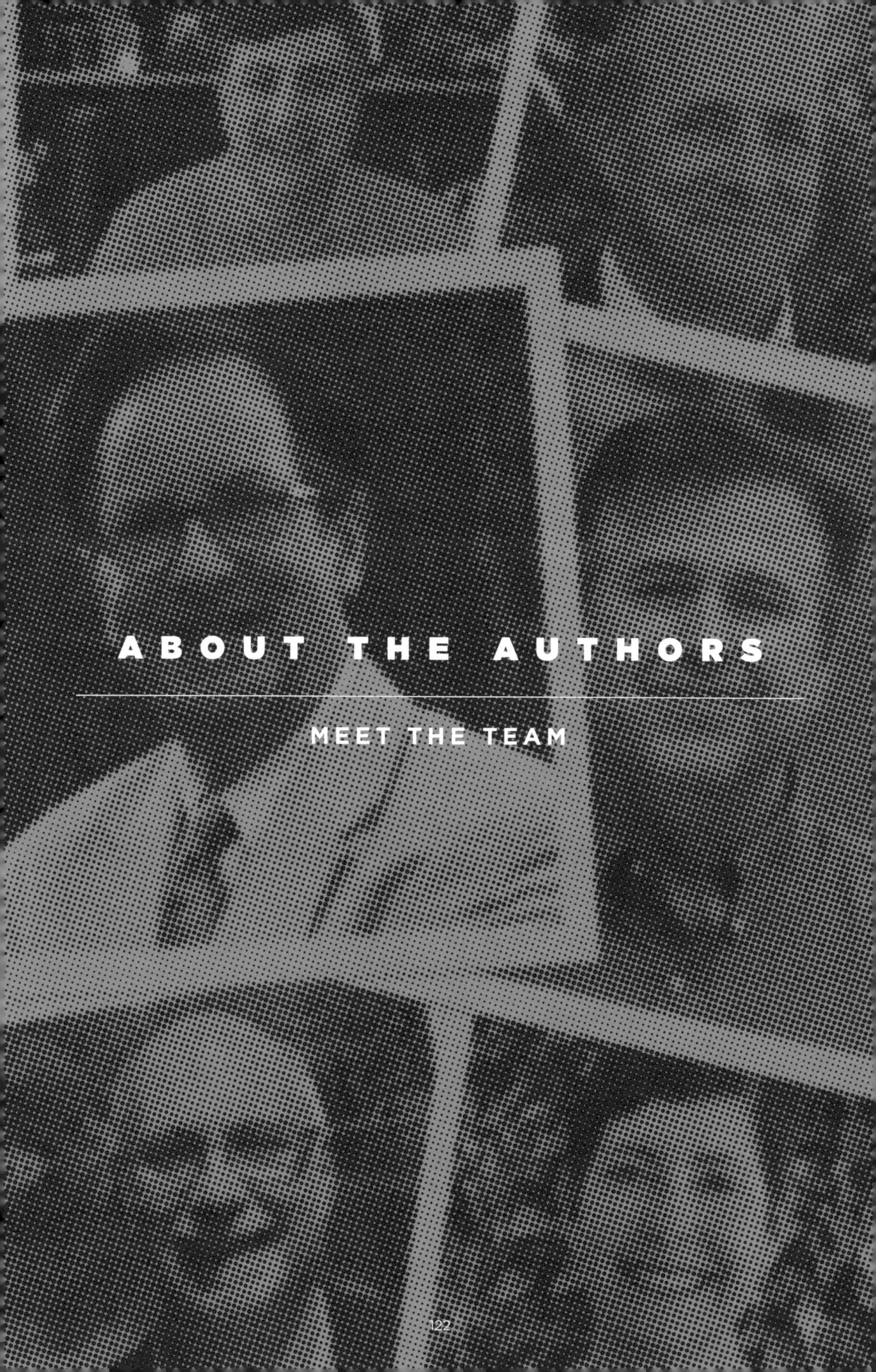

ABOUT THE AUTHORS

MEET THE TEAM

FRANK W. BAKER, STORY + SCRIPT

Frank W. Baker has worked in television news, public education and public television. In 1998 he founded the Media Literacy Clearinghouse website and began work helping teachers and students better understand how to think critically about the media.

Frank has been a frequent presenter at schools, districts and conferences across the United States. His work in media literacy education was recognized by the National PTA and the National Cable TV Association with a national "Leaders In Learning" award in 2007. He also conducted media literacy training with educators in Singapore, Mumbai (India) and Nairobi (Kenya). In 2019, Frank was recognized by UNESCO with its GAPMIL (Global Alliance Partnership for Media & Information Literacy) honor.

He has been published in *Learning & Leading With Technology* (ISTE), *Education Week, Cable in The Classroom, Telemedium, Florida English Journal, Ohio Media Spectrum, Middle Ground: The Magazine of Middle Level Education, Library Media Connection* (LMC), and *Screen Education* (Australia). His first book, *Coming Distractions: Questioning Movies*, was published by Capstone Press. His second book, *Political Campaigns & Political Advertising: A Media Literacy Guide* was published by Greenwood Press. His third book, *Media Literacy in The K-12 Classroom* was published by ISTE (2012). In 2017, Routledge published Baker's *Close Reading the Media: Literacy Lessons and Activities for Every Month of the Year.*

Learn more about Frank at www.frankwbaker.com.

TIM E. OGLINE, CO-PLOT/SCRIPT + ART & DESIGN

Tim E. Ogline is a Greater Philadelphia based writer and illustrator as well as design professional. Tim's first book, *Ben Franklin For Beginners*, has been called "beguiling" by Pulitzer Prize winner Joseph J. Ellis and a "must read" by former Pennsylvania Governor Edward G. Rendell as well as "nothing short of absolutely brilliant" by *Geekadelphia*. He is currently working on a new graphic novel, *Benjamin Franklin's The Way to Wealth and Other Words of Wisdom*.

Ogline is an alumnus of Temple University's Tyler School of Art and has previously taught there as well as at Moore College of Art & Design. Ogline additionally holds an MBA with a concentration in Marketing Management from Temple University's Fox School of Business.

Ogline's illustrations (www.timogline.com) have appeared in *The Wall Street Journal*, *Institutional Investor*, *The Philadelphia Inquirer*, the *Utne Reader*, *Outdoor Life*, *Philadelphia Style*, *Loyola Lawyer*, *How Magazine*, and *Mensa Bulletin* among others.

Tim Ogline's award-winning graphic design practice, Ogline Design (www.ogline.design), has served clients including Pennsylvania Governor Edward G. Rendell, The White House, the National Governors Association, Historic Philadelphia, the Crossroads of the American Revolution Association, the American Association for the Advancement of Science, University of Pennsylvania Graduate School of Education, the Wharton School, Albright College, and many more with creative solutions that have ranged from identity design to publication design to website development.

JOHN SHABLESKI, EDITOR + PROJECT MANAGER

John Shableski is the editor and project manager for this book. His other endeavors include serving as the president of Reading With Pictures and as an advisory board member for Graphic Mundi. He is a nationally recognized expert in the development of the graphic novel category. Along with editorial and strategic planning, his scope of expertise includes the study of industry trends and market development for retail, public library for book publishing along with classroom application of graphic novels.

John has worked with the Will and Ann Eisner Family Foundation and the American Library Association to launch the Will Eisner Graphic Novel Grant program. He was also the architect of The Excellence in Graphic Literature Awards for Pop Culture Classroom. Shableski has additionally served as a consultant for a wide range of organizations, publishers and events: The Norman Rockwell Museum, Fordham University's Teachers College, The New England Comic Arts in Education Conference, Reading With Pictures at Northwestern, Archie Comics, *Heavy Metal Magazine*, Zuiker Press, and the Texas Library Association Texas Maverick's committee.

He has served as an advisory board member for Book Expo America, as a jury member for Comic Con International's Eisner Awards, Penn State University's Lyn Ward Graphic Novel prize and the Children's Jury for the 2021 Excellence in Graphic Literature Award. He has also created over 500 hours of professional development programs for educators, librarians, retailers, publishers and author/creators at industry trade shows, conferences, and conventions across North America including New York Comic Con, Comic-Con International (San Diego) and Miami Book Fair International.

HENRY GOLDBERG, STORY CONSULTANT

Henry D. Goldberg was born in June 1948 to Polish-Jewish parents Felix and Bluma Goldberg, who were Holocaust survivors. He was born in an American-run Displaced Persons camp in Landsberg, Germany.

As a small child he immigrated with his parents to the United States in 1949. They made their home in Columbia, South Carolina where his father got a job as a janitor in a tile store. Henry attended public schools in Columbia and he graduated from the University of Georgia with a Bachelor's Degree in Business Administration in 1970. From 1970 to 1976, Henry served in the South Carolina Air National Guard at the McEntire ANG Base.

In 1972, he married Gloria Goldberg and they have two sons, Jason and Adam. Jason now lives in Charleston and Adam resides in Los Angeles, California. Henry and Gloria Goldberg have three grandchildren.

Henry worked for his father at the Tile Center for twelve years before beginning his own business in 1982. Following in his father's footsteps of entrepreneurship, he is the Founder and President of Palmetto Tile Distributors.

Henry is a strong supporter of the Jewish community. He has served on the Beth Shalom Synagogue Board of Directors for many years. He served two one-year terms of President of the Columbia Jewish Community Center and also as the President of the Columbia Jewish Foundation. He has additionally been a former Board of Trustees Member of the Central Carolina Community Foundation. He is also a staunch supporter of efforts to strengthen Holocaust education and awareness to ensure that the stories of his family and so many others remain alive.

KARL GOLDBERG, STORY CONSULTANT

Karl Goldberg was born on June 26, 1953, in Columbia, South Carolina, just four years after his parents Bluma and Felix Goldberg immigrated to the United States. He graduated from the University of South Carolina in 1976 with a degree in Sociology. During his tenure at USC, Karl spent a semester abroad at a kibbutz in Israel. He then returned to Columbia to work in the family business.

Karl has served on the board of Beth Shalom Synagogue, the Columbia Jewish Community Center, and the committee that plans the Holocaust Memorial Day service. He was Chairman of the Youth Basketball league for the JCC and coached both girls' and boys' basketball teams. He has spent the last twenty years speaking to groups across the state about his parent's experience during the Holocaust. His mission is to educate the public, especially students, about the atrocities of the Holocaust by personalizing his parent's story.

Today, Karl is proud to continue his parent's legacy as an owner and President of The Tile Center Inc., the business his parents started in 1957. He is an avid sports fan, especially following the South Carolina Gamecocks. Karl enjoys boating, fishing, gardening, and traveling. He and his wife, Margo, have two children, Philip Goldberg, and Robin Roth, one granddaughter, and twin girls on the way.

ESTHER GOLDBERG-GREENBERG, STORY CONSULTANT

Esther Greenberg was born in February 1957 in Columbia, South Carolina. She was the youngest of three children, whose parents Bluma and Felix Goldberg survived the Holocaust and immigrated to the United States.

Esther's father Felix founded The Tile Center in 1957, a successful tile business, where Esther still works to this day. Esther's mother Bluma worked in the business for over twenty years. Today, Esther is co-owner of the business.

Esther received a Bachelor of Science degree with a major in Nutrition from the University of Georgia. She then worked as a Registered Dietitian for ten years. She married Ira Greenberg in 1981 and they have three children. Daughters Leah and Rachel reside in Atlanta and Philadelphia respectively. Esther's son Sam lives in Columbia as well. Esther and Ira have two grandchildren.

Esther is also highly involved in the Columbia Jewish Community. She served as President of the Columbia Jewish Federation for two years and has served on its board for many years. She is currently co-chair of the Columbia Holocaust Education Commission, whose mission is to promote Holocaust education throughout South Carolina. Esther often speaks to students and other community groups to tell her parents' story.

STEVEN WILSON, PRESIDENT, IMAGINE AND WONDER

Steven has spearheaded many successes for prominent publishing houses internationally and has been a leader in developing new business avenues, product creation, and sales globally.

Imagine and Wonder, a New York-based publisher launched in 2021, aims to produce titles with a vision that serves to inspire both children and parents. He started publishing age-appropriate children's books which focus on the challenges facing today's youth and hope to spark meaningful ideas and change. Imagine and Wonder publishes activity books, health and wellness guides for children, and tales of endangered animals facing extinction due to climate change and other struggles and their future preservation.

The Imagine and Wonder mission is to make learning activities and reading exciting, challenging and to help accelerate development in children's learning skills. As a father of two daughters, the true goal for Imagine and Wonder is to publish books he would have wanted to read with them.

From the moment Steven was introduced to Frank and Tim and then the Goldberg family, he felt privileged to be part of the telling of Frank and Bluma's story. Steven would like to add a dedication to the memory of Abraham and Helene Weinstock—his grandparents, who perished during the Holocaust.

ACKNOWLEDGEMENTS

This graphic novel could not have been possible without the cooperation and blessing of the Goldberg family: Henry Goldberg, Karl Goldberg, and Esther Goldberg-Greenberg. We are grateful for sharing the story of Bluma Tishgarten Goldberg and Felix Goldberg with us so that we could bring it to you.

It is our hope that we can keep their memory alive and that their story will continue to serve as an example of the endurance of the human spirit as well as an admonition against the horrors resulting from racism and the hatred of the other.

The authors would like to express their sincere gratitude for the participation and assistance of the following individuals:

Richelle Budd Caplan

Dr. Karen Gavigan, Interim Director, School of Information Science, University of South Carolina

Bernd Horstmann, Curator Register of Names/Permanent Exhibition

Vincent E. Slatt, Librarian, United States Holocaust Memorial Museum

Dr. Doyle Stevick, Anne Frank Center, University of South Carolina

Dr. habil. Christoph Thonfeld
Leiter der wissenschaftlichen Abteilung/ Head of Research Department
KZ-Gedenkstätte Dachau/ Dachau Concentration Camp Memorial Site

This work could not have been completed without the patience, love, and support of our families and friends.

From Frank: The Claims Conference created an awareness campaign with the slogan "It Started with Words." How prophetic. It was Felix Goldberg's (of blessed memory) words that started me down the path that resulted in this graphic novel. Thanks to a recommendation from my colleague at the University of South Carolina, I was connected to John Shableski who instantly recognized the importance of the subject matter (and the story)—one that needed to be told. Before long, I was "meeting" artist extraordinaire Tim Ogline and thus began the journey that resulted in this book. It could not have been accomplished without their incredible knowledge, support and patience. And I would be remiss if I did not also acknowledge here the Goldberg family—who opened their hearts—relating to me personal moments with their parents and at the same time enthusiastically endorsing this book from the start. We know young people need new approaches to understanding the Holocaust—and we pray that this graphic novel is just one step in overcoming widespread ignorance.

From Tim: I am forever grateful for the love and support of my family, but especially for my wife Candice and for her patience with me and all the late nights and weekends devoted to this work. She's understood the mission and what it means. And thanks especially to John Shableski for sending me the Facebook message that changed my life... and introduced me to a man I truly admire and have spent the past 18 months with on this amazing collaboration, Frank Baker. We have an astonishing team and I'm thankful to have had the opportunity to work with Frank and John on this book.

From John: Thank you first to my family: Rhonda, Addison, Ashley, Collin and Alaina for your love and support... and patience. A big thank you to this brain trust: Frank Baker and Tim Ogline. It's been an amazing journey. Thanks also to Steven Wilson, our publisher. He made this leap with us possible. And I owe a huge debt of gratitude for the librarians who are the driving force for this thing we call a graphic novel. Librarians are the reason I live and breathe in this publishing world. Kat Kan, Robin Brenner, Eva Volin, Mike Pawuk, Francesca Goldsmith, Michele Gorman, Steve Wiener, Candice Mack, Karen Green, Melissa Jacobs, Amie Wright (along with a whole host of others), you made this book possible. And one last thank you, to my teachers. Not only did you show me a bigger world, many of you literally saved my life.

TIMELINE

EVENTS RELATED TO WORLD WAR II AND THE HOLOCAUST

1914

28 July	World War I begins

1917

2 January	Kingdom of Poland is established
2 January	Felix Goldberg is born near Kalisz, Poland
7 May	RMS Lusitania attacked and sunk by Germany Navy, killing all 1,198 aboard

1918

11 November	World War I ends

1919

28 June	Treaty of Versailles signed in Paris, officially ending the war between Germany and the Allied Powers

1925

18 July	Adolf Hitler's *Mein Kampf* published

1926

12–14 May	The May Coup was a coup d'état carried out in Poland by Marshal Józef Piłsudski
10 June	Bluma Tishgarten is born in Pinczow, Poland

1933

20 January	Adolf Hitler becomes German Chancellor, Hitler appoints Joseph Goebbels as Minister of Propaganda
27 February	German parliament (Reichstag) building in Berlin burned down due to arson
22 March	Dachau Concentration Camp opens
23 March	Enabling Acts passed
1 April	Boycott of Jewish businesses begins
10 May	Book Burning at Berlin Opera Square

1935

15 September	Nuremberg Race Laws announced

1937

15 July	Buchenwald Concentration Camp opens

1938

26 March	Herman Goring warns Jews to leave Austria
13-18 June	First mass arrests of Jews begins
30 September	Munich Conference – resulting in an agreement by Great Britain, France, Italy and Germany that ceded the Sudetenland region of Czechoslovakia to Germany
9–10 November	Kristallnacht (Night of Broken Glass)
15 November	Jewish children expelled from German public schools

1939

27 May	Ship carrying Jewish refugees turned away from Havana, Cuba
1 September	World War II begins
4 September	Nazis invade Pinzcow, Poland
13 September	Felix Goldberg taken POW

1940

9 April	Germany invades Denmark and Norway
6 May	Auschwitz-Birkenau Concentration Camp opens
10 May	Battle of France begins. Netherlands, Belgium, and Luxembourg quickly fall under German control.
14 June	First prisoners arrive at Auschwitz-Birkenau
7 September	Nazi "Blitzkrieg" of London begins (lasting 57 days)

1941

6 April	Germany invades Yugslavia and Greece
22 June	Germany invades Soviet Union
29 – 30 September	Babi Yar (Ukraine) Massacre
7 December	Japan bombs Pearl Harbor, Hawaii
8 December	"A Day That Will Live in Infamy," President Franklin Roosevelt's speech to Congress and the American people
11 December	U.S. Declares War on Germany
12 December	Hitler declares the 'destruction of the Jewish race' to the Nazi Party leadership and orders the Holocaust and the genocide of European Jews.

1942

20 January	High ranking Nazi officials meet at a villa in Berlin, Germany. The Wannsee Conference is where the "Final Solution" is first planned and set in motion.
19 April – 16 May	Warsaw Ghetto uprisings
6 July	Anne Frank and family go into hiding

1944

6 June	(D-Day) Allies invade Normandy, France
4 August	Anne Frank and her family arrested and eventually deported to Auschwitz-Birkenau
16 Dec '44 – 16 Jan '45	Battle of the Bulge (Belgium-Luxembourg)

1945

27 January	Auschwitz-Birkenau liberated by Russian Troops
19 Feb – 26 Mar	Battle for Iwo Jima
11 April	Buchenwald liberated by Allied Troops
15 April	CBS Newsman Edward R. Murrow's Buchenwald Broadcast
24 April	US Congressman and Media tour Buchenwald
7 May	Germany Surrenders
6 August	U.S. drops Atomic Bomb on Hiroshima, Japan
9 August	U.S. drops Atomic Bomb on Nagasaki, Japan
2 September	Japan Surrenders, signals end of WWII
20 November	Nuremberg Trials begin

GLOSSARY

For most of the definitions used in the book, a number of resources were used including dictionary.com, Wikipedia, the US Holocaust Memorial Museum and others. We are grateful for the chance to share those with the reader.

ANTISEMITISM
Hostility toward or discrimination against Jews as a religious or racial group.

BOYCOTT
Withdrawal from commercial or social relations with (a country, organization, or person) as a punishment or protest.

CHEDER
School for Jewish children in which Hebrew and religious knowledge are taught.

CONCENTRATION CAMP
A place where large numbers of people, especially political prisoners or members of persecuted minorities, are deliberately imprisoned in a relatively small area with inadequate facilities, sometimes to provide forced labor or to await mass execution. The term is most strongly associated with the several hundred camps established by the Nazis in Germany and occupied Europe in 1933–45, among the most infamous being Dachau, Belsen, and Auschwitz.

CREMATORIA
Venue for the cremation of the dead.

DEATH MARCH

A forced march of prisoners of war or other captives or deportees in which individuals are left to die along the way.

DELOUSING

Process of ridding (a person or animal) or lice and other parasitic insects.

DIASPORA

The dispersion of any people from their original homeland.

DISPLACED PERSON

A person expelled, deported, or impelled to flee from his or her country of nationality or habitual residence by the forces or consequences of war or oppression.

DP CAMP

Displaced Person camp.

EXTERMINATION

To get rid of by destroying completely.

FINAL SOLUTION

The Nazi policy of exterminating European Jews. Introduced by Heinrich Himmler and administered by Adolf Eichmann, the policy resulted in the murder of 6 million Jewish people in concentration camps between 1941 and 1945.

FORCED LABOR

See SLAVE LABOR.

FORCED LABOR CAMP

During World War II the Nazis operated several categories of Arbeitslager (labor camps) for different categories of inmates. Prisoners in Nazi labor camps were worked to death on short rations and in bad conditions, or killed if they became unable to work. Many died as a direct result of forced labor under the Nazis. (Source: *Wikipedia*)

GENEVA CONVENTION

International treaty to provide for humane treatment of civilians and prisoners of war during wartime.

GHETTOS

Places in which Jews were held as prisoners under duress, usually in overcrowded and unsanitary conditions and with severe shortages of food, water and medicines.

IMMIGRANT
A person who comes to live permanently in a foreign country.

INFERIOR RACE
Persons regarded as less important because they have less status or ability.

JUDE
German word for Jew.

JUDENFREI
Designation for area or region where Jews were forcibly removed or killed.

MEZUZUAH
A parchment inscribed with religious texts and attached in a case to the doorpost of a Jewish house as a sign of faith.

ORTHODOX (JEW)
A Jew who adheres faithfully to the principles and practices of traditional Judaism as evidenced chiefly by a devotion to and study of the Torah, daily synagogue attendance if possible, and strict observance of the Sabbath, religious festivals, holy days, and dietary laws.

POGROM
A violent riot aimed at the massacre or expulsion of an ethnic or religious group, particularly one aimed at Jews.

PREJUDICE
A lack of tolerance and a hostility toward persons or groups typically based on factors such as race, religion, or sexual orientation.

PROPAGANDA
The Nazis effectively used propaganda to win the support of millions of Germans in a democracy and, later in a dictatorship, to facilitate persecution, war, and ultimately genocide. The stereotypes and images found in Nazi propaganda were not new, but were already familiar to their intended audience.

RACISM
A belief that race is a fundamental determinant of human traits and capacities and that racial differences produce an inherent superiority of a particular race.

REFUGEE
A person who has been forced to leave their country in order to escape war, persecution, or natural disaster.

REICHSTAG FIRE DECREE
The Reichstag Fire Decree permitted the regime to arrest and incarcerate political opponents without specific charge, dissolve political organizations, and to suppress publications. It also gave the central government the authority to overrule state and local laws and overthrow state and local governments.

SS (A.K.A. SCHUTZSTAFFEL)

The Nazi special police force. Founded in 1925 by Hitler as a personal bodyguard, the SS provided security forces (including the Gestapo) and administered the concentration camps.

SABBATH (A.K.A. SHABBAT)
In the Jewish religion—the time between Sundown Friday and Sundown Saturday—a time for the cessation of work (for many) and time for prayer and contemplation.

SHOAH
Jewish word for *The Holocaust*.

SHTETL
Small Jewish town or village in eastern Europe.

SYNAGOGUE
Jewish house of worship.

SLAVE LABOR
Labor that is coerced and inadequately rewarded, or the people who perform such labor.

TYPHUS FEVER
A group of diseases caused by bacteria that are spread to humans by fleas, lice, and chiggers... resulting in fever, cough, rash, and aches.

TOLERANCE
Acceptance of and respect for a person or group regardless of race, religion, or sexual orientation.

WORK CAMP
See FORCED LABOR CAMP.

RECOMMENDED RESOURCES

FURTHER READING & STUDY

Your public library or your school library are also excellent places to start in order to find appropriate readings.

Yad Vashem Primary Sources
https://www.yadvashem.org/education/educational-materials/learning-environment/babi-yar/primary-sources.html

Holocaust Encylopedia (United States Holocaust Memorial Museum)
https://encyclopedia.ushmm.org/

Holocaust Study Resources (YIVO Institute for Jewish Research)
https://yivo.org/holocaust-study-resources

University of Southern California Shoah Foundation
https://sfi.usc.edu

Resources (South Carolina Jewish Historical Society)
https://jhssc.org/publications/magazines/

Holocaust Books for YA Readers
https://www.jewishbookcouncil.org/books/reading-lists/holocaust-books-for-young-adults

Age-Appropriate Middle Grade & YA Books about the Holocaust (School Library Journal)
https://www.slj.com/story/Commemorate-Holocaust-Remembrance-Day-with-this-Booklist-libraries-students

The Holocaust: Primary Sources
https://guides.smu.edu/c.php?g=940430&p=6777633

Books About The Holocaust (Common Sense Media)
https://www.commonsensemedia.org/lists/books-about-the-holocaust

Non-Fiction: Holocaust Lit for Young Adults
https://ya-holocaust-lit.weebly.com/non-fiction.html

Student Recommended Book List (Holocaust Museum and Cohen Education Center)
https://hmcec.org/resources/library/

Holocaust Books for Middle School and Jr. High School
https://learnincolor.com/list-holocaust-books-grades-5-9-rated-reviewed.html

Suggested Readings for Students (Virginia Holocaust Museum)
https://www.vaholocaust.org/resources-for-students/suggested-reading-for-students/

Undeniable: The Truth To Remember (CBS News documentary)
https://www.youtube.com/watch?v=NFJnop4XoBk&t=6s

Memory of the Camps (PBS Frontline documentary)
https://www.youtube.com/watch?v=xy_xWKJubuY&t=2s

The Last Survivors (PBS Frontline documentary)
https://www.youtube.com/watch?v=crkVNLgPPV0

America and the Holocaust (PBS The American Experience)
https://www.pbs.org/wgbh/americanexperience/films/holocaust/

Seared Souls: South Carolina Voices from The Holocaust (South Carolina ETV)
https://www.knowitall.org/series/b-seared-souls-south-carolina-voices-holocaust

INDEX

Stories Of Survival
storiesofsurvival.org
WE SURVIVED THE HOLOCAUST: THE BLUMA & FELIX GOLDBERG STORY
Stories of Survival
Stories of Survival
The Story Of Felix And Bluma Goldberg

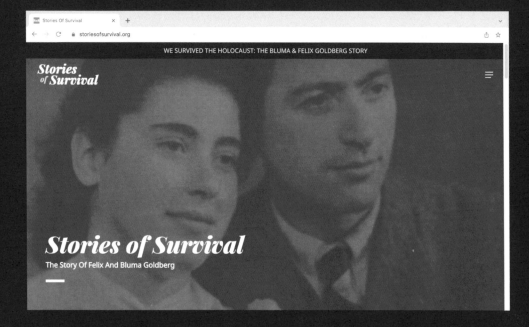

LEARN MORE

VISIT THE STORIES OF SURVIVAL WEBSITE

Scan this QR code with your phone camera for more information about the Bluma and Felix Goldberg and their miraculous story of risk, resilience, and renewal.